Lecture Notes in Computer S

Commenced Publication in 1973
Founding and Former Series Editors:
Gerhard Goos, Juris Hartmanis, and Jan van Leeuwen

Kurt Vanmechelen   Jörn Altmann
Omer F. Rana (Eds.)

Economics of Grids, Clouds, Systems, and Services

9th International Conference, GECON 2012
Berlin, Germany, November 27-28, 2012
Proceedings

 Springer

Volume Editors

Kurt Vanmechelen
University of Antwerp
Department of Mathematics and Computer Science
Middelheimlaan 1, 2020 Antwerp, Belgium
E-mail: kurt.vanmechelen@ua.ac.be

Jörn Altmann
Seoul National University, College of Engineering
Department of Industrial Engineering,
Technology Management, Economics, and Policy Program
599 Gwanak-Ro, Gwanak-Gu, Seoul 151-744, South Korea
E-mail: jorn.altmann@acm.org

Omer F. Rana
Cardiff University
School of Computer Science
Queen's Buildings, Newport Road, Cardiff, CF24 3AA, UK
E-mail: o.f.rana@cs.cardiff.ac.uk

ISSN 0302-9743   e-ISSN 1611-3349
ISBN 978-3-642-35193-8   e-ISBN 978-3-642-35194-5
DOI 10.1007/978-3-642-35194-5
Springer Heidelberg Dordrecht London New York

Library of Congress Control Number: 2012952398

CR Subject Classification (1998): C.2.4, K.4.4, H.4, H.3, H.5, J.1

LNCS Sublibrary: SL 5 – Computer Communication Networks and Telecommunications

Typesetting: Camera-ready by author, data conversion by Scientific Publishing Services, Chennai, India

Printed on acid-free paper

Springer is part of Springer Science+Business Media (www.springer.com)

Preface

The way in which IT resources and services are being provisioned is currently in flux. Advances in distributed systems technology have allowed for the provisioning of services on an unprecedented scale and with increasing flexibility. At the same time, business and academia have started to embrace a model wherein third-party services that can be acquired with minimal service provider interaction replace or complement those that are managed internally.

Organizations have only started to grasp the economic implications of this evolution. As a global market for infrastructure, platform, and software services emerges, the need to understand and deal with these implications is quickly growing. In addition, a multitude of new challenges arise. These are inherently multidisciplinary and relate to aspects such as the operation and structure of the service market, trust, the alignment of cost, revenue and quality-related objectives when taking on a service consumer or provider role, and the creation of innovative business models and value chains.

The 9th International Conference on Economics of Grids, Clouds, Systems, and Services, which has been held in Berlin, brought together researchers and practitioners in the areas of economics, business administration, and computer science who have thoroughly investigated the economics-related issues and solutions associated with these developments and challenges. This volume collects the detailed reports on their findings.

For this year's event, we received over 36 submissions, showing the growing success of GECON and its solid position in this interdisciplinary research landscape. Each submission was assessed by three to five reviewers of the International Program Committee. The structure of this volume follows the seven sessions that comprised the conference program (two of which comprise work-in-progress papers):

- Session A: Market Mechanisms, Pricing, and Negotiation
- Session B: Resource Allocation, Scheduling, and Admission Control
- Session C: Work in Progress on Tools and Techniques for Cost-Efficient Service Selection
- Session D: Market Modeling
- Session E: Trust
- Session F: Cloud Computing in Education
- Session G: Work in Progress on Cloud Adoption and Business Models

For these seven sessions, 18 contributions were selected from all submissions. Twelve of those 18 contributions were marked as full papers. Six papers were integrated in the volume as shorter work-in-progress papers. The acceptance rate of full papers was 33%.

Session A comprised three papers on market mechanisms, pricing, and negotiation. The first paper by Edwin Yaqub, Ramin Yahyapour, Philipp Wieder, and Kuan Lu entitled "A Protocol Development Framework for SLA Negotiations in Cloud and Service Computing" presents a domain-independent framework based on a protocol development lifecycle, comprising four phases (modeling, verification, rule-based implementation, and generic execution). The authors demonstrate the workings of their framework by introducing a bilateral negotiation protocol, showing that it is well-formed, deterministic, and deadlock-free, and analyzing its correctness and state space scalability. The second contribution, "The Use of Provision Point Contracts for Improving Cloud Infrastructure Utilization," by Owen Rogers and Dave Cliff focuses on a pricing method for cloud computing that allows providers to schedule virtual machines more efficiently through the use of provision point contracts (PPCs). They demonstrate an increase in server utilization and a reduction of costs that arise from the use of such contracts. The final contribution of this session is by Felipe Díaz, Elias Doumith, Sawsan Al Zahr, and Maurice Gagnaire entitled "An Economic Agent Maximizing Cloud Provider Revenues Under a Pay-as-you-Book Pricing Model." It offers a solution to the resource provisioning problem for advance reservation under the pay-as-you-book pricing model by handling the extra time required by some jobs at a higher price on a best-effort basis.

Session B is centered on papers that deal with resource allocation, scheduling, and admission control. The first of the three papers is by Wim Depoorter, Kurt Vanmechelen, and Jan Broeckhove entitled "Economic Co-Allocation and Advance Reservation of Network and Computational Resources in Grids." It presents ENARA, a novel economic resource management system with advance reservation and co-allocation support for both network and computational resources. The authors demonstrate that ENARA can significantly increase the user value realized by the infrastructure compared to traditional resource management systems, and present novel approaches to pricing both network and computational resources. The subsequent contribution by Rafael Tolosana-Calasanz, José Ángel Bañares, Congduc Pham, and Omer F. Rana entitled "QoS-adaptive Resource Management on Shared Clouds for Heterogenous Bursty Data Streams" describes an infrastructure for supporting QoS for concurrent data streams. Using profit maximization as the provider's objective, streams are only accepted if they improve the overall revenue. The last contribution, "The ISQoS Grid Broker for Temporal and Budget Guarantees," which has been authored by Richard Kavanagh and Karim Djemame, introduces a broker for ensuring completion of jobs within time and budgetary constraints. The authors also analyze the stability of prices in such a scheme, focusing on the impact of rescheduling approaches in this regard.

Session C, which comprises work-in-progress papers on tools and techniques for cost-efficient service selection, starts with the contribution of Ulrich Lampe, Melanie Siebenhaar, Ronny Hans, Dieter Schuller, and Ralf Steinmetz. "Let the Clouds Compute: Cost-Efficient Workload Distribution in Infrastructure Clouds" proposes an exact and a heuristic-based optimization approach to cost-efficiently allocate resources for task execution across different cloud providers. The paper quantifies both the performance of these approaches and their cost-efficiency. The second contribution by Miranda Zhang, Rajiv Ranjan, Surya Nepal, Michael Menzel, and Armin Haller entitled "A Declarative Recommender System for Cloud Infrastructure Services Selection" presents a declarative approach for selecting cloud-based infrastructure services. The authors analyze the effectiveness and scalability of their approach, presenting a service configuration selection experiment incorporating offerings from Amazon, Azure, and GoGrid. The third and last contribution in this session is authored by Spyridon V. Gogouvitis, Gregory Katsaros, Dimosthenis Kyriazis, Athanasios Voulodimos, Roman Talyansky, and Theodora Varvarigou and is entitled "Retrieving, Storing, Correlating and Distributing Information for Cloud Management." This contribution describes a service management architecture and focuses on the corresponding information model that supports this architecture.

Session D consists of two papers on market modeling. The first contribution by Jörn Künsemöller and Holger Karl entitled "On Local Separation of Processing and Storage in Infrastructure-as-a-Service" investigates the market success of separate processing and storage facilities compared to a combined approach. The results show that stable market constellations with separate service-specific facilities are possible. The second contribution by Netsanet Haile and Jörn Altmann entitled "Value Creation in IT Service Platforms Through Two-Sided Network Effects" analyzes the value creation through service platforms for application users, service developers, and a single-platform provider. Their simulation results demonstrate that the profit of service developers is relatively low compared to the profit of a platform provider, indicating the risk that service developers stop using the service platform for offering their services.

Session E focuses on trust in cloud computing markets. Mario Macías and Jordi Guitart first propose a decentralized approach to the realization of a reputation system for cloud environments. In "Cheat-Proof Trust Model for Cloud Computing Markets," they apply statistical analysis to detect dishonest behavior in peers and validate their model in different settings through simulation. In "Trust Factors for the Usage of Cloud Computing in Small and Medium-Sized Craft Enterprises," Holger Kett, Harriet Kasper, Jürgen Falkner, and Anette Weisbecker subsequently report on the importance of different factors of trust from an SME business perspective. Their analysis is based on a literature review and a survey-based study among SMEs with over 350 respondents.

Session F deals with the adoption of cloud computing in education. "A Cost Analysis of Cloud Computing For Education," by Fernando Koch, Marcos Assuncao, and Marco Netto focuses on the cost efficiency of three different resource allocation strategies, with one strategy specifically tailored to the domain of education. The authors analyze these strategies in terms of quality-of-service and cost metrics and the interrelation between both. A second contribution in this session "Delivering Cloud Services with QoS Requirements: An Opportunity for ICT SMEs," by Alfonso Quarati, Daniele D'Agostino, Antonella Galizia, Matteo Mangini, and Andrea Clematis, evaluates the performance of a broker for hybrid clouds in the context of serving e-learning courses in virtual classrooms and the delivery of a risk-assessment service. The advantages and disadvantages of three allocation policies are evaluated in this regard.

The final session of the conference program includes work in progress on cloud adoption and business models. Francesco Novelli reports on the phases that software companies go through when transitioning from an on-premise to on-demand delivery model, the organizational issues raised as a result of that, and the advisability for such a transition. Although the paper, entitled, "A Mixed-Methods Research Approach to Investigate the Transition from On-Premise to On-Demand Software Delivery" is currently based on a limited number of real-world providers that went to this transition, it provides a valuable insight in these issues. In "Towards a Federated Cloud Ecosystem: Enabling Managed Cloud Service Consumption," Dirk Thatmann, Mathias Slawik, Sebastian Zickau and Axel Küpper report on the adoption of cloud computing in the health sector. They describe an architecture and proof-of-concept implementation of a cloud proxy to deal with the strict compliance constraints and trust issues that are prevalent in this sector. Finally, Monika Kaczmarek and Agata Filipowska present "Business Models for Semantic Content Providers," in which they report on the different offering, revenue, and customer models that are to be considered in the semantic content domain.

As we received a significantly higher number of submissions this year, the reviewing process was backed by a reinforced Program Committee. Therefore, we would especially like to thank our long-term committee members, as well as our ten new committee members for completing their reviews on time and giving valuable feedback to the authors. We would also like to extend our thanks to the Technical University of Berlin for hosting this edition of GECON. Furthermore, we would like to express our gratitude toward Alfred Hofmann from Springer for his support in publishing the GECON proceedings under this year's challenging time constraints.

November 2012

Kurt Vanmechelen
Jörn Altmann
Omer F. Rana
Matthias Hovestadt

Organization

GECON 2012 was organized by the Technology Management, Economics, and Policy Program at Seoul National University, the Department of Mathematics and Computer Science at the University of Antwerp, the School of Computer Science at Cardiff University, and the Department of Complex and Distributed Systems at the Technical University of Berlin.

Executive Committee

Chairs

Jörn Altmann	Seoul National University, South Korea
Matthias Hovestadt	Technical University of Berlin, Germany
Kurt Vanmechelen	University of Antwerp, Belgium
Omer F. Rana	Cardiff University, UK

Program Committee

Ashraf Bany Mohammed	University of Ha'il, Saudi Arabia
Hermant K. Bhargava	UC Davis, USA
Ivona Brandic	Technical University of Vienna, Austria
Rajkumar Buyya	University of Melbourne, Australia
Jeremy Cohen	Imperial College, London
Gheorghe Cosmin Silaghi	Babes-Bolyai University, Romania
Costas Courcoubetis	Athens University of Economics and Business, Greece
Karim Djemame	University of Leeds, UK
Torsten Eymann	University of Bayreuth, Germany
Thomas Fahringer	University of Innsbruck, Austria
Saurabh Garg	IBM Research, Australia
Wolfgang Gentzsch	DEISA, EU
Thomas Hess	Ludwig-Maximilians-Universität München, Germany
Chun-Hsi Huang	University of Connecticut, USA
Bahman Javadi	University of Western Sydney, Australia
Odej Kao	Technical University of Berlin, Germany
Kibae Kim	Technical University of Braunschweig, Germany
Stefan Kirn	University of Hohenheim, Germany
Tobias A. Knoch	Erasmus University, The Netherlands
Bastian Koller	HLRS, Germany
Harald Kornmayer	DHBW Mannheim, Germany

Dimosthenis Kyriazis	National Technical University of Athens, Greece
Richard T.B. Ma	National University of Singapore, Singapore
Jysoo Lee	KISTI, South Korea
Dan Ma	Singapore Management University, Singapore
Steven Miller	Singapore Management University, Singapore
Marco A.S. Netto	IBM Research, Brazil
Dirk Neumann	University of Freiburg, Germany
Karsten Oberle	Alcatel-Lucent Bell Labs, Germany
Dang Minh Quan	CREATE-NET, Italy
Rajiv Ranjan	University of Melbourne, Australia
Peter Reichl	Telecommunications Research Center Vienna, Austria
Rizos Sakellariou	University of Manchester, UK
Satoshi Sekiguchi	AIST, Japan
Arunabha Sen	Arizona State University, USA
Katarina Stanoevska	University of St.Gallen, Switzerland
Burkhard Stiller	University of Zurich, Switzerland
Bruno Tuffin	IRISA/INRIA, France
Dora Varvarigou	National Technical University of Athens, Greece
Gabriele von Voigt	University of Hannover, Germany
Stefan Wesner	HLRS, Germany
Phillip Wieder	GWDG, University of Göttingen, Germany
Ramin Yahyapour	GWDG, University of Göttingen, Germany
Wolfgang Ziegler	Fraunhofer Institute SCAI, Germany

Steering Committee

Jörn Altmann	Seoul National University, South Korea
Kurt Vanmechelen	University of Antwerp, Belgium
Rajkumar Buyya	University of Melbourne, Australia
Thomas Fahringer	University of Innsbruck, Austria
Hing-Yan Lee	National Grid Office, Singapore
Jysoo Lee	KISTI, South Korea
Steven Miller	Singapore Management University, Singapore
Dirk Neumann	University of Freiburg, Germany
Omer F. Rana	Cardiff University, UK

Sponsoring Institutions

Seoul National University, Seoul, South Korea
University of Cardiff, Cardiff, UK
University of Antwerp, Antwerp, Belgium
Technical University of Berlin, Germany
Springer LNCS, Heidelberg, Germany

Table of Contents

Session A: Market Mechanisms, Pricing and Negotiation

A Protocol Development Framework for SLA Negotiations in Cloud
and Service Computing 1
  Edwin Yaqub, Ramin Yahyapour, Philipp Wieder, and Kuan Lu

The Use of Provision Point Contracts for Improving Cloud
Infrastructure Utilisation 16
  Owen Rogers and Dave Cliff

An Economic Agent Maximizing Cloud Provider Revenues under a
Pay-as-you-Book Pricing Model 29
  *Felipe Díaz Sánchez, Elias A. Doumith, Sawsan Al Zahr, and
  Maurice Gagnaire*

Session B: Resource Allocation, Scheduling and Admission Control

Economic Co-allocation and Advance Reservation of Network and
Computational Resources in Grids 46
  Wim Depoorter, Kurt Vanmechelen, and Jan Broeckhove

Revenue-Based Resource Management on Shared Clouds for
Heterogenous Bursty Data Streams 61
  *Rafael Tolosana-Calasanz, José Ángel Bañares, Congduc Pham, and
  Omer F. Rana*

The ISQoS Grid Broker for Temporal and Budget Guarantees 76
  Richard Kavanagh and Karim Djemame

Session C: Work-in-Progress on Tools and Techniques for Cost-Efficient Service Selection

Let the Clouds Compute: Cost-Efficient Workload Distribution in
Infrastructure Clouds 91
  *Ulrich Lampe, Melanie Siebenhaar, Ronny Hans,
  Dieter Schuller, and Ralf Steinmetz*

A Declarative Recommender System for Cloud Infrastructure Services
Selection   102
  Miranda Zhang, Rajiv Ranjan, Surya Nepal, Michael Menzel, and
  Armin Haller

Retrieving, Storing, Correlating and Distributing Information for Cloud
Management   114
  Spyridon V. Gogouvitis, Gregory Katsaros, Dimosthenis Kyriazis,
  Athanasios Voulodimos, Roman Talyansky, and Theodora Varvarigou

Session D: Market Modeling

On Local Separation of Processing and Storage in
Infrastructure-as-a-Service   125
  Jörn Künsemöller and Holger Karl

Value Creation in IT Service Platforms through Two-Sided Network
Effects   139
  Netsanet Haile and Jörn Altmann

Session E: Trust

Cheat-Proof Trust Model for Cloud Computing Markets   154
  Mario Macías and Jordi Guitart

Trust Factors for the Usage of Cloud Computing in Small and Medium
Sized Craft Enterprises   169
  Holger Kett, Harriet Kasper, Jürgen Falkner, and Anette Weisbecker

Session F: Cloud Computing in Education

A Cost Analysis of Cloud Computing for Education   182
  Fernando Koch, Marcos D. Assunção, and Marco A.S. Netto

Delivering Cloud Services with QoS Requirements: An Opportunity
for ICT SMEs   197
  Alfonso Quarati, Daniele D'Agostino, Antonella Galizia,
  Matteo Mangini, and Andrea Clematis

Session G: Work-in-Progress on Cloud Adoption and Business Models

A Mixed-Methods Research Approach to Investigate the Transition
from on-Premise to on-Demand Software Delivery   212
  Francesco Novelli

Towards a Federated Cloud Ecosystem: Enabling Managed Cloud
Service Consumption 223
    Dirk Thatmann, Mathias Slawik, Sebastian Zickau, and Axel Küpper

Business Models for Semantic Content Providers 234
    Monika Kaczmarek and Agata Filipowska

Author Index 245

A Protocol Development Framework for SLA Negotiations in Cloud and Service Computing

Edwin Yaqub, Ramin Yahyapour, Philipp Wieder, and Kuan Lu

Gesellschaft für wissenschaftliche Datenverarbeitung mbH Göttingen (GWDG)
Am Faßberg 11, Göttingen 37077, Germany
{edwin.yaqub,ramin.yahyapour,philipp.wieder,kuan.lu}@gwdg.de

Abstract. As businesses transit towards cloud and service oriented economy, agents are employed to efficiently negotiate service level agreements (SLAs) on services procured automatically to match changes in demand. This 'pay-as-you-go' trading model affords flexibility with reliability, but requires customized and seamless interactions enabled by negotiation protocols that best serve the market domain. To this end, we present a domain-independent framework based on a protocol development lifecycle, comprising four distinct phases namely modeling, verification, rule-based implementation and generic execution.

We illustrate all phases by introducing the *Simple Bilateral Negotiation Protocol* (SBNP) - a multi-tier, multi-round and customizable negotiation protocol. We exemplify its adoption among chains of service providers that serve SaaS, PaaS and IaaS offerings. We show that SBNP is *well-formed, deterministic* and *deadlock-free*. We evaluate state space scalability for SBNP and verify its correctness using *Linear Temporal Logic* (LTL). Finally, we show that rule-based implementation allows for generic execution of multiple protocols on our negotiation platform, which provides businesses the agility to sustain competitive advantage.

Keywords: Service Level Agreement (SLA) Negotiation, Negotiation Protocols, Automated Trading, Cloud Computing, Service Computing.

1 Introduction

Service providers are taking an increasing interest in cloud based technologies [2]. Cloud Computing affords a flexible business model where an increase or decrease in service's demand can be elastically applied to the complete stack of services at the background. This has led organizations to develop and offer cloud-based services using service oriented architectures (SOA) which provide a modular and interoperable view of services as first class tradeable entities. According to NIST [21], Cloud Computing provides three service models: *Software as a Service* (SaaS), *Platform as a Service* (PaaS) and *Infrastructure as a Service* (IaaS). Despite the decoupled ownership that emerges from this divisioning, in practice, a network of QoS-aware services across the three models is often needed to match customer requirements with provider's capabilities. This is achieved by negotiating a *Service Level Agreement* (SLA) using a negotiation protocol.

K. Vanmechelen, J. Altmann, and O.F. Rana (Eds.): GECON 2012, LNCS 7714, pp. 1–15, 2012.

As a new era of service procurement dawns, it is envisioned that markets especially in the area of Utility Computing, Internet of Things (IoT) and Internet of Services (IoS) would require negotiation protocols to expose their offerings to a whole new business landscape where electronic agents are the prime citizens. As these businesses transit towards cloud and service based automated economy, a standard approach to develop and adopt heterogenous protocols in a homogenous manner is indeed needed and therefore provides the motivation for this work.

To cater for broader contracting possibilities, providers advertise their service(s) using a machine readable SLA template [18] which lists negotiable QoS terms (e.g., performance, scalability, availability, redundancy, backup, etc.) - each offering a discrete or continuous range of values to choose from. Thus, SLA template may encapsulate a huge contract space [23] and SLA negotiation is the key to reach an agreement where QoS terms are fixed to single values.

In self organizing and dynamic service economies, negotiations are automated among agents. The rules of their engagement are defined by a negotiation protocol. The SLA@SOI research project [17], developed an SLA Management architecture [24], where an agent is represented using an *SLA Manager Instance* equipped with a generic negotiation platform - the *Protocol Engine* (PE) [6] and a domain specific *Planning and Optimization* component (POC) to realize SLA negotiations. At any time, the POC provides a consolidated view of resource utilization, but it is the negotiation protocols and the PE that provide the glue to coordinate complex interactions in an end-to-end seamless manner. This is essential for service providers who follow the popular trends of *composing* and *aggregating* (often cross-organizational) services [26] on the fly.

Additionally, in Cloud Computing, agents interact in multi-tier service chains due to cross-tier dependencies of *capacital* and *actuating* nature, as shown in Fig. 1. This serves as our lead use case where at the top level, a customer negotiates an SLA with a SaaS provider for business services. SaaS providers fork services for PaaS providers (e.g., OpenShift[1] or CloudFoundry[2] based) and benchmark these in advance to estimate performance and scalability terms [25]. SaaS provider negotiates an SLA with a PaaS provider, shielding itself from hosting and administration complexities while enjoying the required QoS. Consequently, the PaaS provider negotiates an SLA with an IaaS provider (e.g., OpenStack[3] based), acquiring virtual resources for its PaaS cloud and provisions the software on them. Advancements in technology now allow automation at all levels.

Problem Statement. The service chains may have different structures depending on the contracting (or subcontracting) workflow of agents e.g., reactive interactions that are quotation based, proactive interactions that are template based, or a mix of both. Interactions may be governed by a single protocol or encompass a pluralistic hierarchy. Further, messaging may be required in serial,

---

[1] https://openshift.redhat.com

[2] http://www.cloudfoundry.com

[3] http://www.openstack.org

parallel or hybrid fashion. Although considerable literature exists on negotiations in general, most work related to developing and executing custom negotiation protocols has been non-holistic (see Section 6); addressing some issues while ignoring others. Serious stakeholders interested in automated negotiations are confronted with gaps between engineering (design, implementation), functional (correctness) and non-functional (scalability) properties of the protocol that hinder adoption.

Contribution. Addressing these gaps, we present a holistic protocol development framework for SLA negotiations in cloud and service based systems. We claim that the flexibility of our approach empowers organizations to efficiently create, test and introduce *niche* protocols that can enlarge their market share.

The remainder of this paper is organized as follows. In Section 2, we introduce our framework which is based on a Protocol Development Lifecycle (PDLC), comprising four distinct phases namely modeling, verification, rule-based implementation and generic execution. In Sections 3, 4 and 5, we illustrate these phases respectively by introducing a multi-tier, multi-round and customizable negotiation protocol - the *Simple Bilateral Negotiation Protocol* (SBNP). In Section 6, we discuss related work. Finally, we conclude the paper in Section 7.

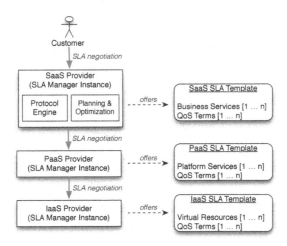

Fig. 1. SLA Negotiation Service Chain

2 Protocol Development Framework

Developing protocols can be a complicated task [22]. Therefore, we base our framework on a systematic Protocol Development Lifecycle (PDLC), as shown in Fig. 2. Firstly, a representation formalism is chosen which can unambiguously model interaction semantics. This is vital for cross-organizational understanding. Secondly, the correctness of a protocol is verified. Ideally, this includes analyzing

Fig. 2. Protocol Development Lifecycle

protocol's memory requirements so scalability limits are evaluated. Thirdly, a reference implementation is needed for adoption and trial. Finally, we show that rule-based implementation allows for generic execution of multiple protocols.

2.1   Negotiation Protocols - State Based Specification

Central to our idea of specifying a negotiation protocol is the negotiation process itself. Negotiation process represents the act of negotiation (or renegotiation). At any point in time, it resides in one of the states from a finite (but extensible) set S={*waiting, initiate, renegotiate, initialized, customize, customized, negotiate, negotiated, decide, cancel, terminated, agreed*} of states. A negotiation protocol therefore, can be expressed as a network of finite state machines (FSM) that communicate in a certain manner under a negotiation session. Interaction between machines takes place by passing messages, methods for which are defined in a negotiation interface. Table 1 describes states, messages to gain entry to these and their alphabetic abbreviation. States are distinguished as *request* and *response* states and messages trigger a transition from the former to the latter.

Table 1. Protocol States, Messages and Alphabets

State	Message	Alphabet	Description
waiting	-	-	Wait for negotiation commencement request
initiate	initiateNegotiation	i	Request to initiate negotiation
renegotiate	renegotiateAgreement	r	Request to renegotiate an existing SLA
initialized	-	-	Response state for *initiate* and *renegotiate*
customize	customizeParameters	u	Request to modify protocol's default parameters
customized	-	-	Response state for *customize*
negotiate	negotiateOffer	o	Request that provides an SLA offer
negotiated	-	-	Response state for *negotiate*
cancel	cancelNegotiation	c	Request to gracefully cancel negotiation session
decide	createAgreement	a	Request to create an SLA of proposed (final) offer
terminated	-	-	Response state that ends negotiation unsuccessfully
agreed	-	-	Response state that ends negotiation successfully
-	successful response	s	A positive response message
-	unsuccessful response	e	A negative response message

Generally, a negotiation process is blocked in the *waiting* state until initiateNegotiation or renegotiateAgreement message arrives, resulting in the *initialized* state which establishes a negotiation session. A customizeParameters message is used optionally for a "customization" mechanism that we introduced in [6], to rationally fix protocol parameters in a mutually consensual manner among the agents before exchanging offers. Parameters (shown in table 2) are then enforced by the negotiation platform throughout the negotiation session.

Objective. Our objective is that in whichever way these machines communicate, they remain synchronized such that deadlocks and livelocks are absent, cycles (if any) are bounded and invalid end states do not occur. Moreover, the interaction must conform to custom requirements. For SBNP, these include that either one or no SLA is created among each negotiating-pair. Further, the negotiation conclusion and SLA creation sequence should rule out under and over commitments when subcontracting. All these factors motivate us to use Communicating Finite State Machines (CFSM) [3][4] formalism.

Table 2. Protocol Parameters

Parameter	Description
Process_Timeout	Life time of negotiation process
Customization_Rounds	Rounds for fixing protocol parameters
Negotiation_Rounds	Rounds for exchanging offers
Max_Counter_Offers	Offers sent as response to received offer
Optional_Critique_OnQoS	Critique on term value e.g., *increase*, *decrease*, *change* or *acceptable*
Quiescence_Time	Inactivity time among negotiating agents
Chain_Length	Allowed length of negotiation service chain

3   Modeling

Given the set of states S and a non-empty finite set of negotiating agents $A = \{a_0, a_1, ...a_n\}$, we define SBNP as a network of CFSM(s) $\mathcal{A}$ such that one machine in this network represents one negotiating agent. In this context, the term agent and machine can be used interchangeably. Agents communicate solely by passing messages over first-in-first-out (FIFO) channels. Then, for all $a \in \{A\}$

$$\mathcal{A} = (\mathcal{A}_a, I, F)$$
$$\mathcal{A}_a = (S_a, \rightarrow) \text{ is a finite state machine}$$
$$S_a \text{ is a set of local states}$$
$$\rightarrow \subseteq S_a \times Act_a \times S_a \text{ is a set of local transitions}$$
$$Act_a \in Act \text{ is a set of local actions}$$
$$I \text{ is a set of global initial states, and}$$
$$F \text{ is a set of global final states.}$$

The transmission over channels is ideally reliable. The set $Act = \{send, receive\}$ is a set of allowed actions in $\mathcal{A}$ consumed by the local transitions that take $\mathcal{A}_a$ from one state to another. The semantics of $send$ for a are $Act_a^! = \{(a_i!^m a_{i+1})\}$ and of its corresponding $receive$ are $Act_a^? = \{(a_{i+1}?^m a_i)\}$ where $0 \leq i < |A|$ and $\{(a_i, a_{i+1}), (a_{i+1}, a_i) \in A \times A\} = Ch$ is a set of outgoing and incoming channels per agent-pair. Intuitively, agent a_i sends a message m to agent a_{i+1} over the channel (a_i, a_{i+1}). Similarly, it receives a message m sent by agent a_{i+1} over the channel (a_{i+1}, a_i). Agent a_{i+1} receives message m from a_i over the channel

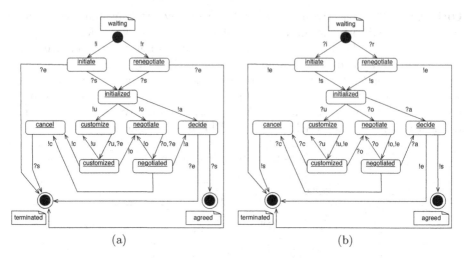

Fig. 3. Simple Bilateral Negotiation Protocol (SBNP) (a) Sender (b) Receiver

(a_i, a_{i+1}) and sends to a_i over the channel (a_{i+1}, a_i). The symbol $m \in \Sigma$ where $\Sigma = \{i, r, u, o, c, a, s, e\}$ is a set of alphabets representing the communicated message, abbreviated as shown in Table 1.

Agents (and hence the FSMs) have the "sender" and "receiver" roles; each of which could be a customer or provider of a service. Negotiation is always initiated by the sender. The behavior of SBNP for sender and receiver, is shown in Fig. 3(a) and 3(b) modeled as a CFSM. As evident, the SBNP provides multi-round negotiation as well as a take-it-or-leave-it interaction. Moreover, a multi-round customization is allowed prior to offer exchange. To realize SBNP for the use case of interest, we propose two formation schemes and give an action-to-agent mapping function for each.

3.1 Exactly Two Agents

The first scheme realizes the trivial scenario where $|A| = 2$. One agent assumes the role of a sender while the other that of a receiver. A sequence of communicative actions are executed by agents as runs of $\mathcal{A}$ on words $w = \alpha_0^! \alpha_1^? \alpha_2^! \alpha_3^? \in Act^*$ where action-to-agent mapping is given by the function:

$$f(\alpha, a) = \begin{cases} (\alpha_0^! \alpha_3^?) \mapsto a_0 \ sender \\ (\alpha_1^? \alpha_2^!) \mapsto a_1 \ receiver \end{cases}$$

3.2 Chain of Agents

The second scheme realizes a service chain spanning an arbitrary number $|A| = n$ of agents and $n > 2$. Each agent represents a single node in a choreographically organized linear topology as shown in Fig. 1. The nodes are classified into three categories: a start node, possibly multiple middle nodes and a last node.

The idea is to use *nesting* to invoke the same action on the next node in the chain and return the response accordingly.

This reveals runs of $\mathcal{A}$ on the words $w = \alpha_0^! \alpha_1^? \alpha_2^! \alpha_3^? ... \alpha_j^? \in Act^*$ where $0 \leq j < (n-1)*4$. We split w into two equal halves; a prefix $\pi = \alpha_0^! \alpha_1^? ... \alpha_k^!$ representing the forward propagation, a suffix $\bar{\pi} = \alpha_{k+1}^! \alpha_{k+2}^? ... \alpha_j^?$ representing the backward propagation and $w = \pi \bar{\pi}$. Here, the send and receive actions are mapped to agents in the chain by the function:

$$
f(\alpha, a) = \begin{cases}
\alpha_0^! \mapsto a_0 & startnode \\
(\alpha_{2l-1}^? \alpha_{2l}^!) \mapsto a_{n'} & middlenode \\
(\alpha_k^? \alpha_{k+1}^!) \mapsto a_{n-1} & lastnode \\
(\alpha_{2l'}^? \alpha_{2l'-1}^!) \mapsto a_{n'} & middlenode \\
\alpha_j^? \mapsto a_0 & startnode
\end{cases}
$$

For π, consider $0 < l < k$ where $0 \leq k < (n-1)*2$ and n' increases within the range $0 < n' < |\mathcal{A}| - 2$. Similarly, for $\bar{\pi}$, consider $0 < l' < j - (k+1)$, where n' now decreases in its range. It can be seen that π and $\bar{\pi}$ are orthogonal copies of each other irrespective of the message m used by the communicative actions.

3.3   Well-Formedness

Considering the two schemes given above, it becomes clear that for SBNP, all $w \in Act^*$ are *proper* as:

- A *receive* action is always preceded by a *send* action in all prefixes σ of w i.e., $|\sigma|_{\alpha^!} \geq |\sigma|_{\alpha^?}$ for all allowed m on all channels in Ch. An m is allowed $\subseteq \sum$ over a state as given by the protocol's FSM.
- Messages are sent and received respecting the FIFO policy at all channels.

All words w runnable on $\mathcal{A}$ follow the same pattern and are proper. Finally, the language accepted by SBNP, $\mathcal{L}(\mathcal{A})$ is made up only of proper words that are also well-formed i.e., $|w_{\alpha^!}| = |w_{\alpha^?}|$ for all allowed m on all channels in Ch in both schemes presented here. This establishes SBNP as a well-formed protocol.

3.4   Determinism

A protocol is deterministic if in any state and any given input, there exits exactly one transition. Like most real world protocols, SBNP is also deterministic.

3.5   Deadlock-Freedom

SBNP is deadlock-free by definition, as in any state, there exists a possible sequence of actions that take the machine to a final state. For SBNP, it means that each negotiation can be concluded, either successfully or unsuccessfully.

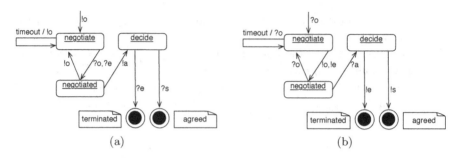

Fig. 4. Timeout at (a) Sender (b) Receiver

4 Verification

The next phase in our PDLC is *Verification* - an automated process that examines the protocol against standard as well as custom behavioral properties. Verification was performed by encoding SBNP in the validation language PROMELA[4] and fed to Spin model checker [9]. Verification may help prevent bugs in design that may go undetected by a human. This became apparent as we attempted to handle unreliability of transmission which causes issues like loss, corruption and duplication of messages in a distributed system, using traditional timeouts.

4.1 Timeouts

Fig. 4(a) shows a partial view of protocol when timeout is applied (only) at sender side to the *negotiate* state for demonstration. A cyclic retransmission of message builds a queue at receiver while the sender may meanwhile transit to the *decide* state, where a single (late arriving) error response of its earlier SLA offer may further transit it to the *terminated* state while the receiver is still active. Moreover, a late arriving agreement request could be accepted by the receiver creating a one-sided SLA while the sender has already aborted. Spin instantly detects these deadlocks as the system may land in invalid end states.

Similarly, Fig. 4(b) shows timeout applied (only) at receiver side to the *negotiate* state - intended to limit counter offer generation time. Here, due to non determinism between either sending an error response or waiting for the next offer, the machine may transit in favor of the latter. This is detected by Spin as a deadlock since both sides end up waiting to receive an input from each other.

If timeouts are applied at both sender and receiver sides simultaneously, Spin's Depth First search shows that above deadlocks are still possible, while its Breadth First search reveals that a livelock is now possible as well. This is because on one side, the sender may continuously timeout, prompting retransmissions while the receiver may remain trapped into its own timeout cycle.

For our implementation, we therefore decided on an alternate solution that offered a safer trade-off. We adopted process level timeout with optional request

---

[4] SBNP validation program encoded in PROMELA is available at
http://sourceforge.net/p/ey-negprotocol/code

level quiescence. If a request or a response is lost, the machine remains quiescent (i.e., blocked but not deadlocked) in its current state until a "Quiescence_Time" parameter times out, after which, each side voluntarily relinquishes the session maintaining system consistency, saving time and resources.

Corrupted and *Duplicated* messages can be identified using the facilities of the negotiation platform. If a message is identified as corrupted, it is simply responded to by an error response. Likewise, if a message is identified as a duplicate i.e., it is found in the list of offers already received, its corresponding counter offer(s) can be resent by simply fetching it from the list of sent offers.

Another important issue in protocol development is that of *unexpected reception*. The unexpected reception is to validation what unspecified reception is to well-formedness. An unexpected reception refers to the arrival of an "unallowed" input m at a state. This is resolved by a flushing mechanism which receives the message, responds back with an error response and maintains the current state. Although not shown in Fig. 3(a) and 3(b) for sake of brevity, unexpected receptions are handled by an "else" self-transition.

4.2 Evaluating Negotiation Complexity

An important but little explored area for negotiation protocols is that of their complexity. SBNP is channel based system whose state space complexity [28] is given by the number of components N and capacity of involved channels K as:

$$\prod_{i=1}^{N}(|\#\text{program locations}| \prod_{x}^{x \in V} |dom(x)|) \prod_{j=1}^{K} |dom(c_j)|^{cap^{c_j}}$$

where V is the set of variables from the verification program, $dom(x)$ is the domain of variable x and $dom(c_j)$ is the domain of channel c_j and depends on the type of messages while the cap^{c_j} refers to the number of messages that may travel over it at one time. The number of program locations refers here to the number of machine states. Considering a single program variable $x \in V$ to hold outgoing and/or incoming message m, $dom(x) = 2$ for start node, 8 for all middle nodes (if any) and 6 for the last node. $dom(c) = 6$ and 2 respectively, for each forward and backward propagating channels per agent-pair.

Fig. 5(a) shows how state space scales when $N = \{2\}$ agents exchange an increasing number of offers $cap^c = \{1, ..., 10\}$. In this case, state space grows exponentially exceeding a million states when 7 offers are exchanged. The large state space however is mostly due to the unreachable states generated by cartesian product. We distill our analysis to reachable protocol states by using Spin which uses partial order reduction optimization to generate only reachable states. An out-of-box verification by Spin generated 129 to 961 states respectively for $N = \{2, ..., 10\}$ agents exchanging a single offer. The verification inspected standard properties like deadlock, invalid end states, acceptance cycles and

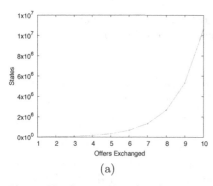
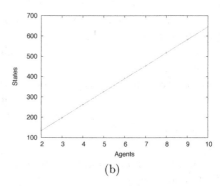

(a)   (b)

Fig. 5. Verification Results: State space scalability with respect to (a) 2 agents exchanging multiple offers (b) multiple agents exchanging 1 offer among each agent-pair

unspecified receptions. These held good for SBNP. The graph in Fig. 5(b) revealed a linear increase in state space establishing SBNP as an efficient protocol when single offer is exchanged, and emphasizing the need for Chain_Length parameter.

4.3   Verifying Correctness

We used Spin to verify SBNP against correctness requirements expressed in LTL. LTL can succinctly represent a behavior spanning a temporal sequence. We abide by the property specification patterns given by Dwyer [10] and avoid the *next* operator which may disobey stutter-invariance under partial order reduction. A brief description of LTL formulae (all of which held good for SBNP) follows.

$\Diamond\Box(one\_or\_no\_sla)$: Eventually, it will always be the case that either one or no SLA is created as a result of negotiation. The proposition $one\_or\_no\_sla$ checks that the condition is satisfied at each agent.

$\Box(l\_agr \rightarrow \Diamond s\_agr)$: It is always the case that if an agreement is reached at the last node, eventually an agreement at the start node will follow. This property implements the Response pattern. Its scalable variant $\Box(l\_agr \rightarrow \Diamond((m\_agr \land \neg s\_agr) \land \Diamond s\_agr))$ extends this behavior to a multi-agent negotiating chain, illustrated here by using the Response Chain (1-stimulus, 2-response) pattern. The property reads that it will always be the case that an agreement at the last node is eventually followed by a sequence of states where firstly, the middle node reaches an agreement and start node has not reached agreement, and secondly, a state eventually follows where the start node also reaches agreement. Thus, SBNP ensures that necessary subcontracting is successfully achieved before an SLA is made with the end customer.

$\Diamond s\_agr \rightarrow (\neg s\_agr \cup (l\_agr \land \neg s\_agr))$: This property implements the Precedence pattern, acts as a converse of the Response property and ensures that an agreement reached eventually at the start node is preceded by an agreement at the last node. Thus, SBNP rules out subcontracting SLAs with third party providers, without ever reaching an SLA with the end customer. Its scalable variant $\Diamond s\_agr \rightarrow (\neg s\_agr \cup ((l\_agr \land \neg s\_agr) \land \Diamond(\neg s\_agr \cup m\_agr)))$ extends the behavior to a multi-agent negotiation chain, by implementing the Precedence Chain (2-cause,1-effect) pattern.

$\square(l\_end \rightarrow \Diamond(s\_end))$: This property examines the negotiation conclusion sequence by implementing the Response pattern. The propositions l_end and s_end capture *agreed* and *terminated* states, where negotiation concludes (successfully or unsuccessfully). The property reads, it is always the case that if the last node concludes the negotiation, eventually, the start node does the same. Its variant $\square(l\_end \rightarrow \Diamond((m\_end \wedge \neg s\_end) \rightarrow \Diamond s\_end))$ extends the sequence to a chain.

$\Diamond s\_end \rightarrow (\neg s\_end \cup (l\_end \wedge \neg s\_end))$: This property examines the negotiation conclusion sequence conversely. It reads that the start node concludes negotiation, preceded by the conclusion of negotiation at the last node. Its variant $\Diamond s\_end \rightarrow (\neg s\_end \cup ((l\_end \wedge \neg s\_end) \wedge \Diamond(\neg s\_end \cup m\_end)))$ extends the behavior to a negotiation chain.

$\square\Diamond((offers\_exchanged \wedge s\_neg) \cup \neg s\_neg)$: This is an essential property for any multi-round negotiation protocol. It reads, always when the agent representing the start node enters *negotiate* state, eventually multiple offers can be exchanged among agents, until the starting agent transits out of *negotiate* state.

5   Implementation and Execution

We aim for a generic negotiation platform that provides a standard software machinery, dedicated to execute multiple protocols within a single *SLA Manager Instance*. The benefits of this approach include ease of maintenance and a common base to test and try heterogenous protocols in a homogenous manner. This requires architectural decisions related to the implementation of the protocol so that the assumptions made by the negotiation platform are met.

5.1   A Generic Negotiation Platform

Under the SLA@SOI project, we developed a generic negotiation platform called the "*Protocol Engine* (PE)" for bilateral protocols [6]. PE orchestrates negotiation on behalf of the agent by executing SBNP or another protocol. For lack of space, here we only list the principles PE is broadly based on.

– Synchronous (web service based) communication is supported where two agents engage in a request-response style messaging that respects Run-to-Completion (RTC) execution model.
– PE maintains a session per negotiation which stores received and sent offers.
– PE is domain-agnostic and loosely couples with the domain-specific POC which implements a negotiation strategy. Interface based design is used to realize this loose coupling which maintains separation of concerns.
– PE is state-ignorant. Hence, it needs not to possess the knowledge to judge unexpected receptions or protocol states - a feature specified in the protocol.
– Timeouts are specified in the protocol and simply enforced by PE.

5.2   Rule-Based Implementation of Negotiation Protocols

We implement negotiation protocols using declarative rules which encode executable logic using *"If-Then"* clauses, providing a natural mapping to describe FSM semantics and bridging the gap between modeling and implementation. Likely, SBNP is encoded as rules in a single document, made publicly available for shared access among agents. The PE passes incoming messages as events to a local Rule Engine which executes the protocol rules in its working memory. The rules follow a simple encoding scheme which inspects the event and current state (in the *If* part) to produce a feedback (in the *Then* part) indicating if the event was successfully or unsuccessfully processed, with possible description of aftermath. The encoding scheme allows a *plug & play* relationship between protocols and the PE. Rule-based approach also brings inherent advantages i.e., the protocol remains human readable as well as machine interpretable.

Primarily, rules enforce protocol's interaction sequence. Additionally, the PE consults POC to process incoming offers and generate counter offers. Listing 1.1 shows an interaction rule belonging to receiver state machine where *initialized* state transits to *negotiate* state upon receipt of an offer.

```
rule "Initialized_To_Negotiate_Transition"
  if
    initializedState : State(name == INITIALIZED, status == RUNNING);
    event : Event(name == OfferArrivedEvent);
  then
    initializedState.setStatus(STOPPED); insert(new State(NEGOTIATE));
    event.setProcessedSuccessfully(true); retract(event);
  end
```

Listing 1.1. Transition Rule

Interaction rules are complemented with domain-sensitive rules that afford providers the agility to sustain their competitive advantage. This includes rules that white list, black list, assign high or low rank to a negotiating party based on past experience and current policy. Domain-sensitive rules allow to soften or harden high level negotiation behavior to rapidly adjust to changing markets[5].

6   Related Work

ICNP [19] is a popular quotation-oriented negotiation protocol for establishing agreement with one out of possibly multiple negotiators. Service providers seem tilted towards bilateral template based offerings. WSAG [15] is a template based specification and protocol, but it provides a limited take-it-or-leave-it interaction. Its extension WSAGN [16] allows for multi-round negotiations, but does not rule out signaling scenarios where both parties may simultaneously send messages which may cause deadlock. WSAG/WSAGN use a FSM to model states of an offer, while we employ CFSM to model the entire negotiation process.

---

[5] SBNP rule file (including interaction and domain-sensitive rules) is available at http://sourceforge.net/p/ey-negprotocol/code

ICNP, WSAG and WSAGN specifications do not provide formal modeling, verification or complexity analysis as we do for SBNP, rather they rely on informal models like sequence diagrams which capture partial behaviors only.

In our previous work [6], we used single state machine to specify a negotiation protocol at a highly abstract level. In this work, we extend our scope into a framework by relating formal modeling and verification to our rule-based implementation and generic execution phases. We demonstrate concrete modeling of a negotiation protocol using CFSM and verify it using Spin [9]. We argue that other protocols can be developed similarly following our example. Other works have used Petri-nets to model trade procedures or business protocols as in [5]. Yeung has used Hoare's CSP to model a contract net protocol for service chains in manufacturing control [7]. Kraenke et al. used a variant of ICNP for logistic service chains and verified it using Spin. Kamel et al. [27] have used Spin to thoroughly validate the GIOP protocol against specification expressed in LTL.

Somewhat closer to our ideas, [14] has developed an XML language that extends WSAG for encoding protocols and a common execution platform, but no formal approach is used or suggested to model or verify protocols. In contrast to XML, we use rules for implementation and do not extend other frameworks. The SeCSe project [29] provides a mechanism to define custom negotiation protocols using a state based design and rule based implementation, but does not address verification of behavior. Further, it is a marketplace that must be entrusted with individual objectives. In contrast, our methodology encourages confidentiality of objectives, a loose coupling of strategies from negotiation platform, while also providing hooks to reveal certain hints if protocol is so customized - a mechanism we introduced in [6] but not adequately addressed in current standards [16][19].

Rules have been used to specify negotiation protocols by Wurman in [12] and Jennings in [13]. These approaches however tend to ignore the demarcation that we emphasize between interaction behavior and the negotiating strategy. Further, in these and other works [11], a protocol's communicative acts are encouraged to be standardized as a separate library (as in [20]), while we represent acts as an interface (similar to [15]) which is more in line with SOA principles [1].

7   Conclusions and Future Work

In this paper, we presented a holistic framework for developing and executing negotiation protocols. We introduced SBNP and showed by its example that CFSM can unambiguously model negotiation protocols. For verification, we advocated Spin model checker and illustrated how correctness specifications expressed as LTL formulae were verified. We evaluated memory scalability and discussed advantages a rule-based implementation and generic execution brings to businesses.

As future extensions of our work, we are interested in developing graphical tools that assist protocol authors in modeling, verification and implementation phases by automatically generating the source code. Further, we are interested in simulating negotiation strategies using our platform to realize optimal SLAs, by relating business objectives of providers to their service offerings.

This requires devising algorithms that correlate cross-tier capacities. Our objective is to investigate the relationship between negotiation strategies and the negotiation protocols in order to derive intelligent guidelines for cloud centered markets.

Acknowledgments. The research leading to these results is partially supported by the European Community's Seventh Framework Programme (FP7/2001-2013) under grant agreement no. 216556.

References

1. Foster, I.: Service-Oriented Science. Science 308, 814–817 (2005)
2. Rangan, K.: The Cloud Wars: $100+ billion at stake, Merrill Lynch Technical Report (2008)
3. Genest, B., Kuske, D., Muscholl, A.: A Kleene Theorem and Model Checking Algorithms for Existentially Bounded Communicating Automata. Inf. Comput. 204(6), 920–956 (2006)
4. Bollig, B., Katoen, J.-P., Kern, C., Leucker, M.: Learning Communicating Automata from MSCs. IEEE Transactions on Software Engineering (TSE) 36(3), 390–408 (2010)
5. Daskalopulu, A.: Model Checking Contractual Protocols. In: 13th Annual Conference, Frontiers in Artificial Intelligence and Applications Series, pp. 35–47 (2000)
6. Yaqub, E., Wieder, P., Kotsokalis, C., Mazza, V., Pasquale, L., Rueda, J.L., Gómez, S.G., Chimeno, A.E.: A Generic Platform for Conducting SLA Negotiations. In: Service Level Agreements for Cloud Computing, Part 4, pp. 187–206. Springer (2011)
7. Yeung, W.L.: Behavioral modeling and verification of multi-agent systems for manufacturing control. Journal of Expert Systems with Applications 38, 13555–13562
8. Mordechai, B.-A.: Principles of the Spin Model Checker, 1st edn. Springer (2008)
9. Holzmann, G.J.: The Model Checker Spin. IEEE Transactions on Software Engineering 23(5), 279–295 (1997)
10. Dwyer, M.B., Avrunin, G.S., Corbett, J.C.: Patterns in Property Specifications for Finite-State Verification. In: 21st IEEE International Conference on Software Engineering (ICSE), pp. 411–420 (1999)
11. Karaenke, P., Kirn, S.: Towards Model Checking & Simulation of a Multi-tier Negotiation Protocol for Service Chains. In: Proc. of the 9th International Joint Conference on Autonomous Agents and Multiagent Systems, AAMAS (2010)
12. Wurman, P.R., Wellman, M.P., Walsh, W.E.: Specifying Rules for Electronic Auctions. AI Magazine 23(3), 15–23 (2002)
13. Lomuscio, A.R., Wooldridge, M., Jennings, N.R.: A Classification Scheme for Negotiation in Electronic Commerce. Journal of Group Decision and Negotiation 12(1), 31–56 (2003)
14. Hudert, S., Eymann, T., Ludwig, H., Wirtz, G.: A Negotiation Protocol Description Language for Automated SLA Negotiations. In: Proc. of the IEEE Conference on Commerce and Enterprise Computing (CEC), pp. 162–169 (2009)
15. Andrieux, A., Czajkowski, K., Dan, A., Keahey, K., Ludwig, H., Nakata, T., Pruyne, J., Rofrano, J., Tuecke, S., Xu, M.: Web Services Agreement Specification, WS-Agreement (2007), http://www.ogf.org/documents/GFD.107.pdf

16. Waeldrich, O., Battré, D., Brazier, F., Clark, K., Oey, M., Papaspyrou, A., Wieder, P., Ziegler, W.: WS-Agreement Negotiation Version 1.0 Specification (2011), `http://ogf.org/documents/GFD.193.pdf`
17. SLA@SOI project (2011), `http://sourceforge.net/projects/sla-at-soi`
18. Kearney, K.T., Torelli, F.: The SLA Model. In: Service Level Agreements For Cloud Computing, Part 4, pp. 43–67. Springer (2011)
19. FIPA Iterated Contract Net Interaction Protocol Specification (2002), `http://www.fipa.org/specs/fipa00030/SC00030H.pdf`
20. FIPA ACL Message Structure Specification (2002), `http://www.fipa.org/specs/fipa00061/SC00061G.pdf`
21. Liu, F., Tong, J., Mao, J., Bohn, R., Messina, J., Badger, L., Leaf, D.: NIST Cloud Computing Reference Architecture. Special Publication 500-292 (2011), `http://www.nist.gov/customcf/get_pdf.cfm?pub_id=909505`
22. Holzmann, G.J.: Design and Validation of Computer Protocols, 1st edn. Prentice Hall (1990)
23. Klein, M., Faratin, P., Sayama, H., Bar-Yam, Y.: Negotiating Complex Contracts. Journal of Group Decision and Negotiation 12, 111–125 (2003)
24. Theilmann, W., Happe, J., Kotsokalis, C., Edmonds, A., Kearney, K., Lambea, J.: A Reference Architecture for Multi-Level SLA Management. Journal of Internet Engineering 4(1), 289–298 (2010)
25. Boniface, M., Nasser, B., Papay, J., Phillips, S.C., Servin, A., Yang, X., Zlatev, Z., Gogouvitis, S.V., Katsaros, G., Konstanteli, K., Kousiouris, G., Menychtas, A., Kyriazis, D.: Platform-as-a-Service Architecture for Real-Time QoS Management in Clouds. In: International Conference on Internet and Web Applications and Services, ICIW (2010)
26. Haq, I.U., Schikuta, E.: Aggregation Patterns of Service Level Agreements. In: Proceedings of the 8th International Conference on Frontiers of Information Technology (2010)
27. Kamel, M., Leue, S.: Formalization and validation of the General Inter-ORB Protocol (GIOP) using PROMELA and SPIN. International Journal of Software Tools for Technology Transfer (STTT) 2, 394–409 (2000)
28. Katoen, J.-P.: Lecture on Model Checking (2005), `http://www-i2.informatik.rwth-aachen.de/Teaching/Course/MC/2005/mc_lec4.pdf`
29. SeCSE project (2008), `http://www.secse-project.eu`

The Use of Provision Point Contracts for Improving Cloud Infrastructure Utilisation

Owen Rogers and Dave Cliff

Department of Computer Science
University of Bristol, Bristol, UK
csorr@bristol.ac.uk, dc@cs.bris.ac.uk

Abstract. The on-demand capability of cloud computing allows consumers to purchase only the computing resources they require, as and when they need it. However, without a view of future demand, cloud providers' faces challenges in optimising the use of their infrastructure. In this paper, we propose a pricing method for cloud computing which allows providers to schedule virtual machines more efficiently through the use of *provision point contracts* (PPCs), commonly used for deal-of-the day websites such as Groupon. We show that the model can achieve a reduction of around 2% on the mean number of servers utilised. This may seem a modest percentage, but it can equate to freeing up thousands of physical servers in a single industrial-scale cloud computing data-centre. Additionally, our pricing model prevents discounts being offered where no increase in server efficiency is likely to be achieved. This suggests that the model can be implemented with little risk of it negatively affecting the efficiency of server provisioning. Finally, our results indicate that the cloud-service users who engage with the PPC method can achieve savings of over 20%.

Keywords: Scheduling, assurance contracts, provision point contracts, pricing.

1   Introduction

On-demand pricing for cloud computing resources, whereby consumers only pay for the resources they use, is generally recognised to offer potential cost saving benefits to consumers [1], [2]. Users have operational control of costs by being able to start and stop resources on demand, and they do not have to engage in the capital expenditure of building their own infrastructure, hiring IT systems support staff, or investing in maintenance of physical machinery. A federated cloud, whereby multiple cloud providers can interoperate, would in principle allow units of available cloud-computing resources to be traded as commodities on an open market, allowing for the price of resources to smoothly vary while the market mechanism enables matching of consumer demand to provider supply [3], [4].

But does on-demand purchasing of cloud-computing resources actually offer benefits to the provider? The on-demand nature of cloud computing means it is difficult for the provider to plan and prepare for the future. How can the provider ensure they are maximising profit and reducing cost if they must provide resources without knowledge of future demand?

K. Vanmechelen, J. Altmann, and O.F. Rana (Eds.): GECON 2012, LNCS 7714, pp. 16–28, 2012.
© Springer-Verlag Berlin Heidelberg 2012

Such knowledge offers benefits to providers in a number of ways. The provider must ensure that there is a physical capability for resource, but when consumers engage in on-demand pricing the providers must predict what usage is required, and ensure that the infrastructure is there.

Knowing when to invest in new infrastructure can be a difficult commercial decision. As manufacturing processes improve and economies of scale increase, the real cost of infrastructure decreases while its technological capability increases. So it is better for the provider to wait for as long as possible before investing in additional capability so they get the best value for money [5]. But how do they know when is the best time?

The provider has variable costs, which are related to the output being generated [6]. How can these be planned? Running a thousand servers instead of just one will require many more support staff and engineers: if too few are employed, failures can mount up and cause service outages or downtime. This downtime is not only costly in terms of SLA (Service Level Agreement) penalty fees and refunds, but also in terms of reputational risk; yet if too many are employed, expenditure is wasted on staff that are surplus to requirements.

It is also difficult to schedule customer instances to servers efficiently, without advance notification of usage. Most cloud computing providers require no duration of execution to be stipulated when the instance is started, and hence efficient scheduling of virtual machine instances that reduces or minimises the number of powered servers is a very tough challenge [7], [8].

In this paper, we propose a pricing model for cloud computing which combines on-demand pricing with a financial technology called a provision point mechanism. We show through simulation that a consumer taking advantage of the combined pricing schemes can reduce their expenditure and that the provider can use the information acquired through the sale of advance reservations to reduce the number of powered servers thereby reducing power costs, management overhead and carbon footprint.

2   Enterprise Infrastructure-as-a-Service

Different applications have different requirements for memory, CPU, and storage. For example, a computationally intensive application (such as image processing) may require more CPU capability than a web application.

Most infrastructure-as-a-service (IaaS) providers allow their customers to choose from a number of different virtual machines to meet these different requirements - these are referred to as instance types.

For the provider, this simply means partitioning up the infrastructure on individual servers into computational units that can then be combined to form different instance types. The number of computational units determines the size of the virtual machine. This is relatively simple for memory and storage which can be partitioned by dividing the total available in the server by the number of units required. However, splitting up a CPU chip between multiple virtual machines isn't quite so straightforward due to the complex scheduling and architecture of multi-core CPUs.

One option is to assign one CPU core to one computational unit, with each unit getting an equal share of memory and storage. In a typical blade-server motherboard housing two quad-core CPUs, this provides a total 8 units of computational power.

The total capacity of units on a server can be split amongst several virtual machines of varying sizes. In many commercial deployments, a virtual machine must be fully contained on a server for it to be able to access the resources assigned to it.

Most providers allow users to start virtual machines as soon as required, and to be subsequently billed for the period the machine was running. The provider might choose to start an instance on the first server where free space is available, with the objective of keeping the numbers of servers in operation to a minimum – a first-fit algorithm [9]. This strategy might be adopted to reduce power costs that vary with the number of powered servers, or to reduce the management overhead of monitoring and managing unused servers.

The optimum situation in this instance is when every computational unit in a server is assigned to a virtual machine before starting an additional server. However, the order that virtual machine requests arrive affects the efficiency of the server. Packing these differently sized virtual machines into the smallest number of servers is an instance of the classic bin-packing problem.

The first-fit algorithm has been shown to use no more than $2 + 1.7b$ bins, where b is the minimum number of bins used in the optimum solution [9]. An online bin-packing algorithm places an item before subsequent items are placed – the first-fit algorithm has been shown to be the optimum online bin-packing algorithm [10].

It is possible to migrate running virtual machines from server to server without affecting the machine's performance and this could provide a mechanism for increasing efficiency. However, performing this on large-scale datacentres is not an option due to the vast quantities of virtual machines and servers in use, and the potential for network bottlenecks as a result of the transfer of huge amounts of data [11].

If the IaaS provider has a forecast of future usage, she can schedule more efficiently by sorting customer requirements in descending order of size, and then assigning these to the first server with available space (offline bin-packing). This is often referred to as the first fit decreasing algorithm, and has been shown to allocate items using no more than $1 + (11/9)b$ bins [12]. An alternative method, known as the lower bound and reduction (LBR) procedure was proposed by Martello and Toth, which they claimed aids in reaching an optimum solution [13]

However, obtaining such a forecast has a number of issues. Firstly, how can we incentivise users to provide a forecast instead of just purchasing the resource on-demand? The obvious solution is to provide them with a benefit, such as cost reduction, offered in return for their forecast.

Secondly, how do you users know what they are likely to use? One of the main benefits of cloud computing is for users to purchase resources on-demand for immediate execution without such a forecast being required. Does forecasting negate one of the major benefits of the cloud?

One solution could be to combine forecasting with on-demand computing. Consumers who can provide some commitment to future resources are rewarded with a cost benefit. Should they need more resources at a later date, they can simply buy more resources on-demand and utilise or integrate these with their reserved resources using the rapid-scalability and integration capability cloud computing provides.

However, what happens if the provider incentivises users to forecast their requirements, but subsequently finds that it is not possible to schedule more efficiently than if virtual instances were purchased on-demand? For example, if the entire user population only needs instances of a certain size, then this will be packed in exactly the same manner regardless whether submitted in an offline or online manner. In this case, the provider would have lost revenue as a result of discounted advance pricing without gaining an advantage.

Provision-point contracts (also known as assurance contracts) could provide the answer. In a provision-point mechanism, members of a group pledge to contribute to an action if a threshold of some order is met. If this threshold is met, the action is taken and the public goods are provided; otherwise no party is bound to carry out the action and monies paid are refunded [14].

Such a mechanism is used by deal-of-the-day website Groupon[1]. Users make requests for special offers by purchasing a coupon. When a threshold is reached, the deal is profitable to the provider and the offer is confirmed.

We propose that such a provision-point mechanism (PPM) can be used for increasing scheduling efficiency by only confirming advance reservations if they are beneficial to the provider. In the next section, we describe the mechanism in more detail.

3   Mechanism

The PPM that we explore in this paper involves three distinct phases, or periods, defined as follows:

Period 1
Users make requests for cloud resources to be consumed in the third period, paying a price P_{res} to make the request.

Period 2
The provider trials a number of bin-packing algorithms with the objective of finding the method that uses the lowest number of servers that contains all requests from all users as submitted in the first period. In our simulations, we use the following algorithms:
- First fit decreasing algorithm (FFD);
- Martello and Toth's lower bound and reduction procedure (LBR);
- Randomised order.

If the provider finds that the randomised order uses fewer servers than the FFD or LBR algorithms, it is likely the distribution of resources is such that pre-scheduling is not beneficial. In this case, the provider will reject all requests and refund any monies paid in the first period.

---

[1] www.groupon.com

Otherwise, the provider confirms all requests and contracts are established.

The provider can potentially use the information gathered to plan other variable costs and requirements such as staffing or electricity.

Period 3

If a contract was established, users are given access to resources as per the best-case allocation found in the second period – users also have the right to purchase further on-demand resources. If not, users must purchase on-demand resources to satisfy all their requirements. The cost of on-demand resources is P_{od}.

Unlike a traditional provision-point mechanism, the discounted rate is only available to those who submitted a reservation request previously.

We now demonstrate our PPM in action, via a series of simulation experiments.

4   Simulation

We constructed a cloud-market simulator[2] to explore the behaviour of user-agents interacting with a provider of cloud computing resources in the PPM manner described above.

4.1   Scenario

Users submit their requests up to 24 hours in advance of when they will be exercised. Potentially, other regimes could be used but we have chosen this so that users have a fair chance of predicting future resource requirements, and the provider has enough notice to benefit from this prediction (e.g. by scheduling workloads, purchasing electricity in advance, etc). A reservation specifies one hour of resource-usage, and can be used in combination with on-demand resources.

The provider communicates whether requests are fulfilled to all users exactly twenty-four hours before the reservation begins.

Users can purchase multiple virtual machines instances of any size from 1 to 8 computational units; one computational unit provides access to one CPU core.

The provider has access to servers with 2 x Quad-Core CPUs. In our simulation:

$$P_{od} = 1.75 \text{ and } P_{res} = 1.$$

These values were chosen as these are derived from our previous work exploring the use of derivative contracts in cloud scheduling [15]. Our objective in this work is to determine if a saving is achievable and if this saving is related to server efficiency.

4.2   User Behaviour

A user's behaviour is determined by two factors: her *market demand profile*, and her *product demand split*.

---

[2] Our cloud-market simulator is written in the *Python* programming language. We intend to release this simulator as open-source code in due course. Until then, copies of the source-code can be made available for non-profit research, on request from the authors.

A user's market demand profile is the demand she will experience at each hour throughout the simulation. Demand varies from 0 to 1, where a demand of 1 means that a user's maximum demand requirement (40 in this simulation) will be needed and 0 is where there is no demand. Five demand profiles profiles were chosen, as illustrated in Figure 1, which shows demand varying over one 30-day month (672 hourly time-periods):

- *Flat* profile represents where demand is constant and easy to predict
- *Random* profile represents unpredictable demand
- *Sine* profiles (with period of 24 hours) represents a typical day where demand will grow through the working day and decrease towards the night
  - o *Flat Sine* represents constant demand varying periodically across each day
  - o *Growing Sine* represents daily periodic demand, growing throughout the month
  - o *Shrinking Sine* represents daily periodic demand, shrinking through the month

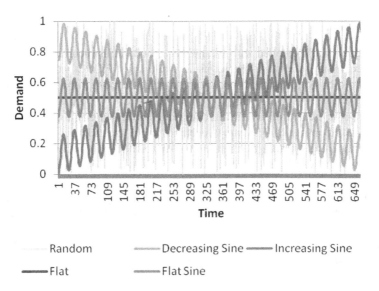

Fig. 1. Demand patterns used in simulation: patterns shown over the course of one month; horizontal-axis units are hours; vertical-axis units are percentage demand

These profiles were chosen with the aim of simulating both the extremes of behaviour, and typical "real-world" demand patterns. Our belief is that by demonstrating success on this data, we can plausibly claim that success of our system would *also* be likely for any other similarly fluctuating pattern of demand.

A user's product demand split (PDS) defines a user's demand for each size of instance type. For example, some users might require smaller instances, while others may require larger ones.

In this simulation, we assume that user i has a product demand split that is non-negative and that follows a normal distribution defined by its mean μ_i, and its standard deviation σ_i: $PDS_i=\max(0,\textbf{N}(\mu_i,\sigma_i))$. The mean represents the instance size that is most likely to be demanded by user i. The standard deviation represents the degree of variation in the distribution of instance sizes demanded by user i. For example, when the mean is 4 and the standard deviation is 0.25, instances of size 4 will almost always be required. When the mean is 3 and the standard deviation is 6, instances of size 6 will be demanded most frequently in the long run, but instances of other sizes will be demanded with similar frequency. Each user's requirements are generated at random from the thresholded normal distribution defined by their individual PDS_i function. This introduces non-determinism into the simulation, to create a more realistic representation of demand.

To determine their future resource demands, a user considers her demand for resources at the same time at which the contract is available to be executed over the past three days. If a resource has been used throughout that period, the user will reserve a resource.

4.3   Execution

The simulation was deployed on commercial cloud infrastructure to increase the speed of generating results. A virtual instance running MySQL was used to hold a table of tests to be performed, defined by the market demand profile and product demand split.

An image was created of an Ubuntu operating system running the Python simulation. Large-sized instances of virtual machines were created using the simulation image. On boot, each virtual machine would automatically connect to the MySQL database and identify experiments that were yet to be performed. Each instance would extract parameter data from the database, and set the status of the record to indicate it was in progress so other instances would not process it. Upon completion of the simulation, the results were deposited in the same record of the database and its status was set to complete. This process continued until there were no more results to obtain.

We performed multiple simulations using homogeneous user populations. In each simulation, all users experienced similar demand patterns.

5   Results and Analysis

Table 1 shows a summarised set of results. Table 2 and 3 show our full set of results, which can be found as an appendix to this paper. Table 2 shows the percentage mean reduction in server usage, comparing the combined pricing model with simple instant creation of on-demand instances. Table 3 shows the percentage mean reduction in consumer's cost per computational unit using the combined pricing model compared to using on-demand only. Note this is the mean cost per computational unit *purchased* rather than *utilised,* so that our results take account of expenditure on virtual machines which are subsequently not used.

Table 1. Summary of main results

Market Profile	Ratio of results where advance scheduling is beneficial	Mean cost saving per computational unit:		Mean server reduction where advance scheduling beneficial
		where advance scheduling beneficial	where advance scheduling not beneficial	
Flat Sin	61%	10.38%	1.89%	0.35%
Increasing Sine	56%	10.04%	2.13%	0.32%
Flat	63%	10.99%	2.03%	0.33%
Decreasing Sine	58%	11.29%	2.58%	0.43%
Random	58%	4.36%	0.59%	0.29%

Table 1 shows that where advance scheduling is beneficial to the provider, consumers are rewarded with mean cost savings of up to 11.29%. Where advance scheduling is found not to be of benefit, the consumers discount is considerably smaller. This protects the provider's revenue by helping to prevent discounted pricing where the provider does not gain any improvement in resource utilisation.

Furthermore, Table 1 shows that when advance scheduling is beneficial to the provider, she reduces the mean number of active servers required by using our pricing method compared to offering on-demand resources only.

Ideally, where advance scheduling is not advantageous to the provider, consumers should receive no discount. However, the provider's method for determining if contracts should be established is not perfect, and occasionally the provider confirms contracts where it is subsequently found that no scheduling advantage is realised.

In Table 2, it can be seen that the model generally increases server utilisation and therefore decreases the number of active servers in all situations tested.

Regardless of the market profile, there are two situations that see the provider decide not to accept future reservations: when the mean instance is 1 or 2, and when the mean is larger (5, 6, 7, and 8) but with a smaller standard deviation.

Larger elements are more difficult to schedule efficiently as they have less flexibility with regards to what sized elements can be situated with them. For example, an element size of 2 can be situated with any size instance except sizes 7 and 8. An element of size 7 can only be situated with an instance of size 1. So when the mean instance is 1 or 2, the provider realizes that advance notification is unlikely to benefit the provider and so does not accept the future reservations.

In a similar manner, when the standard deviation is low for higher instance sizes, there is an abundance of larger elements that are unable to be situated with other instances. In fact, when there are only instances above half the bin size no benefit can be gained by future reservation because every instance requires a server of its own.

The provider realizes that she cannot benefit from the advance reservation and so does not accept the reservation.

Table 3 shows that in these situations, there is little or no difference in the mean cost per computation unit. As a result, the provider has not needlessly lost any revenue by offering discounts for which no benefit is realised.

In the scenarios where the provider *does* offer discounts, the provider makes an improvement in the mean reduced number of active servers by up to 1.8% in our best case scenario.

In all scenarios, server utilisation was never lower than that achieved by scheduling using on-demand only. This suggests the provider has little to lose in terms of server utilisation by implementing such a pricing model.

The regular demand patterns are the most efficient at scheduling, probably as the user's forecasts are more accurate and therefore less inefficiency is created through the random scheduling of on-demand resources. However, the other demand patterns generate utilization benefits for the provider too, despite the crude method used by the users to forecast. It is likely that users would see a growing or shrinking trend in the increasing and decreasing sine wave patterns and would plan accordingly, increasing the accuracy of the forecast and therefore the efficiency of the scheduling.

It was particularly interesting to note the cost savings achieved by the consumers. Consumers are required to pay for the resource if they have reserved it, which might imply that they that pay more on average as a result of reserving resources which they subsequently do not use. However, the results show that consumers will make a saving per computation unit required in spite of sometimes reserving instances that they subsequently do not use. Significant cost savings are achieved by consumers for all markets of up to 22%. The random market still rewards consumers with savings of up to 5%, less than other markets probably due to the purchase of reservations which are subsequently not used. This indicates consumers are likely to take advantage of the model.

6   Discussion

The modest percentage improvement in server utilisation is unlikely to benefit smaller providers of cloud services, who have a limited number of servers. However, this small saving could translate into significant financial benefit for larger providers.

Furthermore, as consumers paid less per computational unit using combined pricing, it is likely that this would act as an incentive, drawing consumers into using the scheme, and giving the provider more accurate information on future demand.

The provider can use this information to reduce cost by:

- reducing the number of *physically located* servers in the datacentre;
- reducing the number of *powered-on* servers in the datacentre.

The former carries more risk than the latter. The provider would prefer to ensure they have enough servers to meet unexpected demand by some margin initially. However, over time as the provider understands patterns of increased growth, she could deploy more servers to meet this demand, which should be less than the demand before combined pricing was implemented.

The latter option is the easiest to implement and is suitable for providers who have already invested in infrastructure. Most commercial cloud providers, including the largest IaaS provider, Amazon Web Services (AWS), are reluctant to publish details about the size of their infrastructure. However, in a recent blog post, Huan Liu at Stanford University reported results from studies of IP address allocations to estimate the number of servers utilised across AWS [16]. He estimated AWS' total number of servers across the world at around 450,000, although many assumptions were made. Combined pricing would reduce the number of servers required by 8100 in our best case scenario of a 1.80% reduction.

Using the online Hewlett-Packard electricity consumption calculator [17], a typical HP Proliant 140 server with two CPUs, would use about 380W at peak. At the typical cost of USD0.062 per kilowatt-hour [18], this translates to running costs on direct electricity consumption (excluding air conditioning, facilities, etc) of around $190 per server per year. The combined pricing scheme used to power-off unused servers would save over $1.6million per annum on direct electricity alone. This could increase significantly if other variable costs such as air conditioning and staffing are also reduced as a result of the pricing scheme's better matching of demand to supply.

Of course, the provider will lose some revenue as a result of offering a discount to consumers. If the cost reduction gained through the reduction in servers is greater than the revenue lost in discounts, then the model is worth implementing. The cost model can be tweaked such that consumers are incentivised whilst the provider makes a net saving through server consolidation.

7   Conclusion

In this paper, we have shown how provision point contracts can be used for advance scheduling of cloud-based virtual instances, so that active servers are reduced compared to using on-demand instances only. Furthermore, we have shown that the provider can protect against some risk by analysing the distribution of resources to determine if servers efficiencies can be achieved, and therefore if the user-population should receive a discount. In our best case scenario, a mean saving of 1.8% on active servers was achieved. However, the provider must have a large number of servers for this saving to be commercially beneficial.

We found that all users make a saving by using advance reservations, despite sometimes purchasing resources in advance that they subsequently do not utilise. This suggests that users would use such a pricing scheme.

Further work is needed to establish the performance of the model across a greater range of scenarios. It would be particularly interesting to use real patterns of demand experienced by cloud providers to analyse the model. However, these results already suggest that a commercial viable implementation may be readily achievable.

Acknowledgments. We thank the UK Engineering and Physical Sciences Research Council (EPSRC) for funding the Large-Scale Complex IT Systems Initiative (www.lscits.org) as well as HP Labs Adaptive Infrastructure Lab for providing additional financial support. We thank Claranet for use of their Virtual Data Centre cloud service.

References

1. Weinman, J.: Time is Money: The Value of "On-Demand",
   http://joeweinman.com/Resources/Joe_Weinman_Time_Is_Money.pdf
2. Armbrust, M., Fox, A., Griffith, R., Joseph, A.D., Katz, R., Konwinski, A., Lee, G., Patterson, D., Rabkin, A., Stoica, I., Zaharia, M.: Above the Clouds: A Berkeley View of Cloud Computing Cloud Computing: An Old Idea Whose Time Has (Finally) Come. Communications of the ACM 53, 50–58 (2010)
3. Buyya, R., Yeo, C.S., Venugopal, S., Broberg, J., Brandic, I.: Cloud computing and emerging IT platforms: Vision, hype, and reality for delivering computing as the 5th utility. Future Generation Computer Systems 25, 599–616 (2009)
4. Mac, M., Rana, O., Smith, G., Guitart, J.: Maximizing revenue in Grid markets using an economically enhanced resource manager, 1990–2011 (2011)
5. Varian, H., Shapiro, C., Farrell, J.: The Economics of Information Technology – An Introduction, Cambridge (2004)
6. Patel, C.D., Shah, A.J.: Cost Model for Planning, Development and Operation of a Data Center. Development 107, 1–36 (2005)
7. Sandholm, T., Lai, K., Andrade, J., Odeberg, J.: Market-based Resource Allocation Using Price Prediction in a High Performance Computing Grid for Scientific AIpplications. In: 15th IEEE International Symposium on High Performance Distributed Computing, pp. 132–143 (2006)
8. Prodan, R., Wieczorek, M., Fard, H.M.: Double Auction-based Scheduling of Scientific Applications in Distributed Grid and Cloud Environments. Journal of Grid Computing, 31-042 (2011)
9. Johnson, D.S., Ullman, J.D., Gareyi, M.R., Grahamii, R.L.: Worst-Case Performance Bounds For Simple One-Dimensional Packing Algorithms. SIAM 3 (1974)
10. Coffman, E., Garey, M., Johnson, D.: Dynamic bin packing. SIAM Journal on Computing 12, 227–258 (1983)
11. Stage, A., Setzer, T.: Network-aware Migration Control and Scheduling of Differentiated Virtual Machine Workloads. In: 2009 ICSE Workshop on Software Engineering Challenges of Cloud Computing, pp. 9–14 (2009)
12. Dosa, G.: The Tight Bound of First Fit Decreasing Bin-Packing Algorithm Is F F D (I) $\leq$ 11 / 9OP T (I) + 6 / 9. Combinatorics, 1–11 (2007)
13. Martello, S., Toth, P.: No Title. Discrete Applied Mathematics 28, 59–70 (1990)
14. Bagnolli, M., Lipman, B.: Provision of Public Goods: Fully Implementing the Core Through Private Contributions. Review of Economics Studies 56, 583–601 (1989)
15. Rogers, O., Cliff, D.: A financial brokerage model for cloud computing. Journal of Cloud Computing: Advances, Systems and Applications 1, 2 (2012)
16. Liu, H.: Huan Liu's Blog, http://huanliu.wordpress.com/2012/03/13/amazon-data-center-size/
17. HP: Online Electricity Consumption Calculator, http://h20000.www2.hp.com/bizsupport/TechSupport/Document.jsp?lang=en&cc=us&taskId=125&prodSeriesId=428936&prodTypeId=15351&objectID=c01510445
18. Barroso, L.A., Hölzle, U.: The Datacenter as a Computer: An Introduction to the Design of Warehouse-Scale Machines. Synthesis Lectures on Computer Architecture 4, 1–108 (2009)

Appendix: Results

Table 2. Percentage mean reduction in server utilization using provision point contracts over on-demand only

Demand	Stdev	Mean							
		1	2	3	4	5	6	7	8
Sine	0.25	0.00	0.00	0.01	0.01	0.00	0.00	0.00	0.00
	0.5	0.00	0.01	0.39	0.20	0.00	0.00	0.00	0.00
	1	0.00	0.00	1.00	0.43	0.02	0.00	0.00	0.00
	2	0.00	0.01	0.12	0.49	0.38	0.06	0.02	0.00
	3	0.00	-0.01	0.13	0.54	0.67	0.30	0.14	0.04
	4	0.00	0.01	0.06	0.46	0.79	0.58	0.38	0.25
	5	-0.01	0.02	0.06	0.45	0.72	0.69	0.55	0.43
	6	0.00	0.02	0.20	0.43	0.66	0.73	0.64	0.62
Increasing Sine	0.25	0.00	0.00	-0.01	0.02	0.00	0.00	0.00	0.00
	0.5	0.00	0.00	0.38	0.14	0.00	0.00	0.00	0.00
	1	0.00	-0.01	0.97	0.32	0.03	0.00	0.00	0.00
	2	0.00	0.00	0.12	0.45	0.31	0.03	-0.01	0.00
	3	0.00	-0.01	0.07	0.38	0.57	0.26	0.14	0.05
	4	0.00	0.01	0.05	0.35	0.60	0.50	0.26	0.19
	5	0.01	-0.01	0.07	0.40	0.60	0.59	0.47	0.33
	6	0.03	-0.01	0.16	0.32	0.59	0.61	0.56	0.49
Flat	0.25	0.00	0.00	-0.01	0.01	0.00	0.00	0.00	0.00
	0.5	0.00	0.01	0.30	0.22	0.00	0.00	0.00	0.00
	1	0.00	0.01	0.80	0.42	0.02	0.00	0.00	0.00
	2	0.00	0.01	0.07	0.52	0.28	0.07	-0.01	0.00
	3	0.00	0.01	0.08	0.44	0.68	0.25	0.10	0.06
	4	-0.01	-0.01	0.09	0.45	0.77	0.58	0.37	0.21
	5	0.02	0.03	0.10	0.46	0.77	0.68	0.53	0.43
	6	0.02	0.06	0.15	0.39	0.72	0.74	0.67	0.58
Decreasing Sine	0.25	0.00	0.01	0.01	0.01	0.00	0.00	0.00	0.00
	0.5	0.00	-0.01	0.37	0.23	0.00	0.00	0.00	0.00
	1	0.00	0.02	1.80	0.48	-0.02	0.00	0.00	0.00
	2	0.00	0.00	0.24	0.64	0.41	0.05	0.03	0.01
	3	0.00	-0.01	0.15	0.56	0.69	0.35	0.15	0.06
	4	-0.01	0.02	0.12	0.55	0.81	0.61	0.39	0.28
	5	-0.03	0.01	0.07	0.53	0.80	0.74	0.62	0.53
	6	0.01	0.06	0.17	0.49	0.75	0.81	0.69	0.64
Random	0.25	0.00	0.00	0.01	0.02	0.00	0.00	0.00	0.00
	0.5	0.00	0.01	0.35	0.18	0.00	0.00	0.00	0.00
	1	0.00	-0.01	1.38	0.35	0.00	0.00	0.00	0.00
	2	0.00	-0.01	0.25	0.38	0.27	0.04	0.00	0.00
	3	0.00	0.00	0.11	0.40	0.45	0.25	0.11	0.00
	4	-0.01	0.02	0.07	0.34	0.52	0.41	0.29	0.19
	5	0.00	0.01	0.08	0.37	0.48	0.44	0.40	0.32
	6	0.02	0.04	0.15	0.34	0.44	0.52	0.47	0.41

Table 3. Percentage mean reduction in consumer's cost per demanded computational unit using provision point contracts over on-demand only

Demand	Stdev	Mean							
		1	2	3	4	5	6	7	8
Sine	0.25	0.00	9.49	0.00	12.76	0.00	0.00	0.00	0.00
	0.5	0.00	5.29	2.92	23.84	0.00	0.00	0.00	0.00
	1	0.02	0.84	19.93	19.30	0.69	0.00	0.00	0.00
	2	0.29	2.05	12.24	13.88	7.98	3.13	0.85	0.05
	3	1.67	5.24	11.10	12.58	10.15	8.11	6.16	3.35
	4	5.04	8.55	10.78	11.32	11.64	10.92	8.82	7.53
	5	8.61	10.74	12.03	11.61	12.02	12.38	10.68	9.84
	6	10.64	12.29	11.47	12.51	12.35	12.84	11.64	11.85
Increasing Sine	0.25	0.00	7.48	0.00	10.95	0.00	0.00	0.00	0.00
	0.5	0.00	5.20	1.85	18.89	0.00	0.00	0.00	0.00
	1	0.00	1.35	17.55	17.57	0.56	0.00	0.00	0.00
	2	0.68	2.40	10.52	12.34	7.13	2.48	0.77	0.19
	3	2.88	5.13	10.55	11.77	10.68	7.58	5.11	2.62
	4	4.36	8.27	11.06	11.46	11.39	10.19	8.66	7.11
	5	8.57	10.38	11.74	11.25	11.76	11.34	10.32	9.47
	6	9.81	10.54	11.61	11.62	11.78	11.59	11.67	10.81
Flat	0.25	0.00	9.05	0.00	13.77	0.00	0.00	0.00	0.00
	0.5	0.00	6.19	2.25	25.31	0.00	0.00	0.00	0.00
	1	0.05	1.07	21.78	21.97	1.15	0.00	0.00	0.00
	2	0.66	2.00	12.98	14.08	6.98	3.07	1.34	0.14
	3	2.68	5.40	11.64	13.09	11.36	8.15	5.31	3.90
	4	5.37	9.36	12.78	13.62	12.91	11.96	9.29	8.54
	5	9.47	12.31	12.58	13.05	13.10	13.62	11.75	10.61
	6	11.23	12.71	13.62	12.83	13.26	13.61	12.86	12.38
Decreasing Sine	0.25	0.00	12.81	0.00	17.03	0.00	0.00	0.00	0.00
	0.5	0.00	4.79	2.26	24.90	0.00	0.00	0.00	0.00
	1	0.00	1.24	20.47	20.42	1.00	0.00	0.00	0.00
	2	0.64	2.00	12.54	13.91	8.09	3.35	1.23	0.51
	3	2.98	6.10	11.83	12.58	11.01	8.62	5.81	3.87
	4	6.56	8.78	12.19	13.00	12.97	11.73	9.28	8.42
	5	9.00	11.82	13.44	12.30	12.73	11.98	12.03	11.41
	6	11.52	12.20	12.31	12.61	13.10	13.70	12.17	12.17
Random	0.25	0.00	2.69	0.00	4.53	0.00	0.00	0.00	0.00
	0.5	0.00	2.03	1.22	8.34	0.00	0.00	0.00	0.00
	1	0.06	0.03	7.60	7.51	0.38	0.00	0.00	0.00
	2	0.12	0.75	4.53	5.56	2.85	1.10	-0.01	0.15
	3	1.22	1.78	4.00	5.17	4.02	3.02	2.44	1.76
	4	1.63	3.21	4.64	4.90	4.68	4.95	3.94	3.05
	5	3.47	4.01	4.83	5.07	4.54	5.38	4.01	4.28
	6	3.98	4.63	4.93	4.93	5.09	4.85	4.54	4.95

An Economic Agent Maximizing Cloud Provider Revenues under a Pay-as-you-Book Pricing Model

Felipe Díaz Sánchez, Elias A. Doumith, Sawsan Al Zahr, and Maurice Gagnaire

Institut Mines-Telecom - Telecom ParisTech - LTCI CNRS
Networks and Computer Sciences Department
46, rue Barrault F 75634 Paris Cedex 13 - France
{felipe.diaz,elias.doumith,sawsan.alzahr,
maurice.gagnaire}@telecom-paristech.fr

Abstract. The Cloud computing paradigm offers the illusion of infinite resources accessible to end-users anywhere at anytime. In such dynamic environment, managing distributed heterogeneous resources is challenging. A Cloud workload is typically decomposed into advance reservation and on-demand requests. Under advance reservation, end-users have the opportunity to reserve in advance the estimated required resources for the completion of their jobs without any further commitment. Thus, Cloud service providers can make a better use of their infrastructure while provisioning the proposed services under determined policies and/or time constraints. However, estimating end-users resource requirements is often error prone. Such uncertainties associated with job execution time and/or SLA satisfaction significantly increase the complexity of the resource management. Therefore, an appropriate resource management by Cloud service providers is crucial for harnessing the power of the underlying distributed infrastructure and achieving high system performance. In this paper, we investigate the resource provisioning problem for advance reservation under a *Pay-as-you-Book* pricing model. Our model offers to handle the extra-time required by some jobs at a higher price on a best-effort basis. However, satisfying these extra-times may lead to several advance reservations competing for the same resources. We propose a novel economic agent responsible for managing such conflicts. This agent aims at maximizing Cloud service provider revenues while complying with SLA terms. We show that our agent achieves higher return on investment compared to intuitive approaches that systematically prioritize reserved jobs or currently running jobs.

Keywords: Cloud computing, Resource provisioning, Advance reservation, Pricing models, Pay-as-you-Book, Economic agents, SLA.

1 Introduction

Cloud computing is a large-scale distributed computing paradigm wherein IT (Information Technology) resources are delivered to end-users as a service. Using virtualization technologies, physical IT resources (*e.g.,* processing power,

K. Vanmechelen, J. Altmann, and O.F. Rana (Eds.): GECON 2012, LNCS 7714, pp. 29–45, 2012.

data storage, network bandwidth, etc.) can be packaged along with an operating system and a set of software into a flexible and scalable virtual machine (VM). End-users can dynamically customize, lease, and release VMs through the Internet according to their needs. Moreover, Cloud computing promises to provide IT resources to end-users as metered services. In analogy to traditional utilities such as water, gas, electricity, etc., Cloud service providers (CSPs) seek to meet fluctuating end-users needs and charge them for resources based on usage rather than on a flat-rate basis.

In Cloud computing, resource provisioning can be performed under on-demand or/and advance reservation plans (*e.g.*, Amazon EC2 and GoGrid). Under on-demand plan, CSPs charge end-users proportional to their resource consumption on a *Pay-as-you-Go* basis (*e.g.*, Amazon EC2 On-Demand Instances). In such a pricing model, resource consumption is measured in fine-grained measurement unit, *e.g.*, data storage consumption is typically measured in gigabytes. Furthermore, Cloud resource provisioning must be elastic, allowing end-users to dynamically lease/release resources to cope with their fluctuating and unpredictable needs. Large scale providers with virtually unlimited resources (*e.g.*, Amazon EC2) can guarantee such elasticity. However, small- and medium-sized providers with relatively limited resources may not be able to instantaneously satisfy all requests.

Another classical resource management strategy is to employ an advance reservation (AR) mechanism. Under AR plan, end-users submit their requests to the CSP beforehand and commit to use the requested service during a given time period by paying a reservation fee. In return, the CSP offers its services at a lower price compared to the on-demand plan. In doing so, the CSP is able to lock resources and thus guarantee that end-users can access the required resources during the reserved time period [1]. Moreover, AR allows the CSP to maximize its resource utilization and yield optimal profits. However, end-users requests are often subject to uncertainties (*e.g.*, job execution time) which may result in under-/over-provisioning problems. In such cases, the CSP has to decide whether or not to satisfy additional requests taking into account available resources and SLAs (Service Level Agreement) agreed with its end-users. To this end, an appropriate resource management by the CSP is crucial for harnessing the power of the underlying distributed infrastructure and achieving high system performance.

In our previous work [2], we studied the problem of Cloud resource provisioning in an on-demand fashion. Indeed, we considered job requests with time-variable capacity requirements whereas the CSP only relies on the capacity requirement upon the request arrival. We investigated different algorithms to solve this resource provisioning problem and compared them in terms of resource utilization as well as VMs dropping and rejection ratios. In this paper, we investigate the problem of Cloud resource provisioning for AR under a *Pay-as-you-Book* pricing model. Our model offers to handle the extra-time required by some jobs at a higher price, on a best-effort basis. Indeed, ARs running for a longer period than expected may lead to resource conflicts with other ARs. In order to resolve such resource conflicts, we propose in this work an economic agent responsible for managing the under-provisioning problem. Our economic agent aims at maximizing the CSP revenues while complying with the SLA terms. Through numerical simulation, we show that our agent achieves higher revenues compared to intuitive approaches that systematically prioritize reserved jobs or currently running jobs.

The remainder of this paper is organized as follows. In Section 2, we provide a detailed state-of-the-art focusing on AR-based resource provisioning approaches. In Section 3, we present our formulation of the resource provisioning problem under a *Pay-as-you-Book* pricing model and emphasize our contribution with regard to related works. We also introduce the economic agent responsible for managing resource conflicts caused by under-estimated jobs. Numerical results and performance evaluation are given in Section 4. We then conclude our paper in Section 5 with some directions for future work.

2   Related Work

Advance reservation has been introduced in Grid and Cloud environments as an efficient way to guarantee the availability of IT resources for use at a specific time in the future. In order to handle AR, the CSP needs some information specifying the quantity of resources required by the job, the ready-time when this job can start its execution, the expected job execution time, and its deadline. Based on the capacity and time requirements of the jobs, we can classify existing studies on AR into:

2.1   Advance Reservation Specified by Cloud Service Providers

This type of AR is tightly related to the subscription-based pricing model, widely proposed by CSPs. Under this pricing model, end-users must commit to use the service for a given time period by paying a one-time fee; in exchange, the CSP guarantees the availability of the required resources at reduced hourly rates. This type of reservation operates on a time-interval basis. At the beginning of each time-interval, the end-user may adjust the amount of resources to be reserved by the CSP for the next time-interval. Conducted research studies can be classified into short-term reservation plans [3, 4] (*e.g.*, fine granularity of 10-minute/1-hour time-intervals) and long-term reservation plans (*e.g.*, several years time-intervals) [5, 6].

In [3], the authors investigated pricing policies for guaranteed bandwidth reservation in the Cloud on a short-term basis such as hours or tens of minutes. Requests are characterized by an estimated average bandwidth requirement, its variability, and the percentage of the traffic flow to be satisfied with guaranteed bandwidth. As for the CSP, it computes the current bandwidth reservation in order to guarantee the required performance in a probabilistic way. It also decides on the reservation fee taking into account the burstiness and the time correlation of the various requests. The authors in [4] investigated a similar problem where a broker is introduced between the CSPs and the end-users. While the broker sells guarantees to end-users individually, it jointly reserves bandwidth from multiple CSPs for the mixed demand, exploiting statistical multiplexing to save reservation cost. The problem was solved using a game theory approach where the equilibrium bandwidth price depends on the demand expectation, its burstiness as well as its correlation to the market.

The long-term reservation plan has been first studied in [5]. The authors considered a single CSP and proposed an algorithm that selects the number of VMs to be reserved by an end-user while deploying a service in the Cloud. In order to cope with request fluctuations and unpredictability, additional resources may be dynamically provisioned with an on-demand plan. The proposed algorithm minimizes the global cost of using a mixture of reserved and on-demand instances by taking advantage of the different pricing models within the same provider. The authors of [6] generalized the problem to the context of multiple CSPs taking into account the uncertainty on end-users future requests and providers resource prices. They formulated the problem as an integer stochastic program and solved it numerically using various approaches.

2.2   Advance Reservation Specified by End-Users

In this type of AR, end-users have a higher flexibility as they can specify, in addition to their capacity requirements, various time constraints associated with the execution of their jobs. Time constraints can be expressed in terms of various parameters such as ready-time, job duration, and job deadline. Thus, end-users have the opportunity to reserve in advance the estimated required resources for the completion of their jobs without any further commitment. In the sequel, we define the AR window as the time-interval delimited by the ready-time and the deadline of a given job request. AR specified by end-users can be classified into three main categories as follows:

a) **Strict Start and Completion Time:** This type of job is characterized by a job duration equal to its AR window. In other words, end-users require the resources at a specified exact time in the future and for a specified duration. This type of jobs does not leave any flexibility to the CSP to reschedule the job at a different time period. Several studies have shown that jobs with strict start and completion time lead to high fragmentation of the resources availability by increasing the number of time intervals that are left unused [7, 8]. These time intervals can be used by other types of requests such as spot and on-demand instances.

The authors of [9] investigated the provisioning of computing, storage, and networking resources in order to satisfy AR requests. They considered several basic services and highlighted how distributed data storage and multicast data transfer can satisfy a larger number of end-users and improve resource utilization of CSPs. The business model of the aforementioned problem has been investigated in [10]. The authors proposed and compared three pricing strategies assessing the expectations of both end-users and CSPs.

b) **Flexible Start But Strict Completion Time:** This type of jobs is characterized by a higher flexibility than the former as the AR window is larger than its execution time. However, these jobs are time-critical and, if accepted, the CSP must ensure that they will complete prior to their firm deadline. Thus, CSPs may use various mechanisms to efficiently arrange, manage, and monitor their resources. For instance, the authors in [1] introduced a model based on computational geometry that allows CSPs to record and efficiently verify the availability of their resources during the SLA negotiation and planning phase. According to this model, when the CSP lacks resources, a flexible alternative solution, referred to as counter-offer, can be generated in order to satisfy the end-user. Hence, the CSP's reputation can be enhanced by improving its ability to satisfy as many end-users as possible leading to higher resource utilization and consequently higher profits. The authors in [11] investigated a negotiation mechanism that allows either parties (CSPs and end-users) to modify the SLA or to make counter proposals in order to converge to a mutually acceptable agreement. In the investigated scenarios, once the SLA has been agreed upon, the CSP has to execute the job at the specified time. Numerical simulations have been carried out to highlight the benefit brought by time-flexible job requests. The authors in [12] investigated the impact of the AR window size on the blocking probability and the resource utilization for various models of inter-arrival and service times under the first-come-first-served scheduling policy.

In [13], the authors investigated the resource provisioning problem in a market-oriented Cloud considering ARs with flexible window size that is a function of the requirements and the budgets of end-users. The aim of this study is to propose a fair management algorithm that guarantees the QoS (Quality of Service) requirements of end-users while increasing the expected benefit of CSPs. For this purpose, the authors introduced a weighted cost function that enables service differentiation relying on time constraints disparity of the requests. An exact linear formulation [13] as well as a heuristic approach [14] have been considered for the numerical performance evaluation. Instead of charging fixed prices, the authors in [15] propose to automatically adjust the price for accessing the resources, whenever necessary, in order to increase the CSP revenues. By charging variable prices, CSPs can give incentives to end-users with less urgent requirements to shift to using the service during off-peak periods and benefit from lower prices. As the prices are adjusted based on the expected workload and the resource availability, ARs submitted a long time in advance are privileged with cheaper prices compared to late ARs.

Similar investigations have been carried out in a slightly different environment. The new environment allows the CSP to modify the execution schedule of already accepted ARs in order to accommodate new requests right up until each execution starts [16]. Such rescheduling of existing jobs is carried out while respecting the deadline constraints specified in the SLA. The authors have shown that this mechanism can mitigate the negative effects of AR and improve the performance of reservation-based schedulers as it tends to reduce the amount of time intervals where resources remain free. Another solution to improve resource utilization is to make use of comprehensive overbooking which is particularly efficient in scenarios with no-show policy, job cancelation [17], and over-estimated execution time of jobs [18]. In this context, rescheduling existing jobs may allow overbooked jobs to get access to the resources during their full execution period if previous jobs do not show up or finish earlier. The Earliest Deadline First scheduler have been investigated to provide probabilistic real-time guarantees for AR over time-shared machines [19]. With this scheduling strategy, an admission control policy is developed where new job requests are accepted if they do not break the QoS constraints of previously accepted reservations. This can be achieved for instance by changing the priority of the running jobs to ensure that the execution completes prior to its deadline.

c) **Flexible Start and Completion Time:** This type of jobs is also characterized by a high flexibility. However, the AR window is not clearly defined. Instead of defining a ready-time and a firm deadline for the execution of each job, the end-user provides a set of time-intervals along with its preferences represented by a utility function. The utility function represents the level of satisfaction that the end-user will experience as a result of the negotiation outcome. This satisfaction may depend on several parameters such as the time of execution, the price of the resources, the delays, the QoS requirements, etc. Usually, not being able to reach an agreement is the worst possible outcome and the end-user receives a null utility as its request is rejected. Dynamic pricing based on resource utilization and end-users classification was introduced in [20]. Such dynamic pricing strategy allows the CSP to adapt the price to set incentives for using the resources during off-peak periods. Two different approaches, which are already well established in other areas, are compared in [21] namely, reservation realized by derivative markets in a perfect competition CSPs environment and yield management techniques assuming an imperfect competition environment. The authors analyze the different requirements in order to apply the proposed approaches in the Cloud and provide models to derive the suitable reservation price. The authors in [22] introduced a bilateral negotiation mechanism for Cloud service reservation that simultaneously considers price and execution time. Numerical simulations have been used to compare the proposed mechanism to traditional pricing models used by current CSPs namely, fixed-prices for on-demand and reserved instances, and variable prices for spot instances. The Time-of-Use pricing policy has been investigated in [23]. According to this policy, the price of accessing resources is totaly independent from the utilization ratio of the requested resources but varies within a day. The optimal pricing strategy that maximizes the end-user satisfaction is derived.

3   Problem Formulation

In this paper, we focus our investigations on VM provisioning and usage for compute-intensive and/or processing-intensive scientific applications. Under this assumption, all VMs are already configured with a considerable amount of CPU resources and dedicated memory space. Once a job is running on a given VM, the underlying resources associated with this VM (*e.g.,* CPU power, memory space, network bandwidth, etc.) are intensively used and cannot benefit from statistical multiplexing. Therefore, an incoming job request only has to express its requirements in terms of VMs without explicitly specifying their configurations. Although the end-users have the illusion of infinite resources within the Cloud, the CSPs are always constrained with limited resource availability. For this purpose, we consider in this study a large data-center, owned by a single CSP, that can host up to $\mathcal{N}$ VMs.

Many scientific applications such as telemedicine, multimedia, or air traffic flow management require the combination and orchestration of several services to meet their requirements. As the resources are being shared by multiple applications which are completely unaware of each other, the use of AR has been proposed as a means to provide time-guarantees on the successful completion of the submitted jobs. The AR mechanism allows end-users to reserve enough resources across independently administrated domains prior to their job's execution. In order to efficiently handle ARs, the CSP needs information regarding the required quantity of resources, the ready-time as well as the execution time of the jobs. As the execution time of the applications may vary from one run to another, it is a tedious task for end-users to provide these values. This is especially true for distributed applications since their execution time highly depends on the interaction between the various implied services.

Due to demand uncertainty, job requests can be classified into under-estimated and over-estimated jobs. Over-estimated jobs will run for a shorter period in comparison to their stipulated execution time. Conversely, under-estimated jobs will run for a longer period than expected. Such inaccuracy in estimating job execution time can result in lower resource utilization and higher rejection rates. However, performance degradation is less severe for job requests characterized by flexible start but strict completion time, or flexible start and completion time. Indeed, these types of jobs can benefit from the backfilling mechanism where the CSP reschedules all the accepted jobs in order to adapt to the changing conditions. For instance, when an over-estimated job leaves the system, the CSP invokes the scheduler in order to achieve larger contiguous idle time periods. These idle periods can facilitate the accommodation of future requests as well as the provisioning of additional time for requests that have exceeded their specified execution time. Thus, instead of aborting the execution of under-estimated jobs, the CSP investigates the feasibility of providing them with extra-time without missing the deadlines of other accepted jobs.

Nevertheless, to the best of our knowledge, demand uncertainty has never been investigated in the context of ARs characterized by strict start and completion time. Previous investigations in this matter assume that the jobs are perfectly known [7–10] or propose to terminate any under-estimated application that is still executing once its reservation period expires. In our study, we offer to handle the extra-time required by some jobs at a higher price on a best-effort basis. Moreover, we propose to manage any resource conflict that may arise between an under-estimated job and another already reserved job while complying with the SLA terms and maximizing the CSP revenues.

3.1   Job Characterization

Scientific applications are typically modeled as workflows consisting of tasks, data elements, control sequences, and data dependencies. A workflow describes the order in which several jobs must be performed by different entities in order to achieve a given outcome. A workflow management engine is responsible for managing and controlling the execution of these jobs. It also allows end-users to specify their requirements using the workflow specification. Thus, the workflow Ω^i of a given end-user $\mathcal{U}^i$ can be modeled by a sequence of jobs ω_j^i, where j denotes the index of the job ω_j^i in the workflow Ω^i ($j = 1 \cdots \mathcal{J}^i$). Each job ω_j^i, characterized by *"strict start and completion time"* (*cf.* Section 2.2a), is represented by a tuple $(n_j^i, \alpha_j^i, \beta_j^i, \gamma_j^i)$, where n_j^i denotes the number of required VMs, α_j^i the ready-time of the job, β_j^i its completion time estimated by the end-user, and γ_j^i its real completion time obtained once executed on the given cluster. A workflow completes when all its jobs are completed. In our study, we have considered a set of $\mathcal{M}$ workflows ($i = 1 \cdots \mathcal{M}$) composed of a sequence of jobs to be executed within a given time interval $[0, \Delta]$.

3.2   Initial Scheduling of Job Requests

Since ARs are made prior to job execution, the CSP can use various scheduling approaches in order to optimize the resource utilization of its infrastructure, and consequently increases its revenues. At this stage, the CSP has only the knowledge of the execution time estimated by end-users. Even though these estimations are often imprecise, the CSP has to decide whether to accept ($\varpi^i = 1$) or reject ($\varpi^i = 0$) each workflow Ω^i depending on its resources availability. As stated previously, a workflow Ω^i is accepted if all its jobs ω_j^i ($j = 1 \cdots \mathcal{J}^i$) can be satisfied.

The initial scheduling problem can be formulated as follows. Given the number $\mathcal{N}$ of VMs and the set of $\mathcal{M}$ workflows, the CSP has to determine, for each accepted workflow, the physical machine that will host it. This should be carried out while respecting the limited resources of the CSP and the fixed ready-time and completion time of end-users jobs. The main objective of the CSP at this stage is to maximize the utilization $\mathcal{G}$ of its resources which can be expressed mathematically as:

$$\mathcal{G} = \frac{1}{\mathcal{N} \times \Delta} \sum_{i=1}^{\mathcal{M}} \sum_{j=1}^{\mathcal{J}^i} \varpi^i \times n_j^i \times \left(\beta_j^i - \alpha_j^i \right). \tag{1}$$

This problem turns out to be similar to the 2-dimensional bin packing problem with rejection. In order to solve this problem, we will use a very straightforward sequential algorithm commonly known as "Decreasing First Fit" (FFD) algorithm. This a simple offline heuristic algorithm that achieves a near-optimal solution for the classical 1-dimensional bin packing problem [24]. The FFD strategy operates in two phases. First, it sorts the workflows in decreasing order of their cumulated reservation time $\left(\sum_{j=1}^{\mathcal{J}^i}(\beta_j^i - \alpha_j^i)\right)$. Then, it processes the workflows according to the previous order, and schedules the jobs of the selected workflow in the first VM with sufficient remaining capacity during their respective reservation intervals. If none of the VMs can (partially or fully) accommodate the incoming workflow, the workflow will be rejected.

3.3   Pay-as-you-Book Pricing Model

Numerous economic models, including microeconomic and macroeconomic principles, have been investigated in the literature for setting the appropriate price for accessing a service. A pricing policy can be derived from various parameters such as the supply-and-demand and their value to the end-users. The commodity market, posted price, tender, bargaining, and auction models are among the commonly used economic models for managing the resources in the Cloud [25]. In this paper, we focus on the *Pay-as-you-Book* pricing model. It is a flat price commodity market model where the CSP specifies its service price and charges end-users for the amount of resources they reserve. Let Γ^R be the hourly rate of a reserved instance. Γ^R is independent of the service quality and the number of jobs. Upon, the acceptance of a workflow Ω^i, the CSP expects the payment of a reward or fee for the successful completion of this reservation. This reservation fee $\mathcal{C}^i$ can be expressed as follows:

$$\mathcal{C}^i = \sum_{j=1}^{\mathcal{J}^i} n_j^i \times (\beta_j^i - \alpha_j^i) \times \Gamma^R. \tag{2}$$

If all the jobs of a given workflow Ω^i finish within their respective reservation period $(\gamma_j^i \leq \beta_j^i)$, the end-user does not have to pay any additional fee. However, it may happen that a job takes more time to execute than initially estimated $(\gamma_j^i > \beta_j^i)$. In this case, the CSP can allocate the required resources for a longer period for a higher hourly rate Γ^O on a best-effort basis $(\Gamma^O > \Gamma^R)$. In other words, the CSP cannot guarantee that the job will continue running until its real completion time γ_j^i. Let θ_j^i be the time when an under-estimated job w_j^i successfully ends $(\theta_j^i = \gamma_j^i)$ or is forced to terminate by the CSP if the resources are reserved for executing another job $(\theta_j^i < \gamma_j^i)$. In this case, the end-user is requested to pay, for each under-estimated job w_j^i, an additional fee $\mathcal{F}_j^i$ equal to:

$$\mathcal{F}_j^i = n_j^i \times (\theta_j^i - \beta_j^i) \times \Gamma^O. \tag{3}$$

When the CSP accepts an AR, the end-user expects to be able to access the agreed resources at the specified ready-time. However, changes may occur between the time when the end-user submits the reservation and this specified ready-time. This can happen for various reasons such as end-users canceling or modifying requests, resource failures, and errors in the estimation of the execution time. Since an AR is considered as a commitment by the CSP, failing to meet this commitment may result in the provider paying the end-user a penalty

$\mathcal{P}_j^i$ larger than the reservation fee. For each rejected job at its ready-time, the CSP is requested to reimburse the end-user an amount $\mathcal{P}_j^i$ equal to:

$$\mathcal{P}_j^i = n_j^i \times (\beta_j^i - \alpha_j^i) \times (\Gamma^R + \Gamma^P), \qquad (4)$$

where Γ^P represents the credit that the CSP has to return to the end-user if it is unable to start the job.

3.4 An Economic Agent for Maximizing CSP Revenues

According to the previous description, we can distinguish three scenarios namely, over-estimated jobs (*cf.* Figure1a), under-estimated jobs without any conflict (*cf.* Figure1b), and under-estimated jobs resulting in a conflict (*cf.* Figure1c) with other ARs. The first two scenarios are trivial since the CSP does not have to intervene and the AR will end normally. For these scenarios, the CSP can keep the reservation fee and will obtain an additional fee for executing any under-estimated job ($\theta_j^i = \max(\beta_j^i, \gamma_j^i)$). However, in the third scenario, a conflict arises as an under-estimated job ω_j^i is competing for the same resources as an incoming AR $\omega_{j'}^{i'}$. Thus, the CSP has to decide at the ready-time $\alpha_{j'}^{i'}$ of the new AR $\omega_{j'}^{i'}$ whether to keep running the under-estimated job ω_j^i or abort it.

Targeting higher revenues, the CSP first has to estimate the average extra-time δ required by such jobs. This can be easily obtained by analyzing the past history of all compute-intensive job executions and hence adjusting δ accordingly. Based on this estimation, the CSP can evaluate the different choices for resolving any conflict. On one hand, if the under-estimated job ω_j^i is kept running, the CSP estimates getting from end-user $\mathcal{U}^i$ an additional fee equal to $F_1 = n_j^i \times (\delta + \beta_j^i - \alpha_{j'}^{i'}) \times \Gamma^O$. However, the CSP has to pay the end-user $\mathcal{U}^{i'}$ a penalty $\mathcal{P}_{j'}^{i'}$ equal to $F_2 = n_{j'}^{i'} \times (\beta_{j'}^{i'} - \alpha_{j'}^{i'}) \times (\Gamma^R + \Gamma^P)$. On the other hand, if the under-estimated job ω_j^i is aborted and the new AR $\omega_{j'}^{i'}$ is executed, the CSP can keep the reservation fee but will not obtain any additional benefit. By comparing the values of F_1 and F_2, the CSP will decide on the best way to resolve this conflict. If the CSP decides to keep the under-estimated job, it should negotiate with the owner of the incoming AR if it accepts to delay its current execution and gets in exchange the penalty specified in the SLA and a new time slot for executing its job. We assume that the end-user can accept such a proposal with a probability ρ.

4 Numerical Results

4.1 Experimental Setup

In our simulations, we consider a single CSP with limited resources that can host up to $\mathcal{N} = 10$ VMs simultaneously. We consider a simulation period of 4 days (or equivalently $\Delta = 96$ hours). In our investigations, we only consider workflows Ω^i

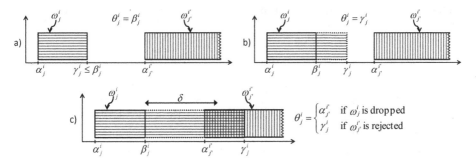

Fig. 1. Possible scenarios of running jobs

with one single job ($\mathcal{J}^i = 1$) requiring a single VM ($n^i_j = 1$). The ready-time α^i_j of a job is chosen uniformly in the interval $[0, \Delta = 96[$ while its estimated execution time μ^i_j follows a negative exponential law of mean $\hat{\mu} = 5$ hours bounded by a maximum duration of 8 hours ($\beta^i_j = \alpha^i_j + \mu^i_j$). The percentage ψ of under-estimated jobs varies in the set $\{20\%, 30\%, 40\%\}$ and the extra-time λ^i_j required by these reservations also follows a negative exponential law of mean $\hat{\lambda}$ equal to 1 or 2 hours ($\gamma^i_j = \beta^i_j + \lambda^i_j$). Without loss of generality, we have fixed the value of Γ^R to 1 and assumed that $\Gamma^O = 3$ and $\Gamma^P = 1$. Finally, the probability ρ of a successful negotiation between the CSP and the end-users has been fixed to 100%.

Under the aforementioned parameters, we have chosen to consider two different AR loads: light loads with $\mathcal{M} = 100$ and heavy loads with $\mathcal{M} = 200$. These AR loads have been inspired from the traces found in [26]. These traces provide, among other information, the submit time, the requested time, the execution time, the identifier, and the status of the jobs.

All experiments have been repeated 1000 times. For each scenario, we report the average values computed over these different runs of:

- The percentage $\mathcal{R}_i$ of ARs that are rejected at the end of the offline initial scheduling.

- The percentage $\mathcal{R}_d$ of ARs that are accepted at the end of the offline initial scheduling but are dropped during their execution because they under-estimated their execution time.

- The percentage $\mathcal{R}_r$ of ARs that are accepted at the end of the offline initial scheduling but are rejected at their ready-time because the CSP decided to keep running an under-estimated job.

- The percentage $\mathcal{R}_a$ of ARs that are accepted and executed during their complete activity period. It is obvious that the following equation holds:

$$\mathcal{R}_i + \mathcal{R}_d + \mathcal{R}_r + \mathcal{R}_a = 1. \tag{5}$$

- The revenues Ξ of the CSP computed as a function of Γ^R, Γ^O, and Γ^P as follows:

$$\Xi = \sum_i \mathcal{C}^i + \sum_{\{\text{extended } \omega_j^i\}} \mathcal{F}_j^i - \sum_{\{\text{rejected } \omega_j^i\}} \mathcal{P}_j^i. \qquad (6)$$

It is worth noting that in our investigations, we assume that the CSP expenses (*i.e.*, CapEx and OpEx) do not change with the number of running jobs. Hence, the CSP profits have the same trend as the CSP revenues and could be deduced accordingly.

- The average utilization ratio χ of the CSP resources during the simulation period Δ. χ is computed in the same way as $\mathcal{G}$ (Eq. (1)) taking into account the aforementioned percentages $\mathcal{R}_d$ and $\mathcal{R}_r$.

As stated previously, the AR mechanism allows end-users to reserve enough resources across independently administrated domains prior to job execution. The end-users may also have QoS requirements that can be expressed in terms of various parameters such as deadlines, security, trust, and budget associated with service invocation. The QoS parameters along with the time and quantity of resources requested by the end-user are encoded in the SLA. Thus, the SLA can be viewed as a formal agreement between the CSP and the end-users specifying the services, priorities, responsibilities, guarantees, etc. of both parties. In this study, the SLA is defined, among other parameters, by:

- The set of workflows $\left\{ \Omega^i = \left\{ \omega_j^i(n_j^i, \alpha_j^i, \beta_j^i), \forall j = 1 \cdots \mathcal{J}^i \right\}, \forall i = 1 \cdots \mathcal{M} \right\}$ to be executed. For each job ω_j^i, the number of required VMs as well as their ready and estimated completion times are also specified.

- The hourly rate Γ^R for running an AR and the hourly rate Γ^O for extending it beyond its estimated completion time.

- The credit Γ^P due by the CSP to the end-user in the case of non-compliance with the SLA terms.

4.2   Reference Scenarios

The goal of this study is to investigate an economic agent responsible for resource management under a *Pay-as-you-Book* pricing model. This economic agent has to achieve *"end-user satisfaction"* by providing QoS guarantees for ARs, *"cost effectiveness"* by efficiently maximizing the CSP revenues, and *"robustness"* by intelligently handling uncertainties such as those in user-estimated execution times. In order to assess the performance of the proposed agent, we will introduce three intuitive strategies that can be adopted by the CSP.

On-Demand Approach: No ARs are made at all and the resource allocation is performed online. Upon the arrival of a new job request ω_j^i, the CSP evaluates its instantaneous resource utilization. If enough free resources are available, the new request is accepted; otherwise, it is rejected. In return, the end-user is expected to pay a higher price Γ^O for accessing the resources as they are not reserved in advance. This approach does not ensure end-user satisfaction with a workflow composed of multiple jobs as there is no guarantee that all its job instances will be accepted. However, as we have considered in our experiments' workflows with a single job, the on-demand approach can be considered as a good reference scenario. Moreover, for workflows with a single job, this strategy is characterized by a null percentage of dropped ARs during their execution ($\mathcal{R}_d = 0$) and a null percentage of rejected ARs prior to their execution ($\mathcal{R}_r = 0$).

Highest Priority to Running Jobs (HPRU): Under this strategy, the CSP will never abort a running job and always try to postpone the incoming AR that causes the conflict to a later period through negotiations. The only incentive for the end-user to accurately estimate its job execution time is motivated by the lower price of reserved instances ($\Gamma^O > \Gamma^R$). This strategy is characterized by a null percentage of dropped ARs during their execution ($\mathcal{R}_d = 0$).

Highest Priority to Reserved Jobs (HPRE): Under this strategy, under-estimated jobs are penalized as they are aborted whenever a conflict arises after they have executed for their estimated execution times. In order to protect their application from forced termination, end-users with critical applications must ensure that the estimated execution times are sufficient for their applications to be completed. This strategy is characterized by a null percentage of rejected ARs prior to their execution ($\mathcal{R}_r = 0$).

4.3 Performance Evaluation

Impact of the Number of Submitted Jobs: In this first scenario, we have fixed the percentage ψ of under-estimated jobs to 20% and the average extra-time required by these jobs to $\hat{\lambda} = 1$.

Table 1. Impact of the number of submitted jobs

| | $\mathcal{M} = 100$ jobs | | | | | $\mathcal{M} = 200$ jobs | | | | |
	$\mathcal{R}_i$	$\mathcal{R}_d$	$\mathcal{R}_r$	χ	Ξ	$\mathcal{R}_i$	$\mathcal{R}_d$	$\mathcal{R}_r$	χ	Ξ
Initial Scheduling	0.10%	0%	0%	35.45%	30500	7.64%	0%	0%	67.51%	58000
On-Demand	0.20%	0%	0%	38.54%	99750	9.68%	0%	0%	67.01%	173250
HPRU	0.10%	0%	8.17%	35.09%	33750	7.64%	0%	10.01%	64.77%	61000
HPRE	0.10%	8.97%	0%	37.15%	32750	7.64%	11.29%	0%	69.64%	61000
Economic Agent	0.10%	6.42%	2.32%	37.03%	35250	7.64%	8.00%	2.91%	69.34%	64750

As expected, the on-demand approach ensures the highest CSP revenues as the end-users are paying a higher price during all the execution of their jobs ($\Gamma^O = 3 \times \Gamma^R$). It also achieves a high overall acceptance ratio $\mathcal{R}_a$ as it does not have to deal with estimation uncertainties. This latter behavior is expected to change in the case of workflows with multiple jobs. We notice that both the HPRU and the HPRE strategies achieve similar revenues Ξ for the CSP.

However, the HPRU strategy achieves the highest acceptance ratio $\mathcal{R}_a$ for AR, while the HPRE has a better performance in terms of resource utilization χ. Our proposed economic agent achieves slightly lower resources utilization compared to the HPRE strategy and keeps the percentage of rejected AR prior to their execution $\mathcal{R}_r$ at an acceptable value. In summary, our proposed economic agent is a trade-off in terms of resource utilization and acceptance ratio between the intuitive HPRU and HPRE strategies, but outperforms both of them in terms of CSP revenues. Indeed, our proposed economic agent achieves an average increase of almost 6% in the CSP revenues. These conclusions still hold independently of the number of submitted jobs.

Impact of the Percentage of under-Estimated Jobs and Their Execution Extra-Time: In this scenario, we vary the percentage ψ of underestimated jobs in $\{20\%, 30\%, 40\%\}$ and the average extra-time $\hat{\lambda}$ required by these jobs in $\{1, 2\}$.

Table 2. Impact of the percentage of under-estimated jobs and their execution extra-time

		$\hat{\lambda}=1$					$\hat{\lambda}=2$				
		$\mathcal{R}_i$	$\mathcal{R}_d$	$\mathcal{R}_r$	χ	Ξ	$\mathcal{R}_i$	$\mathcal{R}_d$	$\mathcal{R}_r$	χ	Ξ
$\psi = 20\%$	Initial Scheduling	7.64%	0%	0%	67.51%	58000	7.43%	0%	0%	67.58%	58000
	On-Demand	9.68%	0%	0%	67.01%	173250	11.12%	0%	0%	68.31%	176250
	HPRU	7.64%	0%	10.01%	64.77%	61000	7.43%	0%	11.21%	65.89%	65000
	HPRE	7.64%	11.29%	0%	69.64%	61000	7.43%	12.81%	0%	70.15%	61500
	Economic Agent	7.64%	8.00%	2.91%	69.34%	64750	7.43%	5.53%	6.51%	69.40%	67500
$\psi = 30\%$	Initial Scheduling	7.44%	0%	0%	67.45%	58000	7.45%	0%	0%	67.49%	58000
	On-Demand	11.10%	0%	0%	68.24%	176250	13.48%	0%	0%	70.66%	180750
	HPRU	7.44%	0%	14.34%	63.60%	62000	7.45%	0%	15.91%	65.22%	67750
	HPRE	7.44%	17.07%	0%	70.61%	62250	7.45%	19.34%	0%	71.38%	63250
	Economic Agent	7.44%	11.89%	4.33%	70.15%	67750	7.45%	9.52%	8.09%	69.98%	71750
$\psi = 40\%$	Initial Scheduling	7.51%	0%	0%	67.54%	58000	7.48%	0%	0%	67.48%	58000
	On-Demand	12.68%	0%	0%	69.52%	179250	15.97%	0%	0%	71.27%	183750
	HPRU	7.51%	0%	18.10%	62.66%	62750	7.48%	0%	19.89%	64.71%	69750
	HPRE	7.51%	22.71%	0%	71.78%	63750	7.48%	25.50%	0%	72.63%	62500
	Economic Agent	7.51%	15.67%	5.59%	71.11%	71000	7.48%	12.36%	10.27%	70.72%	75250

As the initial scheduling does not have any knowledge about the error in estimating the execution time, it achieves the same performance independently of the values of ψ and $\hat{\lambda}$. We notice that the percentage of ARs that are rejected prior to their execution $\mathcal{R}_r$ in the HPRU strategy increases with the percentage of under-estimated jobs. However, this increase is less pronounced than the increase observed in the HPRE strategy for the percentage of dropped ARs during their execution $\mathcal{R}_d$. Finally, our proposed economic agent keeps its superiority and still achieves a trade-off in terms of resource utilization and acceptance ratio between the HPRU and HPRE strategies, but it outperforms both of them in terms of CSP revenues. Indeed, as the percentage of under-estimated jobs increases, the additional gain in the CSP revenues increases from almost 6% for $\psi = 20\%$ to around 12.25% for $\psi = 40\%$. Moreover, as the average extra-time required by the jobs increases, the difference between the HPRU and the HPRE strategies becomes more pronounced as the HPRU strategy achieves higher revenues.

5   Conclusions

Reflecting the recent trend of augmenting Cloud computing with AR provisioning plans, we investigate in this paper the problem of resource provisioning under a *Pay-as-you-Book* pricing model considering ARs characterized by under-estimated execution times. Our model offers to handle the extra-time required by jobs at a higher price, on a best-effort basis. Indeed, the extra-time required by an AR plan may lead to resource conflicts with other AR plans. In order to resolve such resource conflicts, we propose in this work an economic agent responsible for managing the under-provisioning problem. Our economic agent aims to achieve the end-user satisfaction by complying with the SLA terms on one hand as well as the CSP satisfaction by maximizing its revenues through intelligent resource management on the other hand. In this paper, we limited our investigations to compute-intensive applications requesting Virtual Machines. However, this work can be easily generalized to any IaaS resources.

In order to assess the performance of our proposed agent, we have compared our proposed economic agent with two intuitive approaches that systematically prioritize reserved jobs or currently running jobs. Our economic agent achieves a trade-off between the two intuitive strategies in terms of resource utilization and acceptance ratio, but outperforms both of them in terms of CSP revenues. These conclusions still hold independently of the number of submitted jobs, the percentage of under-estimated jobs, and the average duration of the extra-time required. Future studies will extend the results presented in this paper to the case of workflows with multiple jobs. In addition, we intend to enhance the initial scheduling algorithm in order to introduce higher flexibility in the decisions of the economic agent. This economic agent could be be augmented with additional features that implement overbooking techniques. In doing so, the CSP can overcome performance degradation in case of job cancellations.

Acknowledgments. This work is granted by the CompatibleOne project funded by French institutions.

References

1. Lu, K., Roblitz, T., Yahyapour, R., Yaqub, E., Kotsokalis, C.: QoS-aware SLA-based Advanced Reservation of Infrastructure as a Service. In: IEEE CloudCom Conference (November-December 2011)

2. Díaz Sánchez, F., Doumith, E.A., Gagnaire, M.: Impact of Resource over-Reservation (ROR) and Dropping Policies on Cloud Resource Allocation. In: IEEE CloudCom Conference (November-December 2011)

3. Niu, D., Feng, C., Li, B.: Pricing Cloud Bandwidth Reservations Under Demand Uncertainty. In: ACM Sigmetrics/Performance Conference (2012)

4. Niu, D., Feng, C., Li, B.: A Theory of Cloud Bandwidth Pricing for Video-on-Demand Providers. In: IEEE INFOCOM Conference (March 2012)

5. San-Aniceto, I., Moreno-Vozmediano, R., Montero, R., Llorente, I.: Cloud Capacity Reservation for Optimal Service Deployment. In: IARIA Cloud Computing Conference (September 2011)

6. Chaisiri, S., Lee, B.S., Niyato, D.: Optimization of Resource Provisioning Cost in Cloud Computing. IEEE Transactions on Services Computing 5(2) (April-June 2012)

7. Smith, W., Foster, I., Taylor, V.: Scheduling with Advanced Reservations. In: International IPDPS Symposium (2000)

8. Topcuoglu, H., Hariri, S., Wu, M.Y.: Performance-Effective and Low-Complexity Task Scheduling for Heterogeneous Computing. IEEE Transactions on Parallel and Distributed Systems 13(3) (March 2002)

9. Aoun, R., Doumith, E.A., Gagnaire, M.: Resource Provisioning for Enriched Services in Cloud Environment. In: IEEE CloudCom Conference (November-December 2010)

10. Aoun, R., Gagnaire, M.: Towards a Fairer Benefit Distribution in Grid Environments. In: IEEE/ACS AICCSA Conference (May 2009)

11. Venugopal, S., Chu, X., Buyya, R.: A Negotiation Mechanism for Advance Resource Reservations Using the Alternate Offers Protocol. In: International IWQoS Workshop (June 2008)

12. Kaushik, N., Figueira, S., Chiappari, S.: Flexible Time-Windows for Advance Reservation Scheduling. In: IEEE MASCOTS Symposium (September 2006)

13. Aoun, R., Gagnaire, M.: An Exact Optimization Tool for Market-Oriented Grid Middleware. In: IEEE CQR Workshop (May 2009)

14. Aoun, R., Gagnaire, M.: Service Differentiation Based on Flexible Time Constraints in Market-Oriented Grids. In: IEEE GLOBECOM Conference (November-December 2009)

15. Yeo, C.S., Venugopal, S., Chu, X., Buyya, R.: Autonomic Metered Pricing for a Utility Computing Service. Future Generation Computer Systems 26(8) (October 2010)

16. Netto, M.A., Bubendorfer, K., Buyya, R.: SLA-Based Advance Reservations with Flexible and Adaptive Time QoS Parameters. In: International ICSOC Conference (2007)

17. Sulistio, A., Kim, K.H., Buyya, R.: Managing Cancellations and No-Shows of Reservations with Overbooking to Increase Resource Revenue. In: IEEE CCGRID Conference (May 2008)

18. Birkenheuer, G., Brinkmann, A.: Reservation-Based Overbooking for HPC Clusters. In: IEEE CLUSTER Conference (September 2011)

19. Konstanteli, K., Kyriazis, D., Varvarigou, T., Cucinotta, T., Anastasi, G.: Real-Time Guarantees in Flexible Advance Reservations. In: IEEE COMPSAC Conference, vol. 2 (July 2009)

20. Püschel, T., Neumann, D.: Management of Cloud Infrastructures: Policy-Based Revenue Optimization. In: International ICIS Conference (December 2009)

21. Meinl, T., Anandasivam, A., Tatsubori, M.: Enabling Cloud Service Reservation with Derivatives and Yield Management. In: IEEE CEC Conference (November 2010)
22. Son, S., Sim, K.M.: A Price-and-Time-Slot-Negotiation Mechanism for Cloud Service Reservations. IEEE Transactions on Systems, Man, and Cybernetics 42(3) (June 2012)
23. Saure, D., Sheopuri, A., Qu, H., Jamjoom, H., Zeevi, A.: Time-of-Use Pricing Policies for Offering Cloud Computing as a Service. In: IEEE SOLI Conference (July 2010)
24. Yue, M.: A Simple Proof of the Inequality $FFD(L) \leqslant 11/9\ OPT(L) + 1$, $\forall L$ for the FFD bin-packing algorithm. Acta Mathematicae Applicatae Sinica (English Series) 7(4) (1991)
25. Buyya, R., Abramson, D., Giddy, J., Stockinger, H.: Economic Models for Resource Management and Scheduling in Grid Computing. Concurrency and Computation: Practice and Experience 7(13-15) (2002)
26. Parallel Workloads Archive: Logs of Real Parallel Workloads from Production Systems, http://www.cs.huji.ac.il/labs/parallel/workload/logs.html

Economic Co-allocation and Advance Reservation of Network and Computational Resources in Grids

Wim Depoorter, Kurt Vanmechelen, and Jan Broeckhove

University of Antwerp, Middelheimlaan 1, BE-2020 Antwerp, Belgium
{wim.depoorter,kurt.vanmechelen}@ua.ac.be

Abstract. The introduction of economic principles allows Resource Management Systems (RMS) to better deal with conflicting user requirements by incorporating user valuations and externalities such as the usage cost of resources into the planning and scheduling logic. This allows economic RMSs to create more value for the participants than traditional system centric RMSs. It is important for an RMS to take the data requirements of an application into account during the planning phase. Traditional RMSs have been presented supporting co-allocation and advance reservation of both network and computational resources. However, to the best of our knowledge no economic RMSs proposed in the literature possesses these capabilities. In this paper we present ENARA, an economic RMS with advance reservation and co-allocation support for both network and computational resources. We will demonstrate that ENARA can significantly increase the user value compared to an online approach.

Keywords: Resource Management, Co-allocation, Advance Reservation, Grids, Grid Economics, Network Aware, Futures Markets.

1 Introduction

In shared computing environments such as grid systems, Resource Management Systems (RMSs) have to deal with conflicting requirements due to the fact that users of such infrastructures only care about their own self-interest when formulating their requests. We believe that, contrary to traditional RMSs and scheduling approaches in grid systems, the use of economic principles enables the creation of more open and sustainable grid markets oriented towards value maximization. These grid markets charge the users of the system according to their requirements and resulting allocations while taking into account those of other users as well. In this article, we propose and evaluate ENARA, an economic network and resource aware RMS that employs a futures market to trade usage rights on co-allocated and reserved computational resources and network paths. It is important to take data transfers into account when planning applications on a grid system because these transfers can take a considerable amount of time, especially when the data set required by an application is large.

K. Vanmechelen, J. Altmann, and O.F. Rana (Eds.): GECON 2012, LNCS 7714, pp. 46–60, 2012.

We use the GESNET network model to simulate the delays associated with network communication and the transfer of data over the network. We evaluate our RMS in the context of bag-of-task applications with CPU bound jobs and input requirements. A good example is the analysis of data coming from one of the experiments at CERN. All the experiments at CERN produce roughly $15\,PiB$ of data per year. It is clear that the processing even a small part of that data still involves massive input files. We extend our original system model presented by Vanmechelen et al. [1] with data dependencies and network resources.

The system model we use and the broker we developed do not require users to specify a fixed parallelization degree for their applications in contrast to several other existing approaches [2,3,4]. Instead, the ENARA RMS is given the freedom to schedule data transfers and computational workload, as long as it can guarantee that the input files are transferred from storage to the execution site before the computation starts and that the application finishes by a given deadline. In our simulations we explicitly take into account the atomicity of jobs and the limited parallelization degree of an application. We do not require job preemption and migration in the construction of job schedules.

This article is organized as follows. First we take a look at related work in the next section. In section 3 we give an overview of the ENARA system model. We discuss the network (pre)pricing of individual links in section 4. We conclude with an evaluation of our approach. We compare our approach in terms of generated user value to an online network aware scheduling policy.

2   Related Work

There is to the best of our knowledge no other work that combines both economic aware network *and* cpu resource co-allocation and advance reservation. A recurring technique for advance reservation and co-allocation of network resources is the discretization of time to make the scheduling problem more tractable. Depending on the level of granularity, this discretization can induce sizeable internal fragmentation on resources as computational jobs and network transfers typically cannot occupy discretized time slots fully.

Takefusa et al. have proposed an advance reservation-based co-allocation algorithm for distributed computing and network bandwidth [5]. Their online planning approach incorporates both co-allocation and advance reservation, but does not integrate economic principles. The co-allocation problem is solved by discretizing time in laddered time frames and modelling it as a simplified Integer Programming (IP) problem. The MC-T scheme proposed by Stevens et al. also discretizes the time [6] but is less suited for systems to large planning windows due to a limited look-ahead. Work by Dramitinos also proposes a discretized economic advance reservation system [7] for network resources only.

The first two approaches are not economic while the last does not incorporate compute resources. In contrast with our work, all of them make use of discretized time slots.

3   System Model

In this section we give an overview of the elements of our ENARA system. First we introduce the GESNET network layer which is modeled after Lambda Grids. It is this component that provides the necessary features for transferring data and reserving the network paths needed for transporting the input files from their storage locations to the location in the network where the application will be executed. Then we describe how we use *Planning Windows*, how we model *Jobs, Workflows, Data and Requests, Consumers* and *Providers*. We conclude this section with a description of the most important entity in our system model, the *ENARA broker*.

3.1   Network

To accurately take into account the transfer times of data and the cost of these transfers on the network in an advance reservation setting, we have developed the GESNET network model with support for advance reservations and network pricing [8]. GESNET is modeled after Lambda Grids [9] and is built on the *Jung2* library which provides a number of standard graph algorithms [10]. Lambda Grids are fiber optic networks that allow the creation of light paths for setting up dynamically allocated point to point links between two sites in the network. There are multiple wavelengths used in each fiber optic link, dividing it in multiple logical channels. A light path is a path reserved on a set of subsequent links in the network and bound to a specific wavelength. In fact, it is a list of subsequent *channels*. A channel cannot be allocated to more than one light path at a time which contrasts with traditional packet switched networks. As such, Lambda Grids can be seen as frequency divided networks with non-intersecting network planes.

Entities participating in the simulation are placed at specific locations in the network. As such, the communication delay between them will be modelled and incorporated in the simulation. Multiple sites may be located on a single location. We denote the set of storage sites in our simulation with $S = \{s_1, \ldots, s_m\}$ and the set of compute sites with $C = \{c_1, \ldots, c_n\}$. The communication delay between two entities is calculated based on the speed of light in a fiber optic cable over the physical link-distances between the two communicating sites.

GESNET also enables the creation of network paths for file transfer, both ad hoc and as reservations for future use. Future network transfers will be planned either as soon or as late as possible, depending on the properties of the reservation request. In order to do this, GESNET will look through all the network planes for the earliest or latest possible reservation for a transfer of a specific data set from node s to c [8].

3.2   Planning Windows

ENARA uses periodic planning phases with a sliding Planning window PW. When the size of PW is 24 hours for example, the broker can plan one day in the future. The Planning Period PP is defined as the time delta between two consecutive planning phases. Each planning phase, the PW will shift forward by the same amount as the PP. The planning phase itself starts before the beginning of the PW. The specific lead time LT to the planning phase is chosen to be big enough to ensure that the planning phase will have ended before PW starts. During the lead time, we explicitly model both communication delay as provided by our network model as well as the algorithmic overhead induced by our own resource management system and given by the wall clock time difference between the beginning and the end of the planning phase. As such, we can guarantee that ENARA not only establishes appropriate allocations, but also that it does so within a realistic time frame as set by LT. We believe that this is a necessary validation of the practicality and feasibility of scheduling algorithms that is often not incorporated in the simulation model directly but evaluated separately. The Hot Window HW is defined as the time interval that will become unavailable for planning after the current planning phase. As such, when nothing is planned in or can be moved to the HW after the planning phase, the capacity in this HW is effectively lost.

Since PW's can be big in comparison to the time delta between two consecutive planning phases, it is not straightforward to determine whether the system is congested. To assess whether the system is in a state of congestion, we define a Congestion Window CW. A Congestion window can be seen as a kind of "leaky bucket" for planning and as such allows the system to accommodate occasional bursts of high activity.

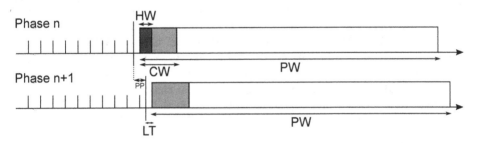

Fig. 1. Planning Windows

All these concepts are illustrated in Figure 1. As can be seen from this figure, the lead time is very small in comparison to the planning window. If we take the scale on the time axis to be 1 hour, PW is 24 h and LT is 30 min. We have marked the 1 h long hot window in dark grey. This is the window that the broker should absolutely try to fill as this capacity cannot be sold anymore in a next planning phase. The congestion window is indicated with light grey and also includes the hot window. It is 3 h long. As can be seen, the planning window is shifted forward when starting the next planning phase. The size of this shift is equal to the planning period.

3.3 Jobs, Workflows, Data and Requests

Jobs are modelled as having a certain processing requirement expressed as a normalized processing time npt (in hours) when executed on a reference architecture. Applications can be modelled as workflows with a number of individual jobs and precedence relations between them. In this work we model bag-of-task applications and we focus on the effects and benefits of network and CPU resource co-allocation and reservation. Typical examples of such applications are parameter sweeps where individual jobs all process the same input data with different parameter values. Applications may potentially require (parts of) big datasets to process. These are modelled by data dependencies in the application model. When an application has a data dependency, the system needs to make sure that the data is transferred to the location of execution before the computational workflow starts.

To execute an application, a consumer submits an **Application Processing Request** (APR) to the RMS. This APR contains the processing workflow, possible input data requirements and the maximum budget $budget(j)$ the consumer is willing to spend for the execution of its application. A workflow consists of n jobs that have to be executed for the application to finish successfully. The normalized processing requirements of the entire workflow of request j is $npt(j) = \sum_{i=1}^{n} npt(i)$ with $npt(i)$ defined as the processing requirements of job i. When a request requires input data, this will be indicated by the presence of a data dependency in the APR. The location and size of this specific file can be found by querying the **File Catalog**. We will denote the size of the input file of request j with $f(j)$, its size with $ds(j) = ds(f(j))\, GiB$ and the storage location(s) of the data as $S(j) = \{s : f(j) \in s\}$. Requests that require input data will be called Data Dependent APRs (DDAPR) from here on. When a request does not require any input data it is called a Data Free APR (DFAPR). In our experiments we assume that data is not cached at the compute locations after an APR is finished due to insufficient storage capacity at the computational resource providers. This means that data needs to be transferred for every DDAPR.

3.4 Consumers

Consumers are modeled as entities that will submit their requests to the broker for planning. For each request, n jobs of randomized length are generated. If the request is a DDAPR, the file $f(j)$ used will be the same for all subsequent requests of a specific consumer. The budget is calculated based on $npt(j)$, $ds(j)$ and the valuations $nv_{cpu}(j)$ for computational resources and $nv_{net}(j)$ for network transfers of the specific consumer. In addition we randomize the budgets with a variance factor var_{budget}. For each subsequent request of a consumer we multiply the base budget with the random factor $RF = (1+rand(-var_{budget}, +var_{budget}))$ with $rand(x, y)$ a uniform random generated value between x and y. The exact formula for the calculation of the request budget is given in Equation 1. We note that $nv_{cpu}(j)$ and $nv_{net}(j)$ are a priori normalized valuations for the application execution and network transfer. These two valuations make it easier to select budget levels for consumers in our experiments and are exclusively used for determining the total request budget and then forgotten. We assume that a real user of the system would only provide an aggregate budget for the execution of its application.

$$budget(j) = (nv_{cpu}(j) * npt(j) + nv_{net}(j) * ds(j)) * RF \qquad (1)$$

Before each planning phase starts, all consumers submit their request to the broker. When a request is successfully planned by the broker, the consumer has to pay both network link and compute resource providers for the usage of their resources. When a request of consumer x is successfully finished, it is added to the set of finished APRs F_x. Consumers will have an implicit value $V(j)$ attached to the execution of their application. The total value planned for a consumer is then defined as $V(x) = \sum_{r \in F_x} V(r)$.

3.5   Providers

Each compute provider manages a number of CPUs. We consider CPUs to be uniform parallel machines. This means that all computational jobs can be executed on all CPUs and that their execution time depends linearly on the relative power of the specific CPU compared with a standard CPU.

When the broker wants to schedule the jobs of the workflow of an APR, it will contact a provider, and ask it to schedule either all jobs or as many jobs as possible by means of a **Request Bid**. The provider will search for free periods in the *PW* of all its CPUs and select the best one for each job by means of a selection policy. In this article, the provider uses a closest to the deadline policy. This ensures that the provider keeps as much free capacity as possible in the beginning of the *PW*, allowing it to schedule in subsequent applications with shorter deadlines. Since the provider will schedule in jobs as close to deadline as possible, it is very likely that after the planning phase no jobs are planned in the Hot Window (*HW*) which is defined as the time interval that will become unavailable for planning after the end of the planning phase. As such the provider will defragment all its CPU schedules and attempt to move or shift reservations forward to fill all compute capacity still available in the *HW* at each specific CPU resource.

3.6   Broker

The ENARA-broker we have developed is capable of scheduling both DDAPRs and DFAPRs. It operates using sliding Planning Windows described in subsection 3.2. In every planning phase, the ENARA-broker will try to plan as many APRs as possible by going through its list of submitted APRs, or *SAPRL*. This list is sorted according to the normalized budget *nb* available to each request. The normalized budget *nb* is a measure for the budget normalized over the expected costs to execute the request's workload and transfer its data. As such it can be used to prioritize APRs from the most to the least valuable. The broker uses a greedy heuristic to try and plan in as much APRs as possible. We use this heuristic approach because our problem domain is NP complete. As such it is not possible to find the optimal allocations in a reasonable time span. Note that in our evaluation, we take both communication delays and overhead of our calculations into account when planning. Therefore, we cannot implement a strategy that may be theoretically correct but not tractable to compute.

Additionally, the ENARA-broker has approximate information of the free capacity of both the network and the compute resources. This allows it to quickly check whether the selected provider and/or the network have enough capacity available just before the planning of an individual APR. As such we have incorporated a fast-fail mechanism in the broker that can reduce both network traffic and computational overhead caused by planning attempts that are bound to fail. We have demonstrated a similar mechanism for APRs without input data [11].

Budget Normalization. In order to normalize APR budgets, the broker uses a `Pre Pricing Algorithm`. For DFAPRs, we can easily calculate their normalized budget as given by Equation 2.

$$nb(j) = budget(j)/npt(j) \tag{2}$$

For DDAPRs however, this is not so straightforward. Their normalized budget depends on the normalized prices that need to be payed for both compute and network resources and on the relative value of these normalized prices. The actual prices are the result of the demand for both network and computational resources and the budgets of individual consumers. However, the actual prices of both computational and network resources are not known until after the planning phase has ended. This means that we have to estimate the expected prices of both computational (np_{cpu}^{E}) and network resources (np_{net}^{E}) before planning the requests.

This is in fact a catch-22 situation since the expected prices in turn will influence the ordering of the APRs, the actual allocations and ultimately the actual prices themselves, which is exactly what we are trying to estimate in the first place. It is therefore important that, when calculating expected prices, we do not create discriminatory prices for individual network paths and computational resources as this would ultimately lead to unbalanced allocations. Note that in each planning phase, we only use the subset of storage sites S that store data requested by the DDAPRs in the *SAPRL*. We do take all compute locations C into account as they have new capacity available in each planning round.

The method of calculating the expected normalized network price np_{net}^{E} and the expected normalized cpu price np_{cpu}^{E} is based on the anticipated congestion of the system for both computational and network resources [8]. It is not discussed here due to space considerations. The distribution of np_{cpu}^{E} over individual links is discussed in section 4. The Gigabyte-to-Workload factor $G2W$ is defined as $np_{net}^{E}/np_{cpu}^{E}$ and is a normalization factor that is used to split the budget of DDAPRs in a separate compute and network budget. The normalized DDAPR budget of request j is defined in Equation 3.

$$nb(j) = \frac{budget(j)}{npt(j) + G2W * ds(j)} \tag{3}$$

The compute budget of a DDAPR is then given by $bc(j) = nb(j) * npt(j)$ and its data budget by $bd(j) = nb(j) * G2W * ds(j)$. This enables the broker to order both DDAPRs and DFAPRs in the submitted APR list ($SAPRL$). The ordering is based on normalized compute budget $nb(j)$ of each request. Since both DDAPRs and DFAPRs are sorted in a single list, we can use a greedy approach for planning.

Planning. The ENARA-broker will iterate over the sorted list of submitted APRs and attempt to schedule in each individual request. For all APRs we define a preferred compute providers list (PPL) which is a sorted list of the providers based on the cost of executing the entire application, including necessary data transfers. All DFAPRs share the same PPL since the location of a compute provider is irrelevant when an application has no input data requirements. For each request we try to plan the individual jobs at the first provider p in the PPL. If p cannot plan all jobs and the request is a DFAPR, the broker tries to plan the remaining jobs with the next provider in the PPL and so on (untill we can plan all jobs). If not all jobs could be planned, we cancel the reservations and remove the DFAPR from the $SAPRL$. If p can plan all jobs of a DDAPR, the broker will attempt to make the necessary network reservations. If it is not successful, all reservations are cancelled and the DDAPR is re-inserted in the $SAPRL$ with an adjusted $nb(j)$. This adjustment is due to the fact that the path price to different network locations *may* be different when the reserve price of a link is higher than the expected price. After planning is finished, the broker will have 2 lists of APRs, the list with planned APRs, $PAPRL$, and the list with unplanned APRs, $UPAPRL$. These may be used in the final pricing phase of the planning process as described in the next subsection.

Pricing. After the broker has planned in all necessary requests, it still needs to price them. For the ENARA broker, we price both compute and network resources with a **Next Highest Losing Bid** strategy (NHLB) as follows. First, we iterate over all requests in the sorted $SAPRL$ and, as long as the current request was planned, we add it to the current set cS. When a request has not been planned, we price all APRs in cS with the normalized budget of the unplanned request and empty cS. We continue iterating over the $SAPRL$ until there are no APRs left. Then we price the remaining request in cS with the reserve price of the providers. The resulting compute price is distributed uniformly over all compute providers that participate in the APR. The distribution for network providers is based on the Extended Minimal Cut List as explained in section 4.2. In this way we become uniform path prices while taking the relative importance of the individual links into account. Note that currently both network and compute resource providers are able to set minimum prices. While it would be possible to dynamically change these during the simulation, we have not experimented with this option.

We use the NHLB pricing strategy because the pricing rule used is closely related to Vickrey auctions. This kind of auction is incentive compatible and the best strategy for a participant is to reveal its true value for the item. For complex systems such as ours, the winner determination is often NP hard. As such it becomes impossible to design a system that on the one hand is incentive compatible, and on the other hand tractable to compute [12]. As such, no hard proof can be given that we have in fact created a system that is incentive compatible. Indeed, there may be situations where participants of the system can in fact gain an advantage by strategic bidding. This should not stop us from applying the most important principles of incentive compatibility to our pricing strategy, namely second price like systems are generally a good choice for participants to reveal their true valuations and are less susceptible to strategic bidding than other pricing systems.

4   Network Pricing

In this section we describe the general approach to pricing individual network links based on their importance. The first subsection deals with the search for links that are responsible for the limitations in transfer capacity between a set of sources S and a set of sinks C in a network. We then explain how the estimated prices translate to the pre-prices of individual resources. More details about the actual algorithms can be found in [8].

4.1   Limiting Links

In this subsection we define the limiting links $LL(S, C)$ $\{l_1, \ldots, l_n\}$ from a set of sources S to a set of sinks C with $S \cap C = \emptyset$ as the set of *all* links where the network capacity $cap_{net}(S, C)$ from S to C decreases when *any* of the links in $LL(S, C)$ is removed. We define $LL(S, C)$ more formally in Equation 4 where the extra parameter g denotes the graph representation of the network.

$$LL(S, C, g) = \{l_1, \ldots, l_n\} \text{ with } \forall l_i \in LL(S, C, g) : \atop cap_{net}(S, C, g) > cap_{net}(S, C, g \setminus l_i) \tag{4}$$

Clearly, the links in $LL(S, C, g)$ are important and should be (pre)priced accordingly. We have designed an algorithm that calculates the Extended Minimal Cut List $EMCL(S, C, g)$ between a set of sources S and a set of sinks C on network graph g [8]. The algorithm first calculates the list of minimal cuts between S and C and then extends the individual minimal cuts with the additional trailing limiting links. The links in the $EMCL(S, C, g)$ are equal to the limiting links defined in Equation 4 and its ordering and composition helps in pricing the links between S and C uniformly.

To further clarify these concepts, we provide an example of an extended minimal cut list based on the network depicted in Figure 2. We take $S = \{1, 2, 3\}$ and $C = \{7, 13, 16\}$. All limiting links are marked with a diamond. Links marked with open diamonds are extending links of a minimal cut. The resulting extended minimal cut list is given in (5).

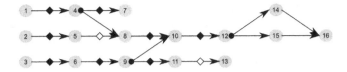

Fig. 2. Extended Minimal Cut List

$$EMCL = \left[\left\{\begin{matrix}(1,4)\\(2,5),(5,8)\\(3,6)\end{matrix}\right\},\left\{\left[\left\{\begin{matrix}(8,10)\\(6,9)\end{matrix}\right\},\left\{\begin{matrix}(4,7)\\(10,12)\\(9,11),(11,13)\end{matrix}\right\}\right]\right\}\right] \quad (5)$$

Extended minimal cut lists are encapsulated in square brackets while extended minimal cuts use curly braces. Extended links are not marked but visible by the fact that the links in an extended link are horizontally separated by commas, for example $(2,5),(5,8)$. As can be seen, the second main extended minimal cut contains an extended minimal cut list all by itself. We can also check that when we remove *any* link in $EMCL$ from the network, its capacity will decrease. The non-limiting links from $\{(4,8),(9,10),(12,14),(12,15),(14,16),(15,16)\}$ are not included in the extended minimal cut list.

4.2   Network Resource Pre-pricing

We estimate both the normalized network (np_{net}^E) and computational resource np_{cpu}^E prices based on the expected congestion on network links and computational resources respectively. All compute resources are uniformly pre-priced based on np_{cpu}^E. For network resources this is slightly more complicated as we have estimated the uniform path price. However, we have to distribute this estimation over the individual links. The distribution of the estimated price is based on the Extended Minimal Cut list.

Due to space considerations, we provide the resulting network link price estimations based on Figure 2 and an estimated network price of $np_{net}^E = 0.8\,EUR/GiB$. We represent the resulting link pre-prices on the graph in Figure 3. It is readily verifiable that any path from a source node to a sink node will be pre-priced at the desired $0.8\,EUR/GiB$. The price distribution matches the importance of the individual links which becomes clear when they are matched with the EMCL in (6). We re-use the relative importance of links when distributing the actual path price over the individual links. Note that we have not taken into account the reserve price for the non-limiting links in order to present the distribution of path prices over the limiting links in the extended minimal cut list more clearly.

$$\left[\left\{\begin{matrix}(1,4)=.4\\(2,5),(5,8)=.2\\(3,6)=.4\end{matrix}\right\}=.4,\left\{\left[\left\{\begin{matrix}(8,10)=.2\\(6,9)=.2\end{matrix}\right\}=.2,\left\{\begin{matrix}(4,7)=.4\\(10,12)=.2\\(9,11),(11,13)=.1\end{matrix}\right\}=.2\right]=.4\right\}=.4\right]=.8 \quad (6)$$

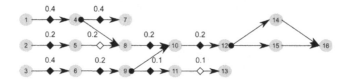

Fig. 3. Extended Minimal Cut List Pricing

5   Results

We now demonstrate with some specific experiments that the different elements of our global approach deliver correct and expected results. We note that variance var of a value v in our experiments is always given as a number in $[0, 1[$ and that for each member of a group, a uniformly random value is chosen in the interval $[v * (1 - var), v * (1 + var)[$ by means of the java `Random nextDouble` method.

For all our experiments we have used a network based on the EGEE topology. We have depicted this network in Figure 4. This figure also contains an example of network prices as calculated by our algorithms. The locations of storage providers are indicated in light grey and the locations of computational resource providers in dark grey. It is readily verifiable that the resulting network path prices are around $0.684\,EUR/GiB$. Note that we have omitted the reserve prices in order to avoid clutter.

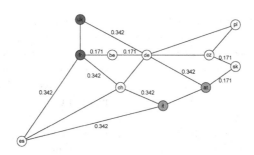

Fig. 4. Simulated Network

5.1   Online vs Offline Network Aware Scheduling

The ENARA broker is an offline scheduling system that periodically plans in all submitted requests in order to generate as much user value and utility as possible. There are however settings where the extra delay caused by this periodic planning is undesirable. As such we have imitated the behaviour of an online FIFO based scheduler that is network aware by randomizing the order in which requests are processed in the planning phase for the ENARA broker. We have named this broker FIFOna. One notable difference with a traditional online system is the fact that applications that cannot be planned immediately will (have to) be resubmitted to the broker. This means that when there is a sudden spike in high-value applications, these applications actually have a higher chance of being scheduled than in a true online FIFO based system.

While FIFOna is quite capable of planning in applications with their data dependencies, it significantly changes the assumptions on which the pricing strategy is based. Since we are not selecting applications based on their normalized budget but rather on their arrival time, we are not assigning the allocations to the highest bidders and as such we cannot use a second pricing approach. Another aspect is that it is much more difficult to estimate the gigabyte to workload factor in an online system, especially when load peaks occur. Because of these two reasons, FIFOna uses a reserve pricing strategy. Therefore we focus in the tests that follow on the value that the system has realized for its users, not on the utility because of the unresolved issues surrounding pricing in an online setting.

The network we use is based on EGEE and is depicted in Figure 4. We have distributed compute and storage sites randomly. The random distribution of compute sites S and storage sites C creates situations with potentially different sizes for the minimal cut between S and C and thus with different network capacities. That is why we have grouped the scenarios with identical network capacities. For these tests, we have chosen 25 scenarios where the minimal cut is 3 links. We set LT to $5\,min$, PP to $15\,min$, PW to $24\,hour$ and CW to $30\,min$ and use $NHLB$ pricing for both computational and network resources. We use 6 providers with 100 cpu nodes each and a reserve price of $0.1\,EUR/hour$ for computational resources and $0.1\,EUR/GiB$ for network link capacity. The number of storage nodes in the network is 2. The simulation bound is $24\,h$. The parameters for the 4 different consumer groups can be found in Table 1. The first group, $Group_N$ are users for which the applications do not have any data dependencies. $Group_D$ are users with applications with data dependencies. The last two groups are groups of a limited number of short deadline consumers that will enter the system in $3\,hour$ intervals as indicated by the reload time rt. They also have a tighter deadline as indicated by the deadline factor df. The number of consumers $|Cons|$ of the short deadline consumer groups is limited to 15. The standard job length is 10 or $20\,min$. We have chosen an input data size $ds = 100\,GiB$ as the time it takes to transfer this amount of data is approximately equal to $15\,min$, which simplifies the parameter choice for our experiments.

Table 1. Experiment Parameters

Param	$Group_N$	$Group_D$	$Group_{HN}$	$Group_{HD}$
$|Cons|$	120	120	15	15
rt	0	0	$3\,hour$	$3\,hour$
$|jobs|$	25	10	25	10
jl	20	10	20	10
df	25	12	3	3
np_{cpu}^E	$0.2EUR/hour$	$0.3EUR/hour$	$0.2EUR/hour * \{1, 10\}$	$0.3EUR/hour * \{1, 10\}$
np_{net}^E	n.a.	$0.3EUR/GiB$	n.a.	$0.3EUR/GiB * \{1, 10\}$

The variation in data size is 5% for these tests. However, we have also performed tests with $var_{ds} = 50\%$ without any negative impact on the resulting allocations. Note that we have chosen var_{jl}, var_{ds}, var_{budget} to be 5% and that we have varied the budget of the short deadline consumers by multiplying the budgets of the normal value consumers with $\{1, 10\}$. This results in two experiments; one where the short deadline consumers have similar valuations than the normal consumers, and one where their valuations are 10 times as high. Consumers keep generating new APRs as long as the simulation runs. For all the experiments executed the ENARA broker could achieve a utilization on both network and computational resources over 97.5%.

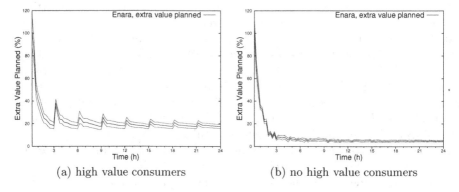

(a) high value consumers   (b) no high value consumers

Fig. 5. Value Planned ENARA vs FIFOna

The relative increase in total value planned for the experiment with high value low deadline groups, is plotted in Figure 5a, together with the deviation. We can observe that offline planning is able to plan just over 17.5% of additional value compared with an online planning approach. In absolute values, the average final consumer value planned for the ENARA system is 118 172 with a deviation of 376 over 25 runs. For the FIFOna system, we obtain an average of 100 477 with a deviation of 1 704 over 25 runs. Note that it would be possible to increase this difference significantly by increasing the number of consumers in groups N and D. Such an enlarged user population would decrease the chances of high-value consumers being planned for the FIFOna broker.

When the low deadline groups have similar valuations than the normal groups, we are in fact testing whether the ENARA system by itself can plan in more value than an online approach. In that case, the difference can only be made by selecting the highest value requests. The results can be seen in Figure 5b. Towards the end of the 24 hour period, the increase in value planned by the ENARA system compared to the online FIFOna planner is approximately 4.7%. This value is very close to the budget variance of 5% and as such a validation of the capacities of the ENARA broker. The average of the final value planned for the ENARA system is 83 800 with a deviation of 455 over 25 runs. For the FIFOna system, we reach an average of 80 012 with a deviation of 233 over 25 runs.

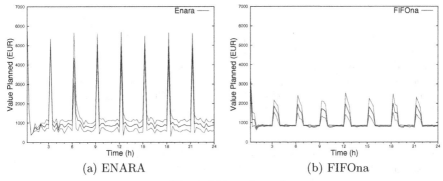

(a) ENARA   (b) FIFOna

Fig. 6. Value planned

In Figure 6 we have plotted the value planned in each planning phase and the deviation over 25 runs of both the offline ENARA system and online FIFOna system. Part (a) and (b) show the results of the experiment with high value low deadline consumer groups. We can make the observation that the ENARA broker plans in all high-value applications immediately as shown by the high peaks every 3 hours while for FIFOna the peaks are much less pronounced. Note that the peaks in the FIFOna system are also wider, which means that it can catch up somewhat with the ENARA broker while the deadlines of the remaining high-value requests have not expired.

We can deduce from the previous graphs that ENARA actively selects the highest value applications when scheduling. This is confirmed in our experiments by the sharp decline in the number of requests planned for the normal value consumers every 3 hours and the simultaneous peak in numbers for the high-value consumers. Since the online FIFOna system cannot perform this active selection, it is not capable of extracting all the additional value from the high-value consumers.

6   Conclusion

In this article we have tackled the advance reservation and co-allocation problem of computational and network resources. By estimating np_{cpu}^{E} and np_{net}^{E} and defining the $G2W$ factor we are able to flatten an inherently two-dimensional problem and use a greedy heuristic for planning both data dependent and data free APRs. We have clearly demonstrated that the ENARA broker is capable of generating higher value for the users of the system compared to an online approach. This is achieved by actively selecting and planning the highest value requests. We have mentioned that the ENARA broker is capable of planning in both network and computational resources at close to 100% utilization, which is a clear indication of the efficiency of the allocation mechanism.

Acknowledgments. This work is partially supported by the Flemish Fund for Scientific Research (FWO) under research grant 1154609N.

References

1. Vanmechelen, K., Depoorter, W., Broeckhove, J.: Market-based grid resource co-allocation and reservation for applications with hard deadlines. Concurrency and Computation: Practice and Experience 21, 2270–2297 (2009)
2. Chun, B.N., Buonadonna, P., AuYoung, A., Chaki, N., Parkes, D., Shneidman, J., Snoeren, A., Vahdat, A.: Mirage: A microeconomic resource allocation system for sensornet testbeds. In: Proceedings of the Second IEEE Workshop on Embedded Networked Sensors, pp. 19–28. IEEE Computer Society (May 2005)
3. Schnizler, B.: Resource Allocation in the Grid – A Market Engineering Approach. PhD thesis, University of Karlsruhe (2007)
4. Stößer, J., Neumann, D.: GreedEx – A scalable clearing mechanism for utility computing. In: Proceedings of the Networking and Electronic Commerce Research Conference, NAEC 2007 (2007)
5. Takefusa, A., Nakada, H., Kudoh, T., Tanaka, Y.: An Advance Reservation-Based Co-allocation Algorithm for Distributed Computers and Network Bandwidth on QoS-Guaranteed Grids. In: Frachtenberg, E., Schwiegelshohn, U. (eds.) JSSPP 2010. LNCS, vol. 6253, pp. 16–34. Springer, Heidelberg (2010)
6. Stevens, T., Leenheer, M.D., Develder, C., Dhoedt, B., Christodoulopoulos, K., Kokkinos, P., Varvarigos, E.: Multi-cost job routing and scheduling in grid networks. Future Gener. Comput. Syst. 25(8), 912–925 (2009)
7. Dramitinos, M., Stamoulis, G., Courcoubetis, C.: An auction mechanism for allocating the bandwidth of networks to their users. Computer Networks: The International Journal of Computer and Telecommunications Networking 51(18), 4979–4996 (2007)
8. Depoorter, W.: Economic and Network Aware Grid Resource Management. PhD thesis, UA (2012)
9. GLIF: Global lambda integrated facility (2012), http://www.glif.is/ (accessed October 8, 2012)
10. Madadhain, J., Fisher, D., Smyth, P., White, S., Boey, Y.: Analysis and visualization of network data using jung. Journal of Statistical Software 10, 1–35 (2005)
11. Depoorter, W., den Bossche, R.V., Vanmechelen, K., Broeckhove, J.: Evaluating the divisible load assumption in the context of economic grid scheduling with deadline-based qos guarantees. In: IEEE International Symposium on Cluster Computing and the Grid, Los Alamitos, CA, USA, pp. 452–459. IEEE Computer Society (2009)
12. Rothkopf, M.: Thirteen reasons why the Vickrey-Clarke-Groves process is not practical. Operations Research 55(2), 191–197 (2007)

Revenue-Based Resource Management on Shared Clouds for Heterogenous Bursty Data Streams

Rafael Tolosana-Calasanz[1], José Ángel Bañares[1], Congduc Pham[2], and Omer F. Rana[3]

[1] Dpto. de Informática e Ingeniería de Sistemas
Universidad de Zaragoza, Spain
{rafaelt,banares}@unizar.es
[2] LIUPPA Laboratory
University of Pau, France
congduc.pham@univ-pau.fr
[3] School of Computer Science & Informatics
Cardiff University, United Kingdom
o.f.rana@cs.cardiff.ac.uk

Abstract. When data from multiple sources (sensors) are processed over a shared distributed computing infrastructure, it is necessary to often provide some Quality of Service (QoS) guarantees to each data stream. Service Level Agreements (SLAs) identify the cost that a user must pay to achieve the required QoS, and a penalty that must be paid to the user in case the QoS cannot be met. Assuming the maximisation of the revenue as the provider's objective, then it must decide which streams to accept for storage and analysis; and how many (computational / storage) resources to allocate to each stream in order to improve overall revenue. We propose an infrastructure for supporting QoS for concurrent data streams to be composed of self-regulating nodes. Each node features an envelope process to accept user streams; and a resource manager to enable resource allocation, admission control and selective SLA violations, while maximizing revenue.

Keywords: Data stream processing, Cloud computing, SLA Management, Admission control, QoS provisioning.

1 Introduction

The number of applications that need to process data continuously over long periods of time has increased significantly over recent years. Often the raw data captured from the source is converted into complex events – which are subsequently further analysed. Such applications include weather forecasting and ocean observation from sensors [1], text analysis (especially with the growing requirement to analyse social media data, for instance), "Urgent Computing" [2], and more recently data analysis from electricity meters to support "Smart

K. Vanmechelen, J. Altmann, and O.F. Rana (Eds.): GECON 2012, LNCS 7714, pp. 61–75, 2012.
© Springer-Verlag Berlin Heidelberg 2012

(Power) Grids" [3]. Data source (sensor) nodes can vary in complexity from smart phones to specialist instruments, and can consist of sensing, data processing and communication components. Data streams in such applications are generally large-scale and distributed, and generated continuously at a rate that cannot be estimated in advance. Scalability remains a major requirement for such applications, to handle variable event loads efficiently. Data elements are streamed from their source to their sink, and may be processed en-route (referred to *in transit* processing), rather than entirely at source /destination [4]. The benefit of such an approach is many fold: (i) to reduce power consumption at source (which may have limited battery capacity) and sink (which may have limited data storage space); (ii) enable the outcome of data analysis to be shared between multiple users; (iii) enable optimization by moving the processing close to the producers and consumers where applicable (consider an example where there are multiple sensors within the same location, and the event processing involves aggregation of events that are emitted by these sensors); (iv) alter the processing rate at intermediate (in transit) nodes to achieve a particular QoS requirement [5]; (v) combine data streams with archived data at intermediate nodes; (vi) enable fault tolerance to be supported at intermediate nodes – thereby providing an overall resilient infrastructure that masks faults generated due to the generation of large data volumes (referred to as data inflation) or failure of resources involved in data processing [6]; (vii) redirect event traffic to different nodes according to network conditions or workload [4].

We assume an Event Processing Network (EPN) is composed of a sequence of stages and datasets are streamed through that sequence (pipeline). Each EPN stage is mapped to a node in the infrastructure, though a node can enact more than one EPN stage. Using this approach, *each node* must be able to *self-regulate* its behaviour dynamically through adaptive resource provisioning, i.e. resources allocated for each incoming stream can be varied dynamically by a node controller. Various existing approaches [3,7,5,8] identify how Cloud infrastructures can be used to support data stream analysis. When multiple applications are executed within the same shared elastic infrastructure, each stream must be isolated from another and for the underlying coordination mechanism to adapt the infrastructure to either: (i) run all instances without violating their particular Quality of Service (QoS) constraints; or (ii) indicate that, given current resources, a particular instance cannot be accepted for execution. The QoS demand of each stream is captured in a Service Level Agreement (SLA) – which must be pre-agreed with each service provider prior to analysis. Such an SLA identifies the cost that a user must pay to achieve the required QoS and a penalty that must be paid to the user if the QoS cannot be met [9].

In previous works, we presented scenarios to validate the use of TB and the adaptation of TB parameters to achieve SLA objectives. In [5], a scenario that shows the role of TB for *shaping* the amount of data that subsequently forwarded to computational resources was presented, allowing for bursts of data while at the same time providing isolation of data streams. In [8], we subsequently demonstrate how a streaming pipeline, with a variation in the amount of data generated (referred to as data inflation/deflation), can be supported and managed using a dynamic control strategy at each node. Finally, in [6], we analyse revenue models for supporting streaming under the presence of faulty computational resources. These papers show main models developed using Petri nets to specify the EPN and architectural components and the engine to enact them[10]. In this paper, we extend previous work [5] by characterising a revenue model for in-transit analysis. We propose the use of the TB model for estimating the resources required to meet the SLA of each incoming data stream, extending our previous use of the TB mechanism for event traffic shaping. The remainder of this paper is structured as follows. Section 2 describes revenue models for in-transit analysis and the characterization of resource requirements for QoS in event processing applications. Section 3 shows the system architecture based on the token bucket model and a rule-based SLA management of QoS. Section 4 shows our evaluation scenario and simulation results. In Section 5, the related work is briefly discussed. Finally, conclusions are given in Section 6.

2   Revenue Models for In-Transit Analysis

In-transit analysis provides a useful abstraction for separating data capture/use and analysis, enabling different actors (i.e. service providers) to be involved in each of these processes. Hence, data capture may be carried out by a different actor compared to subsequent analysis – enabling multiple capabilities from different actors to be combined at different costs. Each actor may differ in their ability to undertake particular types of analysis that meet varying QoS constraints – leading to different payments that must be made to them by a user to achieve the overall operation.

In our formulation of this problem, we can consider a provider centric view of costs incurred to provide function O. Where a shared Cloud infrastructure is being used, a provider may serve multiple users using a common resource pool through a "multi-tenancy" architecture, or offer multiple functions over their shared infrastructure to one or more users. In both cases, the revenue for the provider is the sum of all the prices $Pr()$ charged to n users for accomplishing m operations O, $\sum_{i=1}^{n} \sum_{j=1}^{m} Pr(O_{ij})$. The provider in turn incurs a cost for performing such operations, $c(O_{ij})$, but can also incur a financial penalty $PSLA_{ij}$ for user i when the QoS targets of operation O_{ij}, identified in the SLA of user stream i are not met. If we assume the objective of the provider is to maximise revenue, then it must decide: (i) which user streams to accept for storage and analysis; and (ii) how many resources (including storage space and computational capacity) to allocate to each stream in order to improve overall revenue (generally over a time horizon). Both of these considerations are based on the SLA that a user and provider have agreed to. By minimising the cost either due to allocation of resources or to SLA penalty, we get the benefit function for the provider as: $\sum_{i=1}^{n} \sum_{j=1}^{m} Pr(O_{ij}) - \sum_{i=1}^{n} \sum_{j=1}^{m} min(c(O_{ij}), PSLA_{ij})$ (Eq. 1)

We consider the SLA for each stream to contain: i) a desired QoS level for each operation, $L_{desired_{ij}}$, ii) the minimum QoS level acceptable to that user

$L_{min_{ij}} \leq L_{desired_{ij}}$, and iii) the cost $c(O_{ij})[k]$ for each QoS level L_k defined by the service in the range $[L_{min_{ij}}, L_{desired_{ij}}]$. A provider incurs in a penalty $PSLA_{ij}$, when it fails to meet the minimum level $L_{min_{ij}}$ for O_{ij}. By minimising the cost either due to allocation of resources or to $PSLA_{ij}$, the provider will select an optimal QoS level k_{ij} for each operation O_{ij} specified in the contract such that, (i) the benefit function in Eq. (1) is maximized, and ii) the aggregated number of resources required to provide each operation $O_{ij}[k_{ij}]$ at the required level does not exceed available resources at the provider node.

In general, in order to achieve resource allocation, all resources such as the number of CPUs, disks, I/O bandwidth, buffer sizes and communication bandwidth must be considered. As our QoS guarantees have throughput and delay semantics, only computational resource (number of CPUs or virtual machines allocated to a stream) consumption and buffer occupancy are considered.

3   System Architecture

The resource requirements imposed by each QoS contract level must be known before utility optimization can be made. The utilization of resources are influenced by three components [11,12,13]: (i) the profiling model used for the characterization of the worst-case resource consumption, (ii) the scheduling mechanism used to allocate resources to data streams, and (iii) the accuracy of determining whether there will be enough resources for the aggregated demand. Our system supports the processing of multiple concurrent streams over a shared elastic infrastructure consisting of multiple processing nodes. Each node self-regulates its computing resources to preserve QoS constraints using the three mentioned components and optimizing revenue generation.

3.1   Architectural Components

A node, as depicted in Fig. 1, involves a combination of traffic shaping, computation and data transfer capability. The *Traffic shaping* component regulates the number of data elements entering into the computing resources, according to the established QoS for each data stream. *Traffic shaping* is based on the use of the Token bucket (TB) model [14]. A TB is characterized by 2 parameters: b and R that are respectively the size of the bucket, and the token generation rate. Tokens are generated and introduced in the bucket at the rate of R tokens/s. Data are stored in the TB buffer until they can be forwarded to the computational resources for processing, based on the availability of one or more tokens in the bucket. When data elements arrive at a rate $r < R$, the generated tokens will build up in the bucket for future usage. In this way, a TB supports bursts of traffic up to a regulated maximum (the amount of data sent cannot exceed $Rt + b$) while isolating data streams from one another and enforcing QoS per data stream. A more detailed description of the TB and its use in this architecture can be found in [5]. The R parameter can be defined to be coincident with the average throughput established for a data stream. For revenue generation at a node, the TB model as an envelop process can be used to estimate cost depending on the resources required during each control period T to process the worst case traffic $RT + b$ for each data stream [13]. However, determining the effective number of computational resources (i.e. a pool of virtual machines at an elastic infrastructure), and data storage and processing requirements can be a challenge. The processing rate will depend on the operation, the event processing engine, the machine, and other specific event processing operations [15]. The impact of these parameters on performance (and therefore SLA compliance) can be evaluated through profiling of previous executions. For simplicity, we assume that: (i) resources are homogeneous, and (ii) there is no data size variation within the elements of a stream during processing.

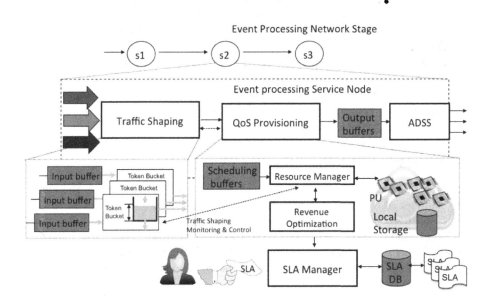

Fig. 1. Workflow System Architecture: the elements of a node

The *QoS provisioning* component manages a number of available computational resources (e.g. a pool of virtual machines in an elastic infrastructure). We are designing the architecture such that any private or public cloud could be incorporated providing that the required adapters are developed. This QoS provisioning component allocates resources to each data stream based on a revenue objective (based on number of required resources to process a data stream in accordance with its SLA, taking account of costs and penalties). It is also possible to define admission control to determine if a node has sufficient resources to support a new data stream without degrading the service of existing ones.

Data in the computational phase is stored in buffers associated with each data stream (we denote these as PU buffers to differentiate them from TB buffers). The PU buffer size can be used to trigger penalization if necessary. For instance, during each control interval T the maximum amount of data that can appear is

$RT + b$. If the PU buffer size is greater than b it means that resources have not been provisioned enough to maintain the QoS level of this data stream. Note that during a time interval b data can be transferred to the processing phase if there are enough tokens in the TB. The *Scheduling buffers* component in Fig. 1 will forward data stored in PU buffers to different intermediate buffers in order to be processed according to a specific scheduling strategy (i.e. whether throughput or latency is being considered) [12].

For a large number of concurrent data streams, the probability for all of them being in the worst case at the same time is low. Once an optimum QoS level has been defined for each data stream different business policies can be used to improve revenue and to provide flexibility in SLA definition, e.g. under-provisioning of resources, selective SLA violations, load shedding (when possible) and an increase in the number of computational resources [16] to name a few. The *Resource Manager* component complements the *Revenue Optimization* process with Business rules that implement these strategies. An explanation of these rules is given in Subsection 3.2. Finally, the Autonomic Data Streaming Service (ADSS) [4] in Fig. 1 handles transmission of data to the following node. It can detect a network congestion between two nodes and react to it by reducing the data transmission rate over the network and temporarily storing data onto disk (thereby avoiding data losses).

3.2   Rule-Based SLA Management

QoS requirements are often defined using the worst case scenario – i.e. the maximum number of resources required to achieve a particular QoS objective. However, some data streams may not use the resources that they have reserved and these unused resources could be used to process other streams to increase revenue. Hence, spare capacity in the system could be reallocated. This is particularly useful to handle periods of bursty behavior on some streams.

To provide service to data flows with maximum throughput performance objectives, we can start by under provisioning resources with a controller constantly monitoring the aggregated input rate and the output rate, and the number of data from each stream in the PU buffers. This controller would allocate additional computational resources when the difference between these rates is over an established threshold in the case of maximum throughput objectives, or the number of data in the PU buffer for a data flow is over a threshold. If this happens, and there are computational resources that can be borrowed from less prioritized data flows, new resources are allocated to the queue. Hence, data flows can be classified according to the benefit and penalty values of their respective QoS levels (assigned by the optimizer): "Gold" – for high penalty and revenue; "Silver" – for medium penalty and revenue, and "Bronze" – for low revenue and no penalty [17]. The controller also monitors the input and output rate for each flow, as well as the TB buffers. We are currently following two main policies, using rules, to improve QoS service: (i) try to minimise the number of computational resources, therefore, this policy prioritises load shedding when possible rather than increasing the number of resources; (ii) try to maximise the accuracy of results, and as a consequence, try to minimise the use of the load shedding mechanism. We implemented the business rules with JESS (Java Expert System Shell) [18]. Each data stream signals the execution of the control loop at a different period for each data stream, or execution can be triggered by an event, such as buffer size over a threshold, or observed throughput degradation. In this way, JESS can support event processing as event-condition-action (ECA) rules [19].

Table 1. Summary of rules in natural language to control data streams and queue provisioning according to Service Level Agreements. **E** represents an event, and **C** a condition (in event-condition-action) terminology.

	Pattern	Action
		Data flow control
1	**E:** B_i over threshold **C:** SLA_i allows control the use of free resources	$\Delta R_i = \sum_{i=1}^{n} NumRes_i * \hat{\delta}_i - \sum_{i=1}^{n} R_i$
2	**E:** B_i over threshold **C:** SLA_i allows control to drop D_i	$B_i = B_i - D_i$
3	**E:** B_i above threshold **C:** Controlled Stream	$\Delta R_i = 0$
		Ranges of QoS control
4	**E:** $\sum_{i=1}^{n}(\lambda_i - R_i)$ over threshold **C:** QoS level allow to borrow N_i resources	$\Delta NumRes = min(\sum_{i=1}^{n} N_i, \sum_{i=1}^{n}(\lambda_i - R_i)/\hat{\delta}_i)$
5	**E:** $\sum_{i=1}^{n}(\lambda_i - R_i)$ over threshold **C:** Queue level allow to pause low level data flows	$\#Paused_{LowLevel} = \sum_{i=1}^{n}(\lambda_i - R_i)/\hat{\delta}$
6	**E:** Overthrow **C:** Controlled Stream	$\Delta NumRes = 0, \#Paused_{LowLevel} = 0$

Table 1 summarizes some of the rules to control each data stream and the resource provisioning at queue level within a node. Rules are shown in natural language for sake of simplicity, representing in a declarative way the pattern with an event and condition part, and the action to be performed. Initial values have been previously estimated for each data stream i. We denote $\hat{\delta}_i$ as an estimate of this output rate, using past executions without considering failures or overheads: $\hat{\delta}_i = AVG(1/t_i)$. In order to maintain the output rate, the minimum number of resources required at node can be obtained from: $Nu\hat{m}Res_i = \sum_{i=1}^{n} R_i/\hat{\delta}_i$. Rule 1 defines the action to be taken when the TB buffer occupancy is over an established threshold and free resources can be used. Rule 2 defines the action to be taken when data shedding is allowed. Rule 3 detects that buffer occupancy is under a threshold and returns to initial TB rates. Finally, rules 4 & 5 detect differences between input and output rates for streams with maximum throughput objectives, and borrow resources from low priority data streams or pauses the streams using dynamic TB parameters adjustments. Rule 6 returns resources from less priority streams or resumes them when the difference between input and output rates is under a given threshold.

4   Evaluation Scenarios

We describe two scenarios to show how our controller can deal with: (i) the addition/removal of resources to the queue that provision "Gold" streams taking resources from "Bronze" streams; (ii) the selective violation of "Silver" data stream SLAs to avoid violations of Gold data streams. We assume that a penalty occurs when the PU buffer occupancy of a data stream is greater than a predefined threshold, which means than not enough resources are provided. We consider that each token allows to pass a data chunk to the processing phase, representing a predefined number of events (e.g. 1 data = 10^3 events), and that a unit of cost is incurred for each unit of processing rate (data/s). The penalty for "Gold" streams will be two times the cost of the required resources to provided the service, and one time for "Silver" streams. These scenarios have been chosen to demonstrate how revenue generation is affected by the choice of a resource allocation strategy (at the TB and the subsequent processing units) within a node, using components discussed in Section 3 and using rules identified in Section 3.2. We note that a number of other scenarios can also be defined, based on the the context of use of the proposed system.

4.1   Scenario 1

In the first scenario, we assume 4 "Gold" (i.e. high priority) customer streams with a period of control of T=10 seconds, 1 stream (ds_1) with R=30 and b=30 and 3 streams (ds_21, ds_22, ds_23) with R=20 and b=20. The maximum number of data to be processed in 10 seconds is 990. We assume that each resource can process 10 data/s (therefore requiring a maximum of 10 processing units). Stream input rates can be irregular and we use the Poisson distribution to control both the probability of bursts (by defining burst inter-arrival time) and a burst duration. We set both the burst inter-arrival time and the burst duration to be between 1 to 6 seconds. With this assumption, we under provision the queue with 5 resources that can support 50 data/s. With the cost assumption ds_1 provides a revenue of 30 units for each control interval, and a penalty of 60 units if data in the PU buffer is over 30, and ds_{2i} will provide a revenue of 20 units and a penalty of 40 units if data in the buffer is over 20 during each control interval. With the provision of 5 resources, we have a fixed cost of 50 units.

Figure 2 shows two simulations of the first scenario, the first one with no variation of processing units, and the second one with the addition of processing units taken from "Bronze" data streams. The three upper graphs show the simulation without addition of procession units. The first graph shows the aggregated input and output rates (continuous lines). This graph shows that the ratio of output to input rate is low, and that the output rate is limited to a maximum of 50 data/s using 5 provisioned resources. This graph also shows (with dotted lines) the TB buffer size $(bTBds_i)$, and the use of rule 3 to drop data from ds_{23} when the TB buffer is over the agreed threshold of 50 data. TB buffer occupancy is therefore used to determine when load shedding can be used. The second figure shows buffer occupancy for each data stream at the resources component

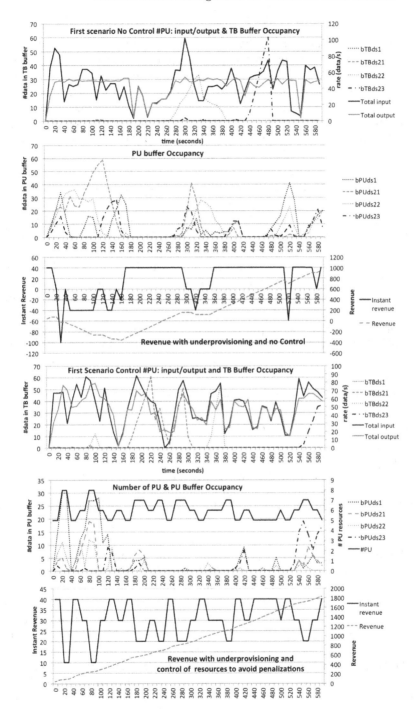

Fig. 2. First scenario: resource management for processing aggregate traffic. The three upper graphs show simulation results without, and the three bottom graphs show results with, addition/removal of resources.

$(bPUds_i)$. Each time $bPUds_1$ is over 30 data and $bPUds_{2i}$ is over 20 data a penalty occurs. The third graph shows the instantaneous revenue, calculated as 90 units of income during each control period minus 50 units of cost to provision 5 resources and the penalties. The graph also shows the accumulated revenue.

The three bottom graphs in Figure 2 shows the simulation with addition of resources. We assume that there are enough resources to be claimed from bronze data streams. The fourth graph shows that the output rate is close to the input rate. In this simulation, rule 3 drops data from ds_21 when the TB buffer is over the agreed threshold of 50 data. The fifth graph shows PU buffer occupancy of each data stream $(bPUds_i)$ and the number of processing units allocated when the difference between aggregated input and output rate is over a threshold (rules 4 and 6). The fifth graph shows periods with the addition of 1 to 3 additional resources borrowed from "Bronze" data streams to handle no initially provisioned resources. This graph shows that in this case no penalization occurs. Finally, the sixth graph shows both the instantaneous revenue in each period of control and the aggregated revenue controlling the provision of resources to "Gold" data streams . When compared with the uncontrolled scenario that shows oscillations in the revenue and periods of negative revenue, the controlled scenario shows regular income instead. It is important to note that we had included in the last graph the cost of adding more processing units to show the revenue of "Gold" data streams. However, if we consider that the cost of these units is supported by "Bronze" data streams, the instantaneous revenue for the controlled scenario is bigger than the instantaneous revenue shown in the last graph. With this consideration the instantaneous revenue would be a constant income of 40.

4.2   Scenario 2

Graphs in Figure 3 show the second scenario. We assume 1 "Gold" data stream $ds1$ with R=30 and b=30 and 3 "Silver" (ds_21, ds_22, ds_23) data streams with R=10 and b=10. The maximum number of data to be processed in 10 seconds is 660. We under provision the node with 4 resources, to be shared between the "Gold" and "Silver" data streams. Here, we assume that ds_1 provides a revenue of 30 units per control interval and a penalty of 60 units if tokens in the PU buffer is over 30. ds_{2i} will provide revenue of 10 and penalty of 10 units per control interval. With 4 resources we have a fixed cost of 40 units. Upper graphs in Figure 3 show PU buffer occupancy and revenue if resource allocation is controlled. The bottom graphs show the use of rules 5 and 6, but in this case, instead of taking resources from "Bronze" streams, a selective violation of "Silver" streams is undertaken to avoid the violation of "Gold" streams. The first graph shows buffer occupancy at the resource component. The uncontrolled scenario shows several periods of "Gold" penalty, 8 control intervals with $(bPUds_1)$ over 30, while the controlled scenario show only 1 penalty interval for "Silver" data streams. The third graph shows PU buffer occupancy and the number of "Silver" data streams that have been been paused to free resources.

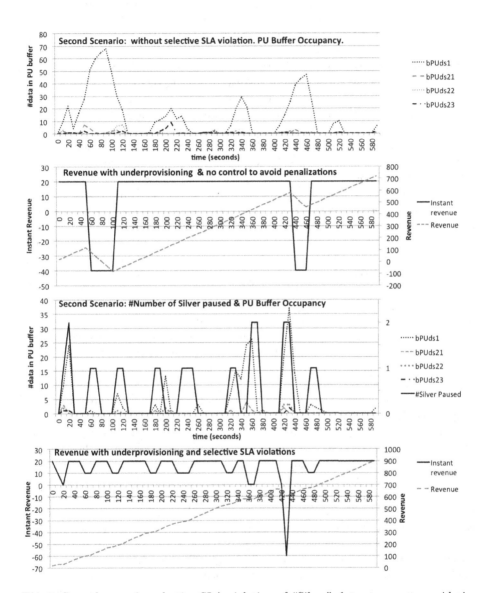

Fig. 3. Second scenario: selective SLA violation of "Silver" data streams to avoid violation of "Gold" data streams. Two upper graphs: without selective SLA violations; two bottom graphs: selective SLA violation.

5 Related Work

Although workflow, streaming and event processing were considered as three separate threads of research in data intensive applications, they share a number of important similarities and challenges such as scalability, fault tolerance and performance that enables them to be considered synergistically [16]. *Data Stream Management Systems* (DSMS) have shifted the emphasis in database systems to directly processing incoming streams instead of storing them first. These efforts focus on data processing performance by restricting the language to graphs of operators with well-defined semantics. Scalability and query distribution are considered in Aurora [20], Borealis [21] and Stream Cloud [22].

On the other hand, *Complex Event Processing* (CEP) has seen a resurgence in the last few years, examples being SPADE/IBM InfoSphere Streams, Esper and DROOLS Fusion [23]. The main difference between them and stream processing systems is that in the former each event is processed at arrival, prioritizing the reaction to event arrival, while stream processing systems work by accumulating and subsequently processing a data set over a time window. Unlike Data Stream Management Systems (DSMS), the notion of QoS is not present in event processing literature [16]. Thus, events are detected based on the best-effort method and most event processing applications are currently implemented by centralized engines.

Scientific workflows have emerged as a paradigm for representing and managing complex distributed computations. Extending state-based workflow management techniques and pipelines with support for streaming data services has recently become relevant [7,24]. The main difference between workflow based stream applications with DSMS and CEP is the focus on the composition of heterogeneous black box services.

TB [14] has been extensively used for network traffic shaping, Foster et al. [25] propose GARA (Globus Architecture for Reservation and Allocation), an architecture providing QoS mechanisms for high-end network applications. Their architecture exploits TB to adapt differentiated rate injection for applications in Globus. Park and Humphrey [26] make use of a TB-based data throttling framework for scientific workflows that involve large data transfers between tasks.

Our approach differs from CEP in general terms in that instead of considering a single data stream, we consider multiple data streams with processing carried out over a shared, elastic infrastructure. In [27], an initial partitioning of the EPN based on semantic dependencies of the EPN operations onto a distributed network of nodes is proposed, along with a mechanism to distribute load among different execution nodes dynamically based on their performance characteristics and the event traffic model. DSMS typically partition their operations onto distributed processing resources, and they incorporate different scheduling heuristics, and QoS depending on the application characteristics. In this work, we make use of TB, the scheduling buffers, and the autonomic computing control loop in order to schedule application data elements onto processing resources. The main advantage of such a combination is that (i) we utilise TB parameters for specifying application QoS; (ii) the TB along with the buffers and the autonomic computing loop is a simple and QoS-driven scheduling heuristic, supporting variable bursts. iii) Besides, in this paper, we integrate the revenue model with our scheduling heuristic.

6 Conclusions

There is emerging interest in processing data streams over shared Cloud infrastructures, with data elements being processed at distributed nodes in transit from source to sink. We consider the execution of simultaneous data stream over such infrastructure, with each stream having particular QoS objectives (throughput or latency, for instance), expressed within an SLA. Our aim is to enforce QoS for each application, and develop revenue models (combining cost of provisioning and penalties incurred due to SLA violations). We propose (i) an architecture that features a Token Bucket (TB) process envelop to support data throttling, (ii) a rule-based control loop to enable resource allocation. The control loop monitors QoS for each application and chooses an action to maximise revenue over a pre-defined control interval. The main advantage of such a combination is that (i) we utilise TB parameters for specifying application QoS; (ii) the TB along with the buffers and the autonomic computing loop is a simple and QoS-driven scheduling strategy, supporting variable bursts of data. We consider three different classes of customers submitting data streams (Gold, Silver and Bronze), with each class providing a different revenue and penalty to the provider. We identify how resource allocation can be dynamically supported between these customer classes.

As future work, we are considering the scalability of the infrastructure. On one hand, each node can naturally scale by incorporating more computational resources on demand at runtime. On the other hand, the scalability of the whole pipeline could be tackled by developing an efficient, and scalable implementation of TB; or by modifying the pipeline topology.

Acknowledgments. This work was partially supported by projects TIN2010-17905 (Spanish Ministry of Education and Science), Aquitaine-Aragon OMNIDATA, and FEDER/POCTEFA 35/08 PIREGRID.

References

1. Allen, G., Bogden, P., Kosar, T., Kulshrestha, A., Namala, G., Tummala, S., Seidel, E.: Cyberinfrastructure for coastal hazard prediction. CTWatch Quarterly 4(1) (2008)
2. Marru, S., Gannon, D., Nadella, S., Beckman, P., Weber, D.B., Brewster, K.A., Droegemeier, K.K.: Lead cyberinfrastructure to track real-time storms using spruce urgent computing. CTWatch Quarterly 4(1) (2008)
3. Simmhan, Y., Cao, B., Giakkoupis, M., Prasanna, V.K.: Adaptive rate stream processing for smart grid applications on clouds. In: Proceedings of the 2nd International Workshop on Scientific Cloud Computing, ScienceCloud 2011, pp. 33–38. ACM, New York (2011)

4. Tolosana-Calasanz, R., Bañares, J.A., Rana, O.F.: Autonomic streaming pipeline for scientific workflows. Concurr. Comput.: Pract. Exper. 23(16), 1868–1892 (2011)
5. Tolosana-Calasanz, R., Bañares, J.Á., Pham, C., Rana, O.F.: Enforcing qos in scientific workflow systems enacted over cloud infrastructures. J. Comput. Syst. Sci. 78(5), 1300–1315 (2012)
6. Tolosana-Calasanz, R., Bañares, J.Á., Pham, C., Rana, O.: Revenue models for streaming applications over shared clouds. In: 1st International Workshop on Clouds for Business and Business for Clouds (C4BB4C), Held at the 10th IEEE International Symposium on Parallel and Distributed Processing with Applications, ISPA 2012 (2012)
7. Zinn, D., Hart, Q., McPhillips, T., Ludaescher, B., Simmhan, Y., Giakkoupis, M., Prasanna, V.K.: Towards reliable, performant workflows for streaming-applications on cloud platforms. In: 11st International Symposium on Cluster, Cloud and Grid Computing (CCGrid 2011), Newport Beach, USA (May 2011)
8. Tolosana-Calasanz, R., Bañares, J.Á., Pham, C., Rana, O.: End-to-end qos on shared clouds for highly dynamic, large-scale sensing data streams. In: IEEE CC-GRID, pp. 904–911 (2012)
9. Petri, I., Rana, O.F., Regzui, Y., Silaghi, G.C.: Risk Assessment in Service Provider Communities. In: Vanmechelen, K., Altmann, J., Rana, O.F. (eds.) GECON 2011. LNCS, vol. 7150, pp. 135–147. Springer, Heidelberg (2012)
10. Kummer, O., Wienberg, F., Duvigneau, M., Schumacher, J., Köhler, M., Moldt, D., Rölke, H., Valk, R.: An Extensible Editor and Simulation Engine for Petri Nets: RENEW. In: Cortadella, J., Reisig, W. (eds.) ICATPN 2004. LNCS, vol. 3099, pp. 484–493. Springer, Heidelberg (2004)
11. Abdelzaher, T.F., Shin, K.G., Bhatti, N.: User-level qos-adaptive resource management in server end-systems. IEEE Trans. Comput. 52(5), 678–685 (2003)
12. Liebeherr, J., Wrege, D.E., Ferrari, D.: Exact admission control for networks with a bounded delay service. IEEE/ACM Trans. Netw. 4(6), 885–901 (1996)
13. Mao, S., Panwar, S.S.: A survey of envelope processes and their applications in quality of service provisioning. IEEE Communications Surveys and Tutorials, 2–20 (2006)
14. Partridge, C.: Gigabit Networking. Addison-Wesley (1994)
15. Mendes, M.R.N., Bizarro, P., Marques, P.: A Performance Study of Event Processing Systems. In: Nambiar, R., Poess, M. (eds.) TPCTC 2009. LNCS, vol. 5895, pp. 221–236. Springer, Heidelberg (2009)
16. Chakravarthy, S., Jiang, Q.: Stream Data Processing: A Quality of Service Perspective Modeling, Scheduling, Load Shedding, and Complex Event Processing, 1st edn. Springer Publishing Company, Incorporated (2009)
17. Macías, M., Fitó, J.O., Guitart, J.: Rule-based sla management for revenue maximisation in cloud computing markets. In: IEEE CNSM, pp. 354–357 (2010)
18. Hill, E.F.: Jess in Action: Java Rule-Based Systems. Manning Publications Co., Greenwich (2003)
19. Etzion, O., Niblett, P.: Event Processing in Action, 1st edn. Manning Publications Co., Greenwich (2010)
20. Cherniack, M., Balakrishnan, H., Balazinska, M., Carney, D., Çetintemel, U., Xing, Y., Zdonik, S.B.: Scalable distributed stream processing. In: CIDR (2003)
21. Abadi, D.J., Ahmad, Y., Balazinska, M., Cetintemel, U., Cherniack, M., Hwang, J.H., Lindner, W., Maskey, A.S., Rasin, A., Ryvkina, E., Tatbul, N., Xing, Y., Zdonik, S.: The Design of the Borealis Stream Processing Engine. In: Second Biennial Conference on Innovative Data Systems Research (CIDR 2005), Asilomar, CA (January 2005)

22. Gulisano, V., Jimenez-Peris, R., Patino-Martinez, M., Valduriez, P.: Streamcloud: A large scale data streaming system. In: 2010 IEEE 30th International Conference on Distributed Computing Systems (ICDCS), pp. 126–137 (June 2010)
23. Etzion, O., Niblett, P.: Event Processing in Action. Manning (August 2010)
24. Biörnstad, B.: A workflow approach to stream processing (2008)
25. Foster, I., Roy, A., Sander, V.: A quality of service architecture that combines resource reservation and application adaptation. In: Proceedings of the 8th International Workshop on Quality of Service. Springer (2000)
26. Park, S.M., Humphrey, M.: Data throttling for data-intensive workflows. In: 22nd IEEE International Symposium on Parallel and Distributed Processing, IPDPS 2008, Miami, Florida USA, April 14-18, pp. 1–11. IEEE (2008)
27. Lakshmanan, G.T., Rabinovich, Y.G., Etzion, O.: A stratified approach for supporting high throughput event processing applications. In: Proceedings of the Third ACM International Conference on Distributed Event-Based Systems, DEBS 2009, 5:1–5:12. ACM, New York (2009)

The ISQoS Grid Broker for Temporal and Budget Guarantees

Richard Kavanagh and Karim Djemame

School of Computing, University of Leeds,
Leeds, LS2 9JT, UK
{screk,k.djemame}@leeds.ac.uk
http://www.comp.leeds.ac.uk

Abstract. We introduce our Grid broker that uses SLAs in job submission with the aim of ensuring jobs are computed on time and on budget. We demonstrate our broker's ability to perform negotiation and to select preferentially higher priority jobs, in a tender market and discuss the architecture that makes this possible. We additionally show the effects of rescheduling and how careful consideration is required in order to avoid price instability. We therefore make recommendations upon how to maintain this stability, given rescheduling.

Keywords: Time-Cost Constrained Brokering, SLA, Negotiation, Job Admission Control, Grid.

1 Introduction

Grids enable the execution of applications in a distributed fashion. It is however, common that such applications are served in a best effort approach only, with no guarantees placed upon the service quality. This is primarily due to the emphasis in production Grids being placed upon the queuing of jobs ready for computation, with the sole intent of maintaining high resource utilisation, rather than user satisfaction. It has also been known for some time that guaranteed provision of reliable, transparent and quality of service (QoS) oriented resources is the next important step for Grid systems [1,2].

In many commercial and scientific settings, guarantees that computation is going to be completed on time are required. It is therefore important to establish during the submission of a job the requirements of the users in terms of completion time and the priority they hold for the work.

In order to motivate our work and illustrate the need for time guarantees we present two scenarios. The first is a commercial scenario, such as animation, where frames may be computed overnight before the animation team arrives, partial completion of the work delays or stops the team from starting the next days work [3]. The second scenario is in an academic environment where it is common before conferences for Grids to become overloaded [4]. To further focus our work and enhance its relevance we consider the types of application

K. Vanmechelen, J. Altmann, and O.F. Rana (Eds.): GECON 2012, LNCS 7714, pp. 76–90, 2012.

running upon the Grid. The focus of our work is hence upon Bag of Task based applications, which are the predominate form of workload in Grids [4].

Given the finite resources available (including budget), it is also wise to prioritise jobs based upon the importance to the end user. In order that this prioritisation is provided correctly an economic approach is used to ensure users give more truthful indications of their priorities [5, 6].

In delivering these time and cost requirements, it presents the added advantage that Grids can be moved away from the best-effort service which limits their importance, as users' would be more willing to pay or contribute resources if results are returned on time, as late results are of limited use [7].

The main contributions of this paper are to:

- Introduce the architecture of the Intelligent Scheduling for Quality of Service (ISQoS) broker. Its focus is upon job submission via the formation of service level agreements, which cover job completion time and cost.
- Demonstrate how a tender market can be formed that actively selects jobs of a higher priority, via their economic properties. We show this as part of a transition from the dominance of the temporal constraints to the budget constraints of a job submission.
- Introduce rescheduling and demonstrate how this can lead to price instability, which is a key factor in a successful Grid market [8]. We therefore make recommendations to counteract this instability.

The remaining part of the paper's structure is as follows, in section 2 We discuss the ISQoS general architecture, which leads on to a more in-depth discussion of the broker's service pricing mechanism and offer evaluation in section 2.2. The pricing of resource and scheduling mechanisms used are then covered in section 2.3, which are the main aspects of this paper's experimentation. The setup for this experimentation can be found in section 3 and the results may be found in section 4. We then discuss related work in section 5 and conclude in 6.

2   The Broker

In this section we discuss the overall architecture of the ISQoS Broker. This broker is primarily aimed at parameter sweep / bag of task applications [9], which are the predominant workload upon the Grid [4].

It uses economic mechanisms and negotiation to find the provider that is most likely to provide QoS in terms of completion time and budget.

The ISQoS Grid architecture is service oriented and is WS-Agreement for Java (WSAG4J) [10] based and presents services to execute jobs. Avoiding classical architectures such as Globus [11] has allowed the focus upon scheduling and the ability to negotiate service level agreements (SLAs). This includes the capacity to perform scheduling for indicative purposes only, i.e. not for committing to work, but merely to generate a candidate schedule for negotiation purposes. The use of scheduling in the architecture also brings it closer in style to the Maui Scheduler [12] and OpenCCS [2] opposed to queuing based methods.

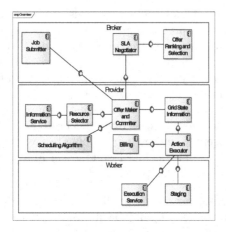

Fig. 1. Overview of Architecture

The broker focuses upon standards such as JSDL [13], but has the capacity to swap out this term language used to describe the work being performed, so long as it is XML based so that it can form part of the agreement. This is achieved by having the part of the XML describing jobs contain an `xsd:any type` for attaching the term language describing the job. This flexibility is also present in the information provider which can use either GLUE [14] or Ganglia [15] based representations of resources.

2.1   Broker Architecture

An overview of the broker's architecture is presented in Figure 1. It primarily consists of three tiers: A broker, a provider and workers. The broker selects the provider to use while the provider commands the workers to execute Grid jobs.

Jobs are submitted via the job submitter of the broker to the offer maker and committer component of each provider. The broker is expected to contact various different resource providers in order to establish a competitive marketplace.

The information submitted to providers includes the job's *resource require-ments*, a *budget* that the user has assigned for the completion of a job, the amount of *markup* the broker makes for the service, which can be used as a notion of minimum available funds for rescheduling and finally its temporal requirements. These will be shown as a *due date* by which the job should be completed by and a *deadline* by when it must be completed.

The resource providers from this information perform initial scheduling of the tasks within a job so they can derive an estimate for completion time and price. They achieve this by using a scheduling algorithm and pricing mechanism that is plugged into the provider. The price is set by the provider's local pricing mechanism which feeds information into the scheduling algorithm. The sched-ules generated are then converted to offers to complete the work, which are then submitted back to the broker. These offers include information about the time and cost for completing the job and the time for completing each task within a job.

The broker from the offers that have been returned, ranks them and filters out poor offers i.e. sort by earliest and filter out unprofitable offers, though various selection mechanisms may be used. The one used in this paper is the ISQoS Hybrid Offer Filter (see Algorithm 1 [16]), with a ranking mechanism based on highest profit first.

Algorithm 1. ISQoS Hybrid Offer Filter

FOR EACH (Offer) {
    Sort the offers based upon the ranking mechanism chosen
    IF Completion_Time <= Due_Date **AND**
    Service_Price <= Budget {
      Accept Offer; **BREAK;**
    } **ELSE** {
      Take the last n accepted offers and find the average rate
      at which profit accumulates and establish the going rate.
      IF Current_offer_profit_rate >=
      (going_rate − acceptable_deviation_below_going_rate) {
        Accept Offer; **BREAK;**
      }
    }
}

The broker then asks the user if it acceptable to proceed with the job at a given price and completion time.

If the offer made to the user is acceptable the broker then submits the bag of tasks that make up the job to the winning provider. In terms of the experimentation in section 4 then any job that has its requirements met is accepted. In the case of a production Grid, the user could resubmit the job with different budget and time requirements in order to ensure the job is accepted.

An accepted job is placed into the schedule and is recorded in the current state of the Grid. The state records the mappings between workers and their jobs as well as other information such as the current resource and job statuses. The workers are represented as objects which maintain a copy of the XML description of the resource and a reference to the XML parser used to interpret the description of the job. This XML description of the job is taken from the agreement which is attached as an xsd:any type, which allows for XML other than JSDL documents to be used. The parser maintains a set of default questions which can be asked about the job i.e. what is the size of the memory available? or the what is the CPU speed?

The descriptions of the tasks are treated in a similar fashion and a basic list of default questions are provided i.e. how much memory is needed. The resource selector for a given task can then be asked to provide the list of acceptable

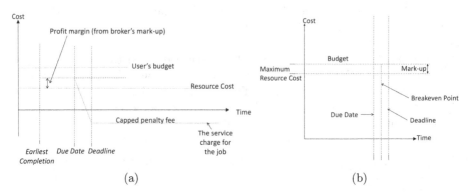

Fig. 2. The generation of offers

workers to the scheduler, without it needing to have a great understanding of what a resource entails.

In terms of a job's breakdown a job is a collection of tasks in the bag, that need executing. Each task has several actions, these equate to: *stage in, execute, stage-out* and *clean* the worker. Stage-out merely holds to the meaning of transferring data away from the worker. Clean removes the task's working area upon a worker node. If the Clean event is the very last action to be performed then the job is submitted for billing.

The action executor merely waits for the next action in the schedule to be ready for execution. At this point it sends a signal to the worker nodes to begin their work.

2.2   Job Pricing and Offer Evaluation

The generation of offers and pricing follows work in [16], but is discussed here to assist understanding of the broker. The broker obtains from each of the providers a resource cost and completion time for the work it submits to tender (see: Section 2.3). The broker in needing to make a profit takes a mark-up from this initial resource cost. This is done as a percentage of the original resource cost as shown in Figure 2a. In order for a budget violation not to occur this must be below the maximum budget, assigned by the user. This gives rise to a notion of *budget slack* or spare budget available and *budget resilience* i.e. the difference between resource cost and the budget available. The latter differs as the broker could notionally decide to use some of its profit to ensure a job complete on time. Hence the profit the broker makes represents the minimum amount of money available, to mitigate problems should it be required.

If a job is returned on time then it achieves its full service price. If it is delayed then it returns a fraction of it based upon how far the completion time is between the due date and deadline (see Figure 2a). The use of the due date and deadline creates a gradient based approach which is known to provide the opportunity for heuristic methods, unlike hard deadlines [17]. Instead of having a penalty to the end user the service charge is stopped at 0 and the broker pays for any resources used that did not fail. This has useful properties in that the breakeven point becomes a fixed point between the due date and deadline [16]. In doing so the offer market is generated which is shown in Figure 2b.

2.3   Scheduling and Resource Pricing

The providers are responsible for giving the broker an estimated completion time and resource cost. They achieve this through a scheduling algorithm and a pricing mechanism, both of which can be swapped out at will. The scheduling algorithms that have been implemented and used in this paper are round robin and a variation of round robin that performs rescheduling (see: Algorithm 2).

Algorithm 2. Round Robin Rescheduling

FOR EACH (Task) {
    Get next worker in round robin order that meets resource
    requirements, skipping the turn of workers that don't meet requirements
    IF Worker.isEmpty() {
      Place Task's Actions; **BREAK**; }
    FOR EACH (ACTION in Task) {
      FIND insertion point **WHERE** (
      Later Actions will not go past their Due Date
      AND No action already started will be moved
      AND No action due to start will be moved);
      Place Action in earliest position possible;
      move existing actions later on;
      BREAK;
    }
}

The rescheduling variant takes the selected workers actions and moves them along as far as their due dates will allow and places new actions in before them. The aim is to have all new jobs start as early as possible and to reduce the dependence upon arrival order in terms of how well a job is served. Actions may not be moved however, if they are due to start or have already started and movement of actions should also not make an action go past its due date.

The resource pricing mechanisms implemented aim to dynamically map the demand for resources to the price. In this paper time for both network and resource usage are billed equally. The charge per second of worker time derives from the count of actions that the provider currently has in its schedule, which is then mapped to a price. In short a provider counts the amount of actions already in the schedule and this maps directly to the price of its resources. This although simple follows demand and as discussed in section 3, is suitable for the experimentation.

3   Experimental Setup

We perform experimentation with the aim of demonstrating the effects of temporal and budget constraints upon machine/task selection, with the intent of creating a mechanism by which job prioritisation may take place. We focus this experimentation upon high load scenarios where correct selection is most required. The configuration of the experiments performed is described next.

We sent 100 jobs with 8 tasks each into a Grid with 2 providers. Each provider had 4 virtual machines, of which one also acted as a head node. Jobs were submitted with a 30 second gap between submissions, from a separate broker virtual machine instance. This is shorter than the time it takes to compute a job, which means the Grid fills and resources become sufficiently scarce as per a time sensitive, high utilization scenario presented earlier. Each provider uses the round robin scheduling algorithm in section 4.1 and a rescheduling based variation in section 4.2. The broker uses the Hybrid Offer Filter, sorting by profit with the highest first with a threshold below the going rate of 0.05.

The virtual machines ran Ubuntu 11.10 (64bit) server, with full virtualization and ran upon 4 physical hosts. The virtual environment was constructed using OpenNebula 2.0 [18] and Xen 4.0.1 [19]. Each head node had 1GB of RAM allocated and worker nodes 768MB. Each processor ran at a speed of 2.4GHz.

The ISQoS Grid uses WS-Agreement for Java v1.0 for the Broker and Provider agreement process. Ganglia 3.2.0 [15] was used as the information provider.

Jobs were setup to be non-data intensive and the stage in/out size was only 1 Megabyte. This mitigates issues with considering the network configuration of the virtual cluster on the cloud testbed. The compute size was given as a value of 3,000. This value derives from a reference processor of 3,000 MHz multiplied by an expected duration of 1 minute, hence on the resources available the tasks are also expected to last approximately 1 minute.

This means that if a job was allocated to a single machine it would take 8 minutes to complete. The due date was therefore set no lower than the submission time + 8, with the knowledge that the Grid would soon be overtaxed. The deadline was set to the due date + 4 minutes. We performed 6 runs of each trace and 95% confidence intervals are shown in the figures in section 4. The first 15 accepted jobs of the traces have been ignored to counteract effects of starting with an unloaded Grid.

We establish three different budgets that jobs could be given: 12,000, 15,000 and 18,000. These values were chosen as they intersected the likely prices that would be generated at different stages of the experiment. A fixed mark-up of 20% was chosen. A resource pricing mechanism was chosen that derived its charge from the count of actions that the provider currently has in its schedule, hence tracking demand. This was chosen as the jobs being submitted were of equal size and there was no great need for a more complex solution. The scheduling algorithm in use was not price aware so a single price could be set for all resources of a given provider. The price with zero actions in the schedule was 1 unit per second and it was increased by 0.125 units for each action added from previously scheduled work.

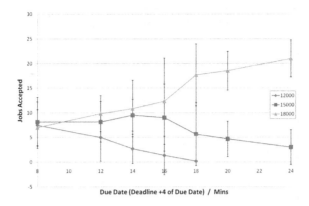

Fig. 3. Transition to Budget Prioritisation - With Round Robin Scheduling

4   Experimental Results

4.1   Transition to Economic Constraints Dominance

In Figure 3 the due date and deadline is gradually incremented. Initially there is no preference based upon budget shown and the temporal constraints take precedence. When the due date is at 12 minutes the lowest budget jobs at 12,000 start to be penalised and by 16 minutes the lowest budget jobs are all but completely rejected. This is because as the due date increases a greater amount of the work is allowed to be queued concurrently on each provider, causing the resource costs to increase to match the demand.

The jobs with the highest budgets are hence accepted more readily in an ever increasing fashion, whilst the middle budget range jobs increases temporarily as the lowest budget jobs are no longer accepted. This clear prioritisation of jobs based upon the budget is seen to be a valuable property of the submission system. This is achieved without any need for jobs to directly compete in an auction style for resources.

In Figure 4, 5 and 6 constraint violations are counted. If the budget causes constraining then a budget violation counter is incremented. A temporal constraint violation is considered to have occurred if the time before the breakeven point is less than zero i.e. where the job is no longer making a profit. This point, where the broker breaks even, is 16.67% of the way between the due date and deadline [16]. It was useful to pick this point as the deadline was unlikely to be ever passed due to the job admission policy in use filtering out unprofitable jobs.

In Figure 4 we see the constraint violations are initially of the temporal type only, this is because the highly restrictive temporal constraints are dominating, ensuring queue lengths do not increase sufficiently, which constrains the service prices. As the due date gets larger the budget constraints become more dominant and service price rises.

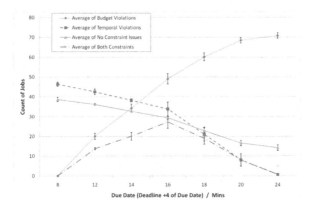

Fig. 4. All Constraint Violations - With Round Robin Scheduling

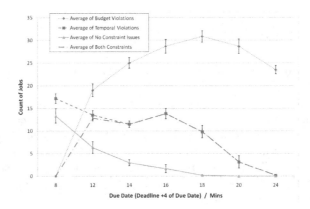

Fig. 5. Constrain Violations with a budget of 12,000 only - With Round Robin Scheduling

In Figure 5 and 6 we show the budget pressures for jobs with a set value. The biasing towards the higher priority/budget jobs is hence demonstrated.

Figure 5 shows that initially jobs are either not meeting the temporal constraints or they are accepted. As the due date is increased the budget constraints become dominant. Though temporal constraints are still being violated, it is also the case that the budget constraints are being violated as well, so practically the budget constraints are taking precedence.

Figure 6 like Figure 5 again shows that initially jobs are either not meeting the temporal constraints or they are accepted. As the due date is increased the budget constraints again become more dominant, but it takes much longer for jobs to be predominantly rejected because of budget violations, which is an indication of the desired property of prioritisation.

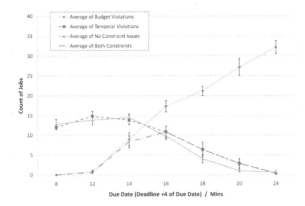

Fig. 6. Constrain Violations with a budget of 15,000 only - With Round Robin Scheduling

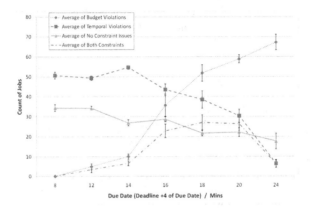

Fig. 7. All Constraint Violations - With Rescheduling

4.2 Introducing Rescheduling

We previously indicated in section 2 that different scheduling algorithms may be selected at provider level. This can introduce more complex situations where rescheduling may be performed. In this case we show how this can have a profound effect upon the market.

In the case where rescheduling is performed similar results can be obtained to the none rescheduling case. There are however notable differences.

Firstly we see in Figure 7 that the budget constraint becomes more dominant than the temporal constraints much later on as compared to Figure 4. This is reflected in the distinction between the amount of jobs accepted of each type, where the lower budget jobs are no longer rejected entirely. This is in part caused by fewer jobs being accepted, leading to a slightly lower resource cost. On average 28/85 jobs without rescheduling and 26/85 with rescheduling, but it is also more significantly down to greater fluctuations in the service price.

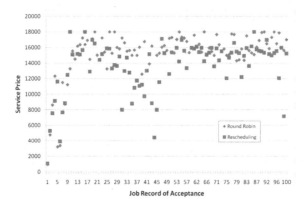

Fig. 8. Effect upon service price of rescheduling (Due Date = 20, Average of all Runs)

We can see from Figure 8 that the service price when rescheduling occurs drops significantly at various stages of the trace. This means the price is sufficiently low for the lower budget jobs to be accepted even when the temporal constraints are at their most relaxed and higher workloads on the server might be expected.

4.3   Price Stability and Selection

In sections 4.1 and 4.2 it was seen that before the budget constraints became dominant, selection pressures did not favour jobs based upon the budget available. Hence should a Grid become overworked then in order to make selection preferences the economic factors should become dominant, by changing the resource/service price. We also saw in section 4.2 how price stability affected the ability of the mechanism to maintain this selection pressure. We therefore suggest various ways that might allow for a more stable price.

The mechanism by which the price is selected may be changed to make an incremental step change from the previous price. This would hence avoid some of the fluctuations and allow for rescheduling. The moderated changes however would have to reflect the completion of spikes in load. Spikes in load can occur for example just before an important conference [4]. The price smoothing mechanism would be required to remain responsive and should not for example artificially maintain a high price at the end of a peak in demand. This is because the system as a whole could either have unrealized profit or utility [20, 6].

The simplest solution would be to ensure that pricing does not rely upon already completed work. This means that any billing event will not affect the price, by removing jobs from the schedule that are used as part of the measure of current load. An example of such a measure would be to take the difference between the current time and the average completion time of all jobs for the provider.

Alternatively billing events would have to purposefully be held apart. In holding these events further apart it would reduce the number of occurrences, where a lot of work is removed from the schedule at the same time. This would require a scheduling algorithm that was geared specifically towards the pricing mechanism. If individual tasks would not be allowed to interweave, then this would help prevent the near simultaneous execution of billing actions. However, if a single very large job completes then regardless of dispersion of billing events the price would fall and potentially harm the selection process.

5   Related Work

Economically oriented Grids have had a long history, including in the early years work such as Nimrod/G [21] and G-Commerce [8]. Nimrod/G is similar in that it also serves parameter sweep/bag of task applications, however ISQoS has a much stronger focus upon QoS provision.

In more recent years work such upon the SORMA project has created the Economically Enhanced Resource Manager (EERM) [22,23]. This includes various features such as: demand forecasting, dynamic pricing, SLA formation and the ability to selectively violate less interesting SLAs [22]. We like EERM use dynamic pricing and SLAs but our SLA focuses upon delivery time of the computed results and cost while encoding the acceptable delay into the agreement, negating some of the need for renegotiation. We also use a negotiation mechanism to advise end users of the current state of the Grid instead of rejecting work that has already been accepted.

In terms of job submission for Bag of Task applications similar work to our own is Venugopal et al. [24] that developed an alternative offers protocol, for job submission using GridBus [25] and Aneka [26]. It however negotiates specific reservations, indicating such as minimum CPU speed and node count in a system centric fashion, whereas ISQoS focuses on agreeing delivery times for jobs against a reference speed processor and specifying leeway that may be used by the provider in terms of cost and completion time, which gives the provider scope for rescheduling without always renegotiating.

The brokering mechanism we present revolves around its pricing mechanism so it is appropriate to discuss the related pricing models and their implementations. Early models focus purely on slowdown such as First Reward & Risk Reward [17] and First Price [27], thus are very system centric.

A major pitfall that has been avoided in ISQoS is that penalty bounds are not always set, such as in [17,27] and LibraSLA [28]. This has issues, as pricing mechanisms should have properties such as budget balance and individual rationality among others [29].

First Profit, First Opportunity & First Opportunity Rate [30] like ISQoS uses the same scheduling algorithm to schedule as they do for admission control. However, our broker's mark-up, gives it rationale for participation in the market while also generating a marked difference in providing a boundary of acceptable QoS. This boundary presents itself in both temporal and budget parameters of the ISQoS model.

The Aggregate Utility [3] model has a lot of flexibility in specifying user requirements but this is at the expense of complexity for the end user.

Resource Aware Policy Administrator (RAPA) [31], focuses upon divisible load but has issues in that it caps the maximum deadline in order to limit the maximum penalty paid as the model lacks flexibility in this regard unlike ISQoS. RAPA is also similar to LibraSLA in that it has hard and soft deadlines and distinguishes between them instead of having a single approach like ISQoS, ensures the decision process need not treat jobs so arbitrarily different. The equivalent of a hard deadline in ISQoS is the due date and deadline being set to the same value.

Finally to cover the topic of market mechanisms further a good catalogue may be found in [20, 32, 33]. A discussion of SLAs and pricing functions may also be found in [34] that covers the subject well. WS-Agreement has previously been used for job submission in cases such as AssessGrid [35], VIOLA's MetaScheduling Service (MSS) [36] and others [37] [1].

6   Conclusion and Future Work

In conclusion we have discussed the architecture of our broker that establishes a tender market. We have focussed upon describing the submission system and the SLA structure, while also showing the effects of changing the scheduling algorithm in use. We have focussed upon job prioritisation and demonstrated how economic constraints can establish this, whilst also showing an initial period of the temporal constraints holding dominance. Given that users will be aiming to set the budget assigned to jobs as low as possible the budget constraints are likely to always have the desired effect. We finally introduced rescheduling and showed how it can lead to price instability by causing the schedule to have several jobs cleared from it due to completion within close succession. Our future work will investigate how to ensure the stability of the resource price, given the possibility of rescheduling.

References

1. Liu, C., Baskiyar, S.: A general distributed scalable grid scheduler for independent tasks. Journal of Parallel and Distributed Computing 69(3), 307–314 (2009)
2. Battre, D., Hovestadt, M., Kao, O., Keller, A., Voss, K.: Planning-based scheduling for sla-awareness and grid integration. In: Bartk, R. (ed.) PlanSIG 2007 The 26th Workshop of the UK Planning and Scheduling Special Interest Group, Prague, Czech Republic, vol. 1, p. 8 (2007)
3. AuYoung, A., Grit, L., Wiener, J., Wilkes, J.: Service contracts and aggregate utility functions. In: 15th IEEE International Symposium on High Performance Distributed Computing (HPDC-15). IEEE, New York (2005)
4. Iosup, A., Epema, D.: Grid computing workloads. IEEE Internet Computing 15(2), 19–26 (2011)

---

[1] A list of WS-Agreement based implementations can be seen at:
https://forge.gridforum.org/sf/wiki/do/viewPage/
projects.graap-wg/wiki/Implementations

5. Buyya, R., Abramson, D., Venugopal, S.: The grid economy. Proceedings of the IEEE 93(3), 698–714 (2005)
6. Lai, K.: Markets are dead, long live markets. SIGecom Exch. 5(4), 1–10 (2005)
7. Kokkinos, P., Varvarigos, E.A.: A framework for providing hard delay guarantees and user fairness in grid computing. Future Generation Computer Systems 25(6), 674–686 (2009)
8. Wolski, R., Plank, J.S., Brevik, J., Bryan, T.: Analyzing market-based resource allocation strategies for the computational grid. International Journal of High Performance Computing Applications 15(3), 258–281 (2001)
9. Buyya, R., Giddy, J., Abramson, D.: An evaluation of economy-based resource trading and scheduling on computational power grids for parameter sweep applications. In: The Second Workshop on Active Middleware Services (AMS 2000), In conjunction with Ninth IEEE International Symposium on High Performance Distributed Computing (HPDC 2000), Pittsburgh, USA. Kluwer Academic Publishers (2000)
10. Hudert, S., Ludwig, H., Wirtz, G.: Negotiating slas-an approach for a generic negotiation framework for ws-agreement. Journal of Grid Computing 7(2), 225–246 (2009)
11. Foster, I.: Globus toolkit version 4: Software for service-oriented systems. Journal of Computer Science and Technology 21(4), 513–520 (2006)
12. Jackson, D.B., Snell, Q.O., Clement, M.J.: Core Algorithms of the Maui Scheduler. In: Feitelson, D.G., Rudolph, L. (eds.) JSSPP 2001. LNCS, vol. 2221, pp. 87–102. Springer, Heidelberg (2001)
13. Open Grid Forum: Job submission description language (jsdl) specification, version 1.0 (2005)
14. Burke, S., Andreozzi, S., Field, L.: Experiences with the glue information schema in the lcg/egee production grid. Journal of Physics: Conference Series 119(6, 062019) (2008)
15. Ganglia Project: Ganglia monitoring system (2012)
16. Kavanagh, R., Djemame, K.: A Grid Broker Pricing Mechanism for Temporal and Budget Guarantees. In: Thomas, N. (ed.) EPEW 2011. LNCS, vol. 6977, pp. 295–309. Springer, Heidelberg (2011)
17. Irwin, D.E., Grit, L.E., Chase, J.S.: Balancing risk and reward in a market-based task service. In: Proceedings of the 13th IEEE International Symposium on High Performance Distributed Computing, pp. 160–169 (2004)
18. OpenNebula Project: Opennebula homepage (2012)
19. Systems, C.: Home of the xen hypervisor (2012)
20. Neumann, D., Ster, J., Weinhardt, C., Nimis, J.: A framework for commercial grids - economic and technical challenges. Journal of Grid Computing 6(3), 325–347 (2008)
21. Abramson, D., Giddy, J., Kotler, L.: High performance parametric modeling with nimrod/g: Killer application for the global grid? In: International Parallel and Distributed Processing Symposium (IPDPS), Cancun, Mexico, pp. 520–528 (2000)
22. Macias, M., Rana, O., Smith, G., Guitart, J., Torres, J.: Maximizing revenue in grid markets using an economically enhanced resource manager. Concurrency and Computation: Practice and Experience 22(14), 1990–2011 (2010)
23. Neumann, D., Stoesser, J., Anandasivam, A., Borissov, N.: SORMA – Building an Open Grid Market for Grid Resource Allocation. In: Veit, D.J., Altmann, J. (eds.) GECON 2007. LNCS, vol. 4685, pp. 194–200. Springer, Heidelberg (2007)

24. Venugopal, S., Xingchen, C., Buyya, R.: A negotiation mechanism for advance resource reservations using the alternate offers protocol. In: 16th International Workshop on Quality of Service, IWQoS 2008, pp. 40–49 (2008)
25. Venugopal, S., Buyya, R., Winton, L.: A grid service broker for scheduling e-science applications on global data grids. Concurrency and Computation: Practice and Experience 18(6), 685–699 (2006)
26. Xingchen, C., Nadiminti, K., Chao, J., Venugopal, S., Buyya, R.: Aneka: Next-generation enterprise grid platform for e-science and e-business applications. In: IEEE International Conference on e-Science and Grid Computing, pp. 151–159 (2007)
27. Chun, B.N., Culler, D.E.: User-centric performance analysis of market-based cluster batch schedulers. In: 2nd IEEE/ACM International Symposium on Cluster Computing and the Grid, p. 30 (2002)
28. Chee Shin, Y., Buyya, R.: Service level agreement based allocation of cluster resources: Handling penalty to enhance utility. In: IEEE International Cluster Computing, pp. 1–10 (2005)
29. Schnizler, B., Neumann, D., Veit, D., Weinhardt, C.: A multiattribute combinatorial exchange for trading grid resources. In: Proceedings of the 12th Research Symposium on Emerging Electronic Markets, RSEEM (2005)
30. Popovici, F.I., Wilkes, J.: Profitable services in an uncertain world. In: Proceedings of the ACM/IEEE SC 2005 Conference on Supercomputing, p. 36 (2005)
31. Han, Y., Youn, C.H.: A new grid resource management mechanism with resource-aware policy administrator for sla-constrained applications. Future Generation Computer Systems 25(7), 768–778 (2009)
32. Buyya, R.: Economic-based Distributed Resource Management and Scheduling for Grid Computing. PhD thesis, Monash University, Melbourne, Australia (2002)
33. Broberg, J., Venugopal, S., Buyya, R.: Market-oriented grids and utility computing: The state-of-the-art and future directions. Journal of Grid Computing 6(3), 255–276 (2008)
34. Wilkes, J.: Utility functions, prices, and negotiation. In: Buyya, R., Bubendorfer, K. (eds.) Market Oriented Grid and Utility Computing. Wiley Series on Parallel and Distributed Computing, pp. 67–88. John Wiley & Sons, Inc. (2008)
35. Djemame, K., Padgett, J., Gourlay, I., Armstrong, D.: Brokering of risk-aware service level agreements in grids. Concurrency and Computation: Practice and Experience 23(13), 1558–1582 (2011)
36. Gruber, R., Keller, V., Thiémard, M., Wäldrich, O., Wieder, P., Ziegler, W., Manneback, P.: Integration of Grid Cost Model into ISS/VIOLA Meta-scheduler Environment. In: Lehner, W., Meyer, N., Streit, A., Stewart, C. (eds.) Euro-Par Workshops 2006. LNCS, vol. 4375, pp. 215–224. Springer, Heidelberg (2007)
37. Sakellariou, R., Yarmolenko, V.: On the flexibility of ws-agreement for job submission. In: 3rd International Workshop on Middleware for Grid Computing, Grenoble, France. ACM (2005)

Let the Clouds Compute: Cost-Efficient Workload Distribution in Infrastructure Clouds

Ulrich Lampe, Melanie Siebenhaar, Ronny Hans,
Dieter Schuller, and Ralf Steinmetz

Multimedia Communications Lab (KOM), TU Darmstadt, Germany
Ulrich.Lampe@kom.tu-darmstadt.de
http://www.kom.tu-darmstadt.de

Abstract. With cloud computing, a virtually inexhaustible pool of computing capacity has become available to IT users. However, given the large number of Infrastructure as a Service offers with differing pricing options, the cost-efficient distribution of workloads poses a complex challenge. In this work-in-progress paper, we formally describe the *Cloud-oriented Workload Distribution Problem* and propose an exact as well as a heuristic optimization approach. Through an evaluation that is based on realistic data from the cloud market, we examine the performance and practical applicability of these approaches.

Keywords: Cloud Computing, Infrastructure, Workload, Distribution, Deployment, Offline, Optimization, Exact, Heuristic.

1 Introduction

With the advent of cloud computing, Information Technology (IT) services have increasingly become commodities over the last few years, resulting in the vision of "IT as the fifth utility" [1]. Combined with aspects such as the elimination of upfront investments and high scalability, the idea to lease computing capacity – rather than provide it in-house – increasingly gains in appeal.

In this work, we assume that a user aims to deploy a *workload* onto leased cloud infrastructure at minimal cost. We define a workload as a set of multiple computational jobs, which are executed on *Infrastructure as a Service* (IaaS) capacities in the form of *Virtual Machines* (VMs). The decision where to place these jobs is complicated by two main factors: First, VMs are discrete compute units that only provide a limited supply of certain resources, such as processor power or local storage space. Second, billing schemes commonly differ between the various cloud providers and involve different price components, such as periodical VM leasing fees and usage-based network traffic fees.

In the work at hand, we refer to this challenge as *Cloud-oriented Workload Distribution Problem* (CWDP). In the following Section 2, the problem is defined in detail. In Section 3, we present exact and heuristic optimization approaches to solve the CWDP. A quantitative evaluation of both approaches is described in Section 4. Section 5 provides an overview of related work. Lastly, Section 6 concludes the paper with a summary and an outlook on future work.

K. Vanmechelen, J. Altmann, and O.F. Rana (Eds.): GECON 2012, LNCS 7714, pp. 91–101, 2012.

2   Problem Statement

As mentioned before, we address the so-called CWDP in the work at hand. We assume that a user has specified a workload, which he/she aims to deploy onto leased cloud infrastructure in the form of VMs. The workload consists of individual computational jobs with given durations, i.e., the initiation and termination times of all jobs are known in advance. Computational jobs may, e.g., represent distributed application components or tasks in a scientific algorithm.

Each job exhibits certain resource demands throughout its execution, e.g., in terms of processor power or network bandwidth. Jobs cannot be split among different VM instances; however, multiple jobs may be combined on one VM instance. In addition, all jobs are non-preemptable, i.e., they have to be continuously executed.

Within the cloud market, different VM types are available to the user from multiple IaaS providers, such as Amazon[1] or Microsoft[2]. Each instance of a VM type supplies a different quantity of resources, e.g., processor power, and imposes a certain usage fee per *fixed-length* leasing period. In addition, surcharges for each unit of resource consumption, e.g., network traffic, may apply.

The objective of the user consists in minimizing his/her total leasing cost. As a constraint, the resource demands of all jobs within the workload have to be satisfied by corresponding resource supplies.

3   Optimization Approaches

In this section, we first introduce formal notations, which subsequently permit to define the CWDP as mathematical optimization model and infer an exact optimization approach. Due to the computational complexity of such exact approach, we additionally present a heuristic optimization approach.

3.1   Formal Notations

In order to map the CWDP into a formal optimization model, we introduce a few formal notations. To begin with, let $J \subset \mathbb{N}$ denote the set of jobs that comprise the workload. For each job $j \in J$, its initiation time $TI_j \in \mathbb{N}$, termination time $TT_j \in \mathbb{N}$, and corresponding duration $D_j \in \mathbb{N}$ are given. The jobs exhibit computational demands, which refer to the set of resource types $R \subset \mathbb{N}$. Specifically, $RD_{j,r}$ denotes the resource demand that job j imposes on a VM instance with respect to the resource type $r \in R$.

The available VM types are given by the set $V \subset \mathbb{N}$. The maximum number of concurrently available instances of VM type $v \in V$, as specified by the respective IaaS provider, correspond to $m_v \in \mathbb{N}$. We further define $RS_{v,r}$ as the supply of resource type r per individual instance of VM type v. $P_v \in \mathbb{N}$ denotes the fixed length of a single leasing period for each VM type v, for which a fixed usage

---

[1] http://aws.amazon.com/ec2/
[2] http://www.windowsazure.com/

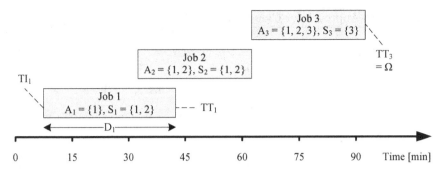

Fig. 1. Example workload with selected formal notations

fee of $CF_v \in \mathbb{R}^+$ will be charged. In addition, $CV_{v,r} \in \mathbb{R}^+$ denotes the cost of resource type r per used resource and time unit.

Based on the above notations, we further define $\Omega = \max_{j \in J}(TT_j)$ as the maximum termination time among all jobs in the workload. In addition, $A_j = \{j' \in J \mid TI_{j'} \leq TI_j\}$ denotes the jobs that are initiated prior to a given job j. Likewise, $S_j = J \setminus \{j' \in J \mid TT_{j'} < TI_j \lor TI_{j'} > TT_j\}$ specifies jobs that are executed simultaneously with j. Please note that both A_j and S_j include j itself (an example is provided in Figure 1).

3.2   Exact Optimization Approach

In order to compute an exact, i.e., cost-minimal, solution to the CWDP, we map the problem statement from Section 2 into its mathematical equivalent. The result is provided in Model 1. Prior to a detailed explanation, we introduce two concepts that are relevant to the understanding of the model.

First, we observe that the lease of a VM instance will always start with the initiation of a job. For a specific VM type v, the lease may consecutively be renewed after one leasing period of the fixed length P_v. The lease will, at the latest, terminate once the final computational job has finished. Thus, based on a given job j, we define a set of (potential) leasing instants $L_{v,j} = \{TI_j, \ldots, TI_j + k \times P_v\}$, where $k = \lfloor (\Omega - TI_j)/P_v \rfloor$. For all jobs in the workload, the set of leasing instants is given by $L_v = \bigcup_{j \in J} L_{v,j}$ accordingly.

For reasons of convenience, we additionally define the set of neighboring leasing instants $N_v(t) = \{l \in L_v \mid l > t - P_v \land l \leq t\}$, which lie within the length of one leasing period P_v before a specified time instant $t \in \mathbb{N}$.

Second, a VM instance must be leased throughout the complete duration of the jobs that have been assigned to it. The existence of such active lease can be verified at certain checkpoints, which temporally coincide with the potential leasing instants that may be relevant to a job. Based on a given job j and the previously defined leasing instants, we define the set of checkpoints as $C_{v,j} = \{TI_j, TT_j\} \cup \bigcup_{j' \in A_j} \{l \in L_{v,j'} \mid l > TI_j \land l < TT_j\}$.

Based on these concepts, the optimization model can be explained in further detail: To begin with, Equation 1 defines the objective, which consists in

Model 1. Exact Approach for Cloud-oriented Workload Distribution

$$\text{Min. } TC(x,y) = \sum_{v \in V, i \in I_v, l \in L_v} y_{v,i,l} \times CF_v \tag{1}$$

$$+ \sum_{j \in J, v \in V, i \in I_v} x_{j,v,i} \times D_j \times RD_{j,r} \times CV_{v,r}$$

subject to

$$\sum_{l \in N_v(c)} y_{v,i,l} \geq x_{j,v,i} \quad \forall j \in J, v \in V, i \in I_v, c \in C_{v,j} \tag{2}$$

$$\sum_{v \in V, i \in I_v} x_{j,v,i} = 1 \quad \forall j \in J \tag{3}$$

$$\sum_{j' \in S_j} x_{j',v,i} \times RD_{j',r} \leq RS_{v,r} \quad \forall v \in V, i \in I_v, j \in J, r \in R \tag{4}$$

$$\sum_{l' \in N_v(l)} y_{v,i,l'} \leq 1 \quad \forall v \in V, i \in I_v, l \in L_v \tag{5}$$

$$I_v = \{1, \ldots, \min(\max_{j \in J}(|S_j|), m_v)\} \tag{6}$$

$$I_v \subset \mathbb{N}$$

$$x_{j,v,i} \in \{0,1\} \quad \forall j \in J, v \in V, i \in I_v \tag{7}$$

$$y_{v,i,l} \in \{0,1\} \quad \forall v \in V, i \in I_v, l \in L_v \tag{8}$$

minimizing the total leasing cost of the cloud infrastructure. The total cost comprises two components, namely the periodical leasing fees for the VM instances and the additional charges for resource consumption.

For that matter, the decision variable $x_{j,v,i}$ indicates whether a job $j \in J$ has been assigned to a VM instance of type $v \in V$ with the running index $i \in I_v$ or not. In a similar manner, the decision variable $y_{v,i,l}$ indicates whether the VM instance of type v with the running index $i \in I_v$ has been leased at the time instant $l \in L_v$ or not. Both x and y are defined as binary variables in Equations 7 and 8. Whereas x is the main decision variable, y can be interpreted as an auxiliary decision variable.

Equation 2 links the two decision variables. More precisely, it defines that if an assignment of a task to a certain VM instance has been made, as indicated by variable x, each checkpoint needs to be matched by a corresponding active lease, as represented by variable y.

Equation 3 ensures that each task is assigned to precisely one VM instance. Equation 4 guarantees that the resource demands of all tasks that are executed simultaneously are met by corresponding resource supplies. Equation 5 ensures that the lease of a VM instance cannot be renewed until the previous lease has expired. Equation 6 defines a set of valid instance indices for each VM type. The definition is based on the notion that, in the worst case, the largest set of simultaneous jobs within the workload, i.e., $max_{j \in J}(|S_j|)$, may be deployed on individual VM instances of the same type; yet, in any case, no more than the maximum number of VM instances, i.e., m_v, can be used.

As can be seen, Model 1 constitutes a special case of a linear program, namely a *Binary Integer Program* (BIP). Such BIP can be solved using well-known methodologies from the field of operations research, such as *branch and bound* [2]. Unfortunately, the computational complexity of such exact methods can be very high. In the worst case, the complexity grows exponentially with the number of decision variables. In the specific case of the CWDP, the worst case complexity corresponds to $\mathcal{O}(2^{|J|^2 \times |V| + |J| \times \sum_{v \in V} L_v})$. Accordingly, an exact solution to the CWDP can most likely not be computed within reasonable time if a workload features multiple jobs, or long job durations that result in a large number of potential leasing instants.

3.3   Heuristic Optimization Approach

In the previous Section 3.2, we have explained that the complexity of computing an exact solution to the CWDP rapidly increases with the number of jobs in the workload. This indicates the need for a heuristic optimization approach, which potentially trades reductions in computation time against possibly sub-optimal solutions.

The heuristic presented in this work is based on an approach that we have previously proposed for the cost-efficient distribution of software services [3]. Because this previous work assumed an online (i.e., at run time), rather than an offline distribution (i.e., at design time), a number of adaptations had to be made. In both cases, however, the principal mechanism is inspired by heuristic solutions to the well-known *knapsack problem* [4].

Our heuristic approach encompasses two phases, *VM packing* and *VM selection*, which are iteratively repeated until a valid solution to the CWDP has been computed. The principle idea is to select a subset of jobs in each iteration and assign it to a new instance of the most cost-efficient VM type. A schematic overview of the complete heuristic in the form of pseudo code is provided in Algorithm 1 and will be explained in the following.

In accordance with Section 3.2, x denotes the main decision variable. Again, $x_{j,v,i}$ indicates whether a job j has been assigned to a VM instance of type v with the running index i or not.

As a preparatory step for the main algorithm, we initialize the current instance index i_v for each VM type v (lines 1–3).

In the first phase, *VM packing*, we create a so-called *packing list* for each VM type. A packing list $PL_v \subseteq J$ represents a subset of jobs that have not been assigned yet and would fit onto a new instance of type v. Initially, we assume an empty packing list. Subsequently, we scan the set of jobs, J, in the order of initiation times. If the current job j would additionally fit onto a new VM

Algorithm 1. Heuristic Approach for Cloud-oriented Workload Distribution

1: **for all** $v \in V$ **do**	23: $\hat{u} \leftarrow 0$
2: $\quad i_v \leftarrow 1$	24: $\hat{v} \leftarrow$ null
3: **end for**	25: **for all** $v \in V$ **do**
4: **repeat**	26: $\quad$ **if** $i_v \leq m_v$ **then**
5: $\quad$ **for all** $v \in V$ **do**	27: $\quad\quad u_v \leftarrow$ compUtil(v, PL_v)
6: $\quad\quad$ **if** $i_v \leq m_v$ **then**	28: $\quad\quad$ **if** $u_v > \hat{u}$ **then**
7: $\quad\quad\quad PL_v \leftarrow \emptyset$	29: $\quad\quad\quad \hat{u} \leftarrow u_v$
8: $\quad\quad\quad$ **repeat**	30: $\quad\quad\quad \hat{v} \leftarrow v$
9: $\quad\quad\quad\quad \delta \leftarrow$ false	31: $\quad\quad$ **end if**
10: $\quad\quad\quad\quad$ **for all** $j \in J \setminus PL_v$ **do**	32: $\quad$ **end if**
11: $\quad\quad\quad\quad\quad$ **if** checkFit$(v, PL_v \cup \{j\})$ **then**	33: **end for**
12: $\quad\quad\quad\quad\quad\quad u \leftarrow$ compUtil(v, PL_v)	34: **if** $\hat{v} \neq$ null **then**
13: $\quad\quad\quad\quad\quad\quad u' \leftarrow$ compUtil$(v, PL_v \cup \{j\})$	35: $\quad$ **for all** $j \in PL_{\hat{v}}$ **do**
14: $\quad\quad\quad\quad\quad\quad$ **if** $u' > u$ **then**	36: $\quad\quad x_{j,v,i_{\hat{v}}} \leftarrow 1$
15: $\quad\quad\quad\quad\quad\quad\quad PL_v \leftarrow PL_v \cup \{j\}$	37: $\quad$ **end for**
16: $\quad\quad\quad\quad\quad\quad\quad \delta \leftarrow$ true	38: $\quad J \leftarrow J \setminus PL_{\hat{v}}$
17: $\quad\quad\quad\quad\quad\quad$ **end if**	39: $\quad i_{\hat{v}} \leftarrow i_{\hat{v}} + 1$
18: $\quad\quad\quad\quad\quad$ **end if**	40: **end if**
19: $\quad\quad\quad\quad$ **end for**	41: **until** $J = \emptyset \vee \hat{v} = \emptyset$
20: $\quad\quad\quad$ **until** $\delta =$ false	
21: $\quad\quad$ **end if**	
22: $\quad$ **end for**	

instance of type v and increase the utility of the packing list, it is added to the packing list. Utility, in this respect, is defined as the ratio between the aggregated durations of all jobs and the corresponding leasing cost. It is computed using the function compUtil. The process of scanning the set of jobs is repeated until no more changes to any packing list could be made, as indicated by the variable δ. This repetition is necessary because a certain job may only increase the utility after a subsequent job has already been added to the packing list (lines 5–22).

In the second phase, *VM selection*, we determine the favorite, i. e., most cost-efficient, VM type, based on the previously created packing lists. In accordance with the previous phase, cost-efficiency is represented by a utility value. The favorite VM type is denoted by $\hat{v}$, with a utility of $\hat{u}$. For each VM type v, we initially assume a utility of zero; VM types for which the maximum number of instances has been reached are excluded from the process. We compute the overall utility value u_v, based on the previously compiled packing list PL_v. If the utility value u_v exceeds the maximal value $\hat{u}$, v is assumed as the new favorite VM type $\hat{v}$ (lines 23–33).

In the following, we check whether a favorite VM type $\hat{v}$ could be identified. This may not be the case if the maximum number of instances of each VM type has been reached, or none of the available VM types is suitable to execute one of the remaining jobs. If a favorite VM type $\hat{v}$ exists, however, we assign all jobs in the packing list $PL_{\hat{v}}$ to a new instance with the index $i_{\hat{v}}$. Finally, we remove the assigned jobs from the set J and increment the instance count $i_{\hat{v}}$ (lines 34–40).

Both phases are iteratively repeated until all jobs have been assigned or no favorite VM type can be identified. In the latter case, a portion of the jobs could not be successfully assigned, thus yielding an invalid solution.

From an analytical point of view, the heuristic has substantial advantages over the exact solution in terms of computational complexity. Specifically, the creation of the packing list is the most complex part; given that the number of resource types is constant and thus negligible, the worst-case complexity of the complete algorithm is polynomial and corresponds to $\mathcal{O}(|J|^4 \times |V|)$.

4   Evaluation

Both previously presented optimization approaches have been prototypically implemented as a Java program, which serves as the basis of our evaluation. For solving the BIP in the exact optimization approach, we apply the *IBM ILOG CPLEX Optimizer*[3].

4.1   Design and Setup

With the evaluation, we aimed to quantitatively assess the performance of the two optimization approaches. Performance, in this respect, is represented by two dependent variables: First, *computation time* represents the scalability of the two approaches and indicates their practical applicability to large-scale CWDPs. Second, *total cost* indicates the solution quality with respect to the objective of cost-efficient workload distribution.

For the evaluation, we created ten classes of CWDPs, each containing 100 individual problems. In classes $A1$ to $A5$, we treated the number of jobs as independent variable, i. e., $|J| \in \{4, 8, 12, 16, 20\}$, assuming a fixed number of VM types, i. e., $|V| = 6$. In classes $B1$ to $B5$, we assumed the number of VM types as independent variable, i. e., $|V| \in \{2, 4, 6, 8, 10\}$, treating the number of jobs as fixed, i. e., $|J| = 12$. Thus, we vary those two variables that have been analytically identified as influential to the computational complexity of both optimization approaches.

For the definition of the VM types, we used the specifications provided by Amazon for its Elastic Compute Cloud (EC2). Each type exhibits specific resource supplies with respect to three resource types (namely processor, memory, and storage), where the consumption is covered by differing hourly leasing fees. In addition, we regarded network traffic – which imposes additional usage-based fees – as fourth resource type, i. e., $|R| = 4$.

The workloads were randomly generated by drawing the initiation times and durations of the jobs from the uniform distributions $U(1, 120)$ and $U(1, 60)$ respectively, assuming minutes as time unit. The resource demands of the individual jobs were also randomly drawn, assuming the resource supplies of an Amazon EC2 *Standard Medium* VM as upper limit.

---

[3] http://www.ibm.com/software/integration/optimization/cplex-optimizer/

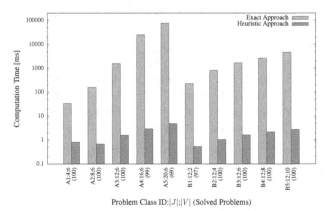

(a) Absolute computation times (note the logarithmic scale)

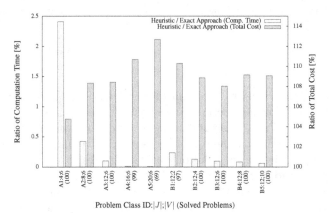

(b) Ratios of computation times (left ordinate) and total costs (right ordinate)

Fig. 2. Evaluation results for both optimization approaches

Each CWDP was solved using both optimization approaches, using a desktop computer with an Intel Core 2 Quad Q9450 processor and 8 GB of memory, operating under Microsoft Windows 7. In the process, we imposed a timeout of 300 seconds (i. e., 5 minutes) per problem and optimization approach. Only such problems that could be successfully solved by both approaches within this timeout period were considered in the following analysis.

4.2   Results and Discussion

As can be observed in Figure 2a, the exact optimization approach quickly reaches absolute computation times in the magnitude order of seconds (classes $A3$ and $B2$ to $B5$, which involve 12 jobs) or even ten seconds (classes $A4$ and $A5$, which involve 16 and 20 jobs), and also results in various timeouts (specifically for class

A5). In accordance with our qualitative analysis in Section 3.2, the absolute computation times exhibit an exponential growth with an increasing number of jobs (classes $A1$ to $A5$). The same applies for a growing number of VM types, even though the effect is less pronounced (classes $B1$ to $B5$).

In contrast, for the heuristic approach, the absolute computation times are in the order of milliseconds or below across all evaluated classes. In relative terms, the heuristic achieves reductions in computation time of more than 97.5% compared to the exact approach (cf. Figure 2b). This gap further increases with a growing number of jobs (classes $A1$ to $A5$), which, in accordance with our analysis from Section 3.3, indicates a superior scalability of the heuristic approach. With an increasing number of VM types (classes $B1$ to $B5$), the benefits of the heuristic approach are less accentuated. However, this is also of limited practical relevance, because the number of available VM types will usually be restricted.

Lastly, as it can be seen in Figure 2b, the reduction in computation time is traded against reductions in solution quality. Depending on the problem size, the increase in total cost for the distribution of the workload ranges between approximately 5% and 13%. The gap between both optimization approaches appears to grow with an increasing number of jobs (classes $A1$ to $A5$), but not with a growing number of VM types (classes $B1$ to $B5$). Accordingly, the proposed heuristic should be seen as a first step toward efficiently solving large-scale CWDPs. That is, it primarily provides a valid baseline solution, which should subsequently be refined by a specific improvement procedure.

In summary, our evaluation indicates that the exact optimization approach is solely applicable to small CWDPs involving around 20 jobs in practice. In comparison, the heuristic approach exhibits a more favorable runtime behavior, which renders it potentially suitable for larger CWDPs involving hundreds or thousands of jobs. However, the heuristic also results in notable increases in the total cost of workload distribution. Thus, a future direction of our research will consist in the development of improvement procedures, which permit enhancements in solution quality while sustaining the low computational complexity of a heuristic solution approach.

5   Related Work

In recent years, the distribution of workloads in cloud and grid environments has been a vivid field of research. Substantial efforts have also been undertaken in the related field of *workflow* distribution. Given space limitations, we only present a brief overview of the most similar works.

To start with, in our own previous work, e. g., [3], we have examined the Software Service Distribution Problem (SSDP). This challenge concerns the distribution of software services within IaaS clouds. Specifically, we have proposed both an exact and a heuristic *online* approach that permits to cost-efficiently allocate software service requests to different VM types at run time. When interpreting software services as computational jobs within a workload, the approach proposed in this work can be seen as a benchmark, which permits to compute a theoretically optimal ex-post, *offline* solution to the SSDP.

Li et al. [5] have studied the distribution of VMs among PMs in order to serve predictable peak loads. Their objective consists in load balancing among the PMs; for that purpose, the authors propose four different algorithms, which are extensively evaluated. While there is a number of similarities between the work by Li et al. and our research, a major difference lies in the objective of cost-efficiency. In addition, we consider fixed-length VM leasing periods, different price components, and multiple resource types in the distribution process.

Genez et al. [6] have examined the problem of cost-efficient workflow deployment in hybrid clouds under consideration of service level agreements. They propose an exact optimization approach based on Integer Linear Programming (ILP), as well as different heuristic approaches that are based on the principle of ILP relaxation. In contrast to our work, Genez et al. take into account temporally movable and inter-dependent jobs. However, the authors only consider a restricted set of resource types and do not regard fixed-length leasing periods of VMs.

Byun et al. [7] have presented a system for the deployment of workflows within grids and clouds. The authors introduce a heuristic approach for the minimization of leasing costs; they do not provide an exact approach though. Byun et al. consider job dependencies and flexible start times, which are not regarded in our work. However, while they consider fixed-length leasing periods, the authors assume identical leasing instants for all compute hosts, whereas our work permits independent leasing instants for the individual VMs.

In summary, to the best of our knowledge, this work is the first to address the distribution of workloads, i.e., set of jobs, onto VMs under the conjoint consideration of fixed-length leasing periods, as well as fixed and variable price components. Due to the prevalence of these characteristics in actual IaaS cloud offers, our approach permits to compute accurate, i.e., truly cost-optimal, distribution schemes. However, in contrast to the large body of research on workflow deployment, our work does neither explicitly regard dependencies between jobs nor the potential to temporally shift jobs. The consideration of these aspects will be part of our future work.

6   Summary and Outlook

Cloud computing has made a large pool of computing capacity available at comparatively low prices. This permits end users to execute workloads using leased infrastructure rather than costly dedicated hardware. However, given the differing pricing schemes for IaaS offers, which commonly also feature fixed-length leasing periods, the cost-efficient distribution of such workloads among VMs is a challenging task.

In the work at hand, we have addressed this *Cloud-oriented Workload Distribution Problem* (CWDP). As a first major contribution, we have formally described the problem in the form of an mathematical optimization model, which can serve for the computation of exact solutions to the CWDP. As a second major contribution, we have introduced a heuristic optimization approach.

We have quantitatively evaluated both optimization approaches with respect to computation time and solution quality, i. e., resulting total leasing cost. We found that the exact solution approach is hardly applicable to workloads involving more than 20 jobs due to its computational complexity. In comparison, the proposed heuristic allows reductions in computation time of more than 97.5%, which renders it potentially suitable for solving large-scale CWDPs. However, the heuristic solutions also lead to substantial increases in total leasing costs of up to 13% in our experimental evaluation, as compared to an optimal distribution scheme.

Thus, the primary goal of our future work consists in the development of heuristic improvement procedures that are specifically tailored to the CWDP. In addition, we aim to substantially extend the evaluation of the proposed approaches through the consideration of additional variables. Lastly, as it has been outlined in Section 5, we plan to consider characteristics that are common in the area of workflow deployment, such as flexible job initiation times.

Acknowledgments. This work has partly been sponsored by E-Finance Lab e. V., Frankfurt am Main, Germany (`http://www.efinancelab.de`).

References

1. Buyya, R., Yeo, C., Venugopal, S., Broberg, J., Brandic, I.: Cloud Computing and Emerging IT Platforms: Vision, Hype, and Reality for Delivering Computing as the 5th Utility. Future Generation Computer Systems 25(6), 599–616 (2009)
2. Hillier, F., Lieberman, G.: Introduction to Operations Research, 8th edn. McGraw-Hill (2005)
3. Lampe, U., Mayer, T., Hiemer, J., Schuller, D., Steinmetz, R.: Enabling Cost-Efficient Software Service Distribution in Infrastructure Clouds at Run Time. In: 2011 IEEE Int. Conf. on Service Oriented Computing & Applications, pp. 82–89 (2011)
4. Domschke, W., Drexl, A.: Einführung in Operations Research, 6th edn. Springer (2004) (in German)
5. Li, W., Tordsson, J., Elmroth, E.: Virtual Machine Placement for Predictable and Time-Constrained Peak Loads. In: Vanmechelen, K., Altmann, J., Rana, O.F. (eds.) GECON 2011. LNCS, vol. 7150, pp. 120–134. Springer, Heidelberg (2012)
6. Genez, T., Bittencourt, L., Madeira, E.: Workflow Scheduling for SaaS/PaaS Cloud Providers Considering two SLA Levels. In: 2012 IEEE Network Operations and Management Symposium, pp. 906–912 (2012)
7. Byun, E., Kee, Y., Kim, J., Maeng, S.: Cost Optimized Povisioning of Elastic Resources for Application Workflows. Future Generation Computer Systemss 27, 1011–1026 (2011)

A Declarative Recommender System for Cloud Infrastructure Services Selection

Miranda Zhang[1], Rajiv Ranjan[1], Surya Nepal[1], Michael Menzel[2], and Armin Haller[1]

[1] Information Engineering Laboratory, CSIRO ICT Centre
{miranda.zhang,rajiv.ranjan,surya.nepal,armin.haller}@csiro.au
[2] Karlsruhe Institute of Technology, Karlsruhe, Germany
menzel@fzi.de

Abstract. The cloud infrastructure services landscape advances steadily leaving users in the agony of choice. Therefore, we present CloudRecommender, a new declarative approach for selecting Cloud-based infrastructure services. CloudRecommender automates the mapping of users' specified application requirements to cloud service configurations. We formally capture cloud service configurations in ontology and provide its implementation in a structured data model which can be manipulated through both regular expressions and SQL. By exploiting the power of a visual programming language (widgets), CloudRecommender further enables simplified and intuitive cloud service selection. We describe the design and a prototype implementation of CloudRecommender, and demonstrate its effectiveness and scalability through a service configuration selection experiment on most of today's prominent cloud providers including Amazon, Azure, and GoGrid.

Keywords: Cloud Computing, Infrastructure Service.

1 Introduction

Cloud computing [1,2,3] assembles large networks of virtualized services: infrastructure services (e.g., compute, storage, network, etc.) and software services (e.g., databases, message queuing systems, monitoring systems, load-balancers, etc.). It embraces an elastic paradigm in which applications establish on-demand interactions with services to satisfy required Quality of Service (QoS) including cost, response time and throughput. However, selecting and composing the right services meeting application requirements is a challenging problem.

Consider an example of a medium scale enterprise that would like to move its enterprise applications to cloud. There are multiple providers in the current cloud landscape that offer infrastructure services in multiple heterogeneous configurations. Examples include, Amazon [10], Microsoft Azure [12], GoGrid [13], Rackspace, BitCloud, and Ninefold, among many others. With multiple and heterogeneous options for infrastructure services, enterprises are facing a complex task when trying to select and compose a single service type or a combination of service types. Here we are concerned with simplifying the selection and comparison of a set of infrastructure service offerings for hosting the enterprise applications and

K. Vanmechelen, J. Altmann, and O.F. Rana (Eds.): GECON 2012, LNCS 7714, pp. 102–113, 2012.

corresponding dataset, while meeting multiple criteria, such as specific configuration and cost, emanating from the enterprise's QoS needs. This is a challenging problem for the enterprise and needs to be addressed.

Existing approaches in helping a user to compare and select infrastructure services in cloud computing involve manually reading the provider documentation for finding out which services are most suitable for hosting an application. This problem is further aggravated by the use of non-standardized naming terminologies used by cloud providers. For example, Amazon refers to compute services as EC2 Compute Unit, while GoGrid refers to the same as Cloud Servers. Furthermore, cloud providers typically publish their service description, pricing policies and Service-Level-Agreement (SLA) rules on their websites in various formats. The relevant information may be updated without prior notice to the users. Hence, it is not an easy task to manually obtain service configurations from cloud providers' websites and documentations (which are the only sources of information).

In order to address the aforementioned problems, we present a semi-automated, extensible, and simplified approach and system for cloud service selection, called CloudRecommender. We indentify and formalize the domain knowledge of multiple configurations of infrastructure services. The core idea in CloudRecommender is to formally capture the domain knowledge of services using a declarative logic-based language, and then implement it in a recommender service on top of a relational data model. Execution procedures in CloudRecommender are transactional and apply well-defined SQL semantics for querying, inserting, and deleting infrastructure services' configurations. The CloudRecommender system proposed in this paper leverages the Web-based widget programming technique that transforms drag and drop operations to low-level SQL transactions. The contributions of this paper can be summarized as follows:

- A unified and formalized domain model capable of fully describing infrastructure services in cloud computing. The model is based and has been successfully validated against the most commonly available infrastructure services including Amazon, Microsoft Azure, GoGrid, etc.
- An implementation of a design support system (CloudRecommender) for the selection of infrastructure cloud service configurations using transactional SQL semantics, procedures and views. The benefits to users of CloudRecommender include, for example, the ability to estimate costs, compute cost savings across multiple providers with possible tradeoffs and aid in the selection of cloud services.
- A user-friendly service interface based on widgets that maps user requirements based on form inputs to available infrastructure services, express configuration selection criteria and view the results.

The remainder of the paper is organized as follows. A discussion on our formal domain model for cloud infrastructure services and our cloud selection approach using CloudRecommender is presented in Section 2. Due to space limitation, Section 3 only included a simple experimental evaluation of the proposed approach, but more details can be found at [20]. A review of related work is provided in Section 4 before we conclude in Section 5.

2   A System for Cloud Service Selection

We propose an approach and system for cloud service configuration selection, CloudRecommender. The system includes a repository of available infrastructure services from different providers including compute, storage and network services, as shown in figure 1(a). Users can communicate with the system via a Web-based widget interface. The CloudRecommender system architecture consists of three layers: the configuration management layer, the application logic layer and the User interface (widget) layer. Details of each layer will be explained in the following sub-sections.

Fig. 1(b) shows the deployment structure of the CloudRecommender system. For persistence we have chosen MySQL for its agility and popularity, but any other relational database can be plugged in. Furthermore, many APIs provided by cloud providers (such as Amazon) and open source cloud management frameworks (e.g. jclouds) are written in Java. Thus, Java is chosen as the preferred language to implement the application logic layer to ease future integration with external libraries. The widget layer is implemented using a number of JavaScript frameworks including jQuery, ExtJS and YUI. CloudRecommender also exposes RESTful (REpresentational State Transfer) APIs (application programming interface) that help external applications to programmatically compose infrastructure cloud services based on the CloudRecommender selection process.

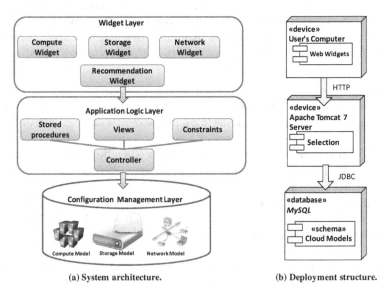

(a) System architecture.   (b) Deployment structure.

Fig. 1. System architecture and deployment structure

2.1   Configuration Management Layer

The configuration layer maintains the basic cloud domain model related to compute, storage, and network services. We defined a Cloud Computing Ontology to facilitate the discovery of services based on their functionality and QoS parameters. The ontology is defined in the Web Ontology Language (OWL) [19] and can be found at: w3c.org.au/cocoon.owl. All common metadata fields in the ontology like Organisation, Author, First Name etc. are referenced through standard Web Ontologies (i.e. FOAF and Dublin Core). To describe specific aspects of cloud computing, established domain classifications have been used as a guiding reference [16], [18]. The resulting ontology consists of two parts, the Cloud Service Ontology and the Cloud QoS Ontology.

Cloud Service Ontology: A *CloudService* (maps to *cloud_service_types* in the relational model in Figure 2) can be of one of the three types, Infrastructure-as-a-Service (IaaS), Platform-as-a-Service (PaaS) or Software-as-a-Service (SaaS). For the CloudRecommender system the cloud infrastructure layer (IaaS), providing concepts and relations that are fundamental to the other higher-level layers, is the one currently relevant. Cloud services in the IaaS layer can be categorised into: Compute, Network, and Storage services (see Table 1).

Cloud QoS Ontology: At the core of the Cloud QoS ontology is a taxonomy of *ConfigurationParameters* and *Metrics (Values)*, i.e. two trees formed using the RDF(s) subClassOf relation where an *Configuration Parameters*, for example, PriceStorage, PriceCompute, PriceDataTransferIn (Out) etc. and a Metric, for example, ProbabilityOfFailureOnDemand, TransactionalThroughput, are used in combination to define Cloud QoS capabilities (e.g. features, performance, costs, etc.). The resulting ontology is a (complex) directed graph where, for example, the Property *hasMetric* (and its inverse *isMetricOf*) is the basic link between the *ConfigurationParameters* and Metric trees. For the metrics part of the QoS, we reference existing QoS ontologies [17] whereas for the *ConfigurationParameters* concepts the ontology defines its independent taxonomy, but refers to external ontologies for existing definitions. Each configuration parameter (see Table 1) has a name, and a value (qualitative or quantitative). The type of configuration determines the nature of service by means of setting a minimum, maximum, or capacity limit, or meeting certain value. For example, "RAM capacity" configuration parameter of a compute service can be set to the value 2GB.

For our CloudRecommender service we implemented the Cloud Service Ontology in a relational model and the Cloud QoS ontology as configuration information as structured data (entities) (as shown in Figure 2), which can be queried using a SQL-based declarative language. We collected service configuration information from a number of public cloud providers (e.g., Windows Azure, Amazon, GoGrid, RackSpace, Nirvanix, Ninefold, SoftLayer, AT and T Synaptic, Cloud Central, etc.) to demonstrate the generic nature of the domain model with respect to capturing heterogeneous configuration (see Table 2) information of infrastructure services. Our model is generic enough to capture all the existing cloud-based infrastructure services. The proposed model is flexible and extensible enough to accommodate new services with minimal changes to our implementation. In future work, we also intend to extend the model with capability to store PaaS and SaaS configurations.

Relationships between concepts representing services are carefully considered and normalized to avoid update anomalies. Services from various providers often have very different configurations and pricing models. Distinct and ambiguous terminologies are often used to describe similar configurations.

Regardless of how providers name their services, we categorize infrastructure services based on their basic functionality. Unit conversions were performed during instantiation of concepts. For example, an Amazon EC2 Micro Instance has 613 MB of memory which is converted to approximately 0.599 GB. Another example is the CPU clock speed. Amazon refers to it as "ECUs". From their documentation [10]: *"One EC2 Compute Unit provides the equivalent COMPUTE capacity of a 1.0-1.2 GHz 2007 Opteron or 2007 Xeon processor. This is also the equivalent to an early-2006 1.7 GHz Xeon processor referenced in our original documentation"*. In 2007, AMD and Intel released both dual-core and quad-core models of the Opteron and Xeon chips, respectively. So it is obviously not clear what an Amazon EC2 Compute Unit compares to. To eliminate this ambiguity, we obtained the compute service clock speed by trying out the actual instance under Linux OS and run "more /proc/cpuinfo" on it. We'd like to get those kinds of information automatically in the future through APIs (if available). Table 2 depicts the configuration ambiguities of compute and storage services of different providers.

Table 1. Infrastructure service types and their configurations

Service	Configurations Parameters	Range/possible values
	cores	>=1
	speed	>0
	RAM capacity	>0
	local storage capacity	>=0
	physical location of cloud	North America,South America,Africa,Europe,Asia,Australia
	cost per hour of usage per month	>=0
	per period cost	>= 0
	period length in days	> 0
	overage cost	>= 0
Compute	plan type	Pay As You Go, Prepaid
	network storage size min and max range	>=0
	cost per GB per Month	>=0
	location of host cloud	North America,South America,Africa,Europe,Asia,Australia
	type of requests	put,copy,post,list,get,delete,search
	cost of request	>=0
	plan type	Pay As You Go, Reduced Redundancy
Storage	Reduced Redundancy storage cost	>=0
Network	data transfer in cost, data transfer out cost	>=0

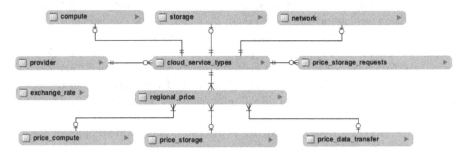

Fig. 2. Conceptual data model representing infrastructure service entities and their relationships

Table 2. Depiction of configuration heterogeneities in compute and storage services across providers

Provider	Compute		Storage	Plans other than Pay As You Go		Trail
	Terminology	Unit	Terminology	Compute	Storage	Period or Value
Windows Azure	Virtual Server	/hr	Azure Storage	Commitment Plan, Member Offer		90 day
Amazon	EC2 Instance	/hr	S3	Reserved, Spot, Marketplace	Reduced Redundancy	1 year
GoGrid	Cloud Servers	/RAM hr	Cloud Storage	Prepaid (1, 6 or 12 month)		Various from time to time, current value: 100 AUD
RackSpace	Cloud Servers	/RAM hr	Cloud Files	Managed Cloud		
Nirvanix			CSN			
Ninefold	Virtual Server	/hr	Cloud Storage	SimplePlan		50 AUD
SoftLayer	Cloud Servers	/hr	Object Storage	Monthly		1 month
AT and T Synaptic	Compute as a Service	vCPU per hour + /RAM hr	Storage as a Service	Committed Allocation Pool		
Cloudcentral	Cloud Servers	/hr				

(Red) Blank cells in the table mean it is not available. Some providers offer their services under a different pricing scheme than pay-as-you-go. In Table II we refer to these schemes as other plans.

Another example of disparity between different Cloud providers is the way in which "on Demand instances" are priced. GoGrid's plan, for example, although having a similar concept to Amazon's On Demand and Reserved Instance, gives very little importance to what type or how many of compute services a user is deploying. GoGrid charges users based on what they call RAM hours – 1 GB RAM compute service deployed for 1 hour consumes 1 RAM Hour. A 2 GB RAM compute service deployed for 1 hour consumes 2 RAM Hour. It is worthwhile mentioning that only Azure clearly states that one month is considered to have 31 days. This is important as the key advantage of the fine grained pay-as-you-go price model which, for example, should charge a user the same when they use 2GB for half a month or 1 GB for a whole month. Other vendors merely give a GB-month price without clarifying how short term usage is handled. It is neither reflected in their usage calculator. We chose 31 days as default value in calculation.

Table 3. Depiction of configuration heterogeneities in request types across storage services

Provider	Storage	Requests		
		Upload	Download	Other
Windows Azure	Azure Storage	storage transactions	storage transactions	
Amazon	S3	PUT, COPY, POST, or LIST Requests	GET and all other Requests	Delete
GoGrid	Cloud Storage	Transfer protocols such as SCP, SAMBA/CIFS, and RSYNC		
RackSpace	Cloud Files	PUT, POST, LIST Requests	HEAD, GET, DELETE Requests	
Nirvanix	CSN		Search	
Ninefold	Cloud Storage	GET, PUT, POST, COPY, LIST and all other transactions		
SoftLayer	Object Storage	Not Specified/Unknow		
AT and T Synaptic	Storage as a Service	Not Specified/Unknow		

Regarding storage services, providers charge for every operation that an application program or user undertakes. These operations are effected on storage services via RESTful or SOAP API. Cloud providers refer to the same set of operations with different names, for example Azure refers to storage service operations as transactions. Nevertheless, the operations are categorized into upload and download categories as shown in Table III. Red means an access fee is charged, green means the service is free, and yellow means it is not specified and usually can be treated as green/free of charge. To facilitate our calculation of similar and equivalent requests across multiple providers, we analyzed and pre-processed the price data, recorded it in our domain model and used a homogenized value in the repository (configuration management layer). For example, Windows Azure Storage charges a flat price per transaction. It is considered as transaction whenever there is a "touch" operation (a Create, Read, Update, Delete (CRUD) operation over the RESTful service interface) on any component (Blobs, Tables or Queues) of Windows Azure Storage.

For providers that offer different regional prices, we store the location information in the price table. If multiple regions have the same price, we choose to combine them. In our current implementation, any changes to existing configurations (such as updating memory size, storage provision etc.) of services can be done by executing customized update SQL queries. We also use customized crawlers to update provider information's periodically. However, in future work we will provide a RESTful interface and widget which can be used for automatic configuration updates.

2.2   Application Logic Layer

The request for service selection in CloudRecommender is expressed as SQL queries. The selection process supports an application logic that builds upon the following declarative constructs: criterion, views and stored procedures. The CloudRecommender builds upon SQL queries which are executed on top of the relational data model.

Criterion: Criterion is a quantitative or qualitative bound (minimum, maximum, equal) on the configuration parameters provided by a service. Cloud services' configuration parameters and their range/values listed in Table I form the basis for expressing selection goal and criteria (e.g., select a cheapest (goal) compute service where (criterion) 0<Ram<=20, 0<=local storage<=2040, number of hours to be used per month = 244). An example query is shown below in Fig 3:

```
27    SELECT *
28    FROM `compute_service_price`
29    left join compute_choice_criterias
30    on `Memory(GB)` >= compute_choice_criterias.ram_low
31    and `Memory(GB)` <= compute_choice_criterias.ram_high
32    and `Local Storage(GB)` >= compute_choice_criterias.local_storage_low
33    and `Local Storage(GB)` <= compute_choice_criterias.local_storage_high
34    where if(all_provider_considered, 1, find_in_set(`Provider Name`,provider_LIST))
```

Fig. 3. Example query in procedure

Procedures: We have implemented a number of customized procedures that automate the service selection process. A number of routines are prepared to process a user service selection request. List of inputs are stored in a temporary table to be passed into the procedures. As such, there is no limit to the size of the input list. Final results are also stored in temporary tables, which are automatically cleared after the expiration of user session.

Table 4. CloudRecommender model parameters

Notations	Meaning
$P = \{p_1, ..., p_p\}$	Set of p service providers
$R_{p_i} = \{r_{p_i,1}, ..., r_{p_i,n}\}$	Regions of provider p_i
$CS = \{cs_1, ..., cs_n\}$	Set of n compute services
$SS = \{ss_1, ..., ss_m\}$	Set of m storage services
$TS = \{ts_1, ..., ts_o\}$	Set of o network (data transfer) services
$t_{s_i,j}$	j-th price tier for a cloud service $s_i \in CS \cup SS \cup TS$
$CR_{s_i} = \{cr_{s_i,1}, ..., cr_{s_i,n}\}$	Set of criteria related to service $s_i \in CS \cup SS \cup TS$
Query	A service selection query
N	Number of rows in a relational entity
M	Number of column in a relational entity

2.3   Computational Complexity of Service Selection Logic

We will discuss the computational complexity of our service selection logic next. For p providers each with cs_i(compute) + ss_i(storage) + ts_i (network) services, the selection logic has to consider $\sum_{i=1}^{p} cs_i \times ss_i \times ts_i$ choices. We give the detailed discussion of model parameters in Table IV. We can nomally reduce the number of options significantly in the early stage if a user has strict requirements. In the worst case scenario, the logic needs to compute a full cross join (cartesian product). The number of choices varies depending on the number of regions (R_{p_i}) with different prices offered by each provider (r_i), and the number of different price tier (t_i) for each service (Price tier example: AWS S3 charges \$0.125 per GB for the first 1 TB / month of usage, \$0.093 for the next 49 TB, etc.). Depending on the estimated usage, the larger the usage, the more price tiers will be involved. Let us assume that each provider offers approximately the same service in each region to simplify the derivation of the computational complexity. As such, the total number of offers can be represented in a more detailed formula:

$$\sum_{i=1}^{p} \left(\sum_{l=1}^{cs_i} t_l\right) \times \left(\sum_{m=1}^{ss_i} t_m\right) \times \left(\sum_{n=1}^{ts_i} t_n\right) \times r_i \tag{1}$$

The queries of the selection logic work as follows. After filtering out criteria-violating services, resulting services are combined via JOIN operation(s) with final costs calculated. In worst case scenario where a few or no criteria are defined, the combination of the services is a full CROSS JOIN over all existing services. Therefore, the selection queries, to our best knowledge, have the upper bound computational complexity of

$$O_{query}(|cr_{compute}| \sum_{i=1}^{p} |cs_i| \times |cr_{storage}| \sum_{i=1}^{p} |ss_i| \times |cr_{network}| \sum_{i=1}^{p} |ts_i|) \tag{2}$$

where cr are criteria and cs, ss and ts are pre-computed views with a singular effort to create the views from JOIN statements. However, in case the database system lacks support for cached views in a worst case the effort multiplies with the effort of the views' JOIN. Modern database can use HASH JOIN O(N + M) and MERGE JOIN O(N*Log(N) + M*Log(M)) which are faster than O(N * M).

2.4   Widget Layer

This layer features rich set of user-interfaces (see Fig 4) that further simplify the selection of configuration parameters related to cloud services. This layer encapsulates the user interface components in the form of four principle widgets including: Compute, Storage, Network, and Recommendation. The selection of basic configuration parameters related to compute services including their RAM capacity, cores, and location can be facilitated through the Compute widget. It also allows users to search compute services by using regular expressions, sort by a specific column etc. Using the Compute widget, users can choose which columns to display and rearrange their order as well. The Storage widget allows users to define configuration parameters such as storage size and request types (e.g., get, put, post, copy, etc.). Service configuration parameters, such as the size of incoming data transfer and outgoing data transfer can be issued via the Network widget. Users have the option to select single service types as well as bundled (combined search) services driven by use cases. The selection results are displayed and can be browsed via the Recommendation widget (not shown in Fig. 4.).

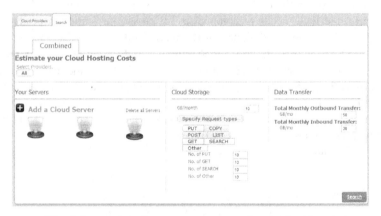

Fig. 4. Screen shot of compute, storage, and network widgets

3   Experiments and Evaluation

In this section, we present the experiments and evaluation that we undertook.

In our infrastructure service selection scenario, we revisit the example of a medium scale enterprise we explained earlier. The enterprise wants to migrate its data to the cloud with the aim of storing and sharing it with other branches through public cloud storage (note that security issues are dealt within the enterprise applications). At this stage, we assume the business analyst of the enterprise has a good estimation of the data storage and transfer (network in/network out) requirements. By using CloudRecommender, the analyst would like to find out which of the public cloud providers would be most cost-effective in regards to data storage and transfer costs. For this selection scenario, the analyst inputs the following anticipated usage information for the storage and network services: (i) Data size of 50 GB, 1000 copy requests and 5000 get requests and (ii) data transfer in size of 10 GB and data transfer out size of 50 GB.

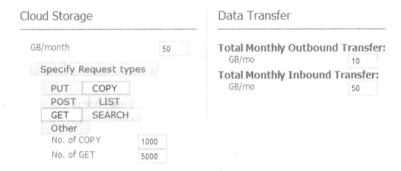

Fig. 5. Service selection criteria set by business analyst

As shown in Fig. 5., the analyst specifies service selection criteria via the storage and network widgets. Programmatically, the above request can also be submitted via the RESTful service interface of the CloudRecommender as shown below in Fig. 6.

Fig. 6. An example REST call

4   Related Work

Prior to CloudRecommender, there have been a variety of systems that use declarative logic-based techniques for managing resources in distributed computing systems. The focus of the authors in work [4] is to provide a distributed platform that enables cloud providers to automate the process of service orchestration via the use of declarative policy languages. The authors in [5] present an SQL-based decision query language for providing a high-level abstraction for expressing decision guidance problems in an intuitive manner so that database programmers can use mathematical programming technique without prior experience. We draw a lot of inspiration from the work in [6] which proposes a data-centric (declarative) framework to orchestrate infrastructure services. The goal of this work is to improve SLA fulfilment ability of cloud service providers. COOLDAID [7] presents a declarative approach to manage configuration of network devices and adopts a relational data model and Datalog-style query language. NetDB [8] uses a relational database to manage the configurations of network devices. However, NetDB is a data warehouse, not designed for cloud service selection and composition. Puppet [9] manages the configuration of data-centre resources using a custom and user-friendly declarative language for service configuration specifications. Puppet simplifies the management of data centre resources for providers. Though branded calculators are available from individual cloud providers, such as Amazon [14], Azure [15], and GoGrid, for calculating service leasing cost, it is not easy for users to generalize their requirements to fit different service offers (with various quota and limitations) let alone computing and comparing costs. Some of the recent research such as [11] has focused on cloud storage service (IaaS level) representation based on an XML schema. However, the proposed declarative model is preferable over hard coding the sorting and selection algorithm (as used in [11]) as it allows us to take the advantage of optimized SQL operations (e.g. select and join).

In contrast to the aforementioned systems, CloudRecommender is designed with a different application domain – one that aims to apply declarative (SQL) and widget programming technique for solving the cloud service configuration selection problem. Facing a new challenge of handling heterogeneous service configuration and naming conventions in cloud computing, CloudRecommender also defines and uses a unified domain model.

5   Conclusion and Future Work

In this paper, we proposed a declarative system (CloudRecommender) that transforms the cloud service configuration selection from an ad-hoc process that involves manually reading the provider documentations to a process that is structured, and to a large extend automated. Although we believe that CloudRecommender leaves scope for a range of enhancements, yet provides a practical approach. We have implemented a prototype of CloudRecommender and evaluated it using an example selection scenario. The prototype demonstrates the feasibility of the CloudRecommender design and its practical aspects.

Our future work includes: (1) extending the CloudRecommender to support the selection of more cloud service types such as PaaS services (e.g., database server, web server, etc.) to further validate our hypothesis and explore new opportunities; (ii) exploring integration of cloud service benchmarking databases such as CloudHarmony to CloudRecommender for facilitating run-time selection based on dynamic QoS information including throughput, latency, and utilization; and (iii) deploying and evaluating the CloudRecommender as a REST service so that it can be easily integrated to any existing cloud service orchestration systems.

Acknowledgments. Initial research on the infrastructure service data models was done when Dr. Rajiv Ranjan was employed at University of New South Wales (UNSW) on a strategic eResearch grant scheme.

References

1. Nurmi, D., Wolski, R., Grzegorczyk, C., Obertelli, G., Soman, S., Youseff, L., Zagorodnov, D.: The Eucalyptus Open-Source Cloud-Computing System. In: Proceedings of the 2009 9th IEEE/ACM International Symposium on Cluster Computing and the Grid (2009)
2. Armbrust, M., Fox, A., Griffith, R., Joseph, A.D., Katz, R., Konwinski, A., Lee, G., Patterson, D., Rabkin, A., Stoica, I., Zaharia, M.: A View of Cloud Computing. Communications of the ACM 53(4), 50–58 (2010)
3. Wang, L., Ranjan, R., Chen, J., Benatallah, B.: Cloud Computing: Methodology, Systems, and Applications. Taylor & Francis (2011)
4. Liu, C., Loo, B.T., Mao, Y.: Declarative Automated Cloud Resource Orchestration. In: Proceedings of the 2nd ACM Symposium on Cloud Computing, Cascais, Portugal (2011)
5. Brodsky, A., Bhot, M.M., Chandrashekar, M., Egge, N.E., Wang, X.S.: A decisions Query Language (DQL): High-level Abstraction for Mathematical Programming over Databases. In: Proceedings of the 2009 ACM SIGMOD International Conference on Management of Data, Providence, Rhode Island, USA (2009)
6. Liu, C., Mao, Y., Van Der Merwe, J.E., Fernández, M.F.: Cloud Resource Orchestration: A Data-Centric Approach. In: The Biennial Conference on Innovative Data Systems Research (CIDR 2011), Asilomar, CA, pp. 241–248 (2011)
7. Chen, X., Mao, Y., Mao, Z.M., Van Der Merwe, J.E.: Declarative Configuration Management for Complex and Dynamic Networks. In: Proceedings of the 6th International Conference on Emerging Networking Experiments and Technologies (CoNEXT), Philadelphia, Pennsylvania, USA (2010)
8. Caldwell, D., Gilbert, A., Gottlieb, J., Greenberg, A., Hjalmtysson, G., Rexford, J.: The Cutting Edge of IP Router Configuration. SIGCOMM Comput. Commun. Rev. 34(1), 21–26 (2004)
9. Puppet: A Data Center Automation Solution, http://www.puppetlabs.com/ (accessed on June 22, 2012)
10. Amazon EC2 Instance Types, http://aws.amazon.com/ec2/instance-types/ (accessed September 26, 2012)
11. Ruiz-Alvarez, A., Humphrey, M.: An Automated Approach to Cloud Storage Service Selection. In: Proceedings of the 2nd International Workshop on Scientific Cloud Computing, San Jose, California, USA (2011)
12. Microsoft Azure Cloud, http://www.windowsazure.com/ (accessed June 22, 2012)
13. GoGrid Cloud, http://www.gogrid.com/ (accessed June 22, 2012)
14. Amazon Price Calculator, http://calculator.s3.amazonaws.com/calc5.html (accessed June 22, 2012)
15. Windows Azure Calculator, http://www.windowsazure.com/en-us/pricing/calculator/ (accessed June 2012)
16. Mell, P., Grance, T.: The NIST Definition of Cloud Computing, Gaithersburg (2011)
17. Papaioannou, I.V., Tsesmetzis, D.T., Roussaki, I.G., Anagnostou, M.E.: A QoS Ontology Language for Web-services. In: 20th International Conference on Advanced Information Networking and Applications, AINA, p. 6 (2006)
18. Youseff, L., Butrico, M., Da Silva, D.: Toward a Unified Ontology of Cloud Computing. In: Grid Computing Environments Workshop, pp. 1–10 (2008)
19. W3C, OWL 2 Web Ontology Language (2009), http://www.w3.org/TR/owl2-overview/
20. Zhang, M., Ranjan, R., Menzel, M., Haller, A., Nepal, S.: A Declarative Recommender System for Cloud Infrastructure Services Selection (2012), http://arxiv.org/abs/1210.2047

Retrieving, Storing, Correlating and Distributing Information for Cloud Management

Spyridon V. Gogouvitis[1], Gregory Katsaros[1], Dimosthenis Kyriazis[1],
Athanasios Voulodimos[1], Roman Talyansky[2], and Theodora Varvarigou[1]

[1] Dept. of Electrical and Computer Engineering National Technical
University of Athens, Athens, Greece
{spyrosg,gregkats,dimos,thanosv}@mail.ntua.gr, dora@telecom.ntua.gr
[2] SAP Research Israel, Ra'anana, Israel
roman.talyansky@sap.com

Abstract. The emergence of Cloud technologies ultimately affected the
service computing ecosystem introducing new roles and relationships as
well as new architectural and business models. The increase of the capabilities and potentials of the service providers raised the need for managing the information being available in an efficient way. In this paper we
introduce a service management architecture as well as the corresponding
information model, which is the placeholder for the information needed
to perform management operations. The design of the proposed model
was based on the case of a storage service being provided through a cloud
infrastructure, but the approach is implemented in a flexible and modular fashion in order to support any service provided through a cloud
environment.

Keywords: Cloud management models, information services, storage
clouds.

1 Introduction

Cloud computing as a whole is rapidly evolving and becoming one of the most
challenging paradigms of Information Technology. Its usefulness for users and
enterprises in general is clearly recognized [1], mainly due to the varying business models it can facilitate. Indeed, their reliance on this paradigm is reaching
unexpected levels. To this end, more and more cloud providers are contributing
towards a quite young, but relatively broad cloud ecosystem. On the other hand,
this massive availability of resources and services resulted in an increase in the
information generation that the current data models and representations cannot
always capture.

Notwithstanding, the rapid evolution of the cloud, along with the new and
emerging needs of customers, pose additional challenges with respect to the management of such environments, given the involvement of various entities, such as
stakeholders at different levels (i.e. users, providers, brokers, etc) with, in many

K. Vanmechelen, J. Altmann, and O.F. Rana (Eds.): GECON 2012, LNCS 7714, pp. 114–124, 2012.
© Springer-Verlag Berlin Heidelberg 2012

cases, disparate interests, documents capturing information such as Service Level Agreements (SLAs) and application descriptors, virtualized resources, to name a few. Thus, providers of cloud service models, e.g. Platform as a Service (PaaS) and Infrastructure as a Service (IaaS), deal with huge amounts of information that needs to be collected, managed and evaluated. For this reason, consistent cloud-enabled data models representing the aforementioned multiple entities and their interrelationships are required.

Furthermore, there is a spreading need for efficiently collecting, gathering and storing monitoring information from the underlying cloud infrastructure. This information can range from application-related metrics, such as Web based services response time or HPC jobs completion deadline, to infrastructure-related metrics such as power consumption or resource capacity and utilization. In any case, all this information should be assessed in order to provide Business Level Parameters (BLPs). Thereafter, these pieces of data can be considered in a synergistic way in decision making processes.

In this paper, an information management system and its corresponding data model that considers all the necessary information flows within a cloud environment are presented. Our analysis was based on a cloud storage service but could be extended for any service offered through clouds, since the proposed model is directly extensible by adding structures to describe any kind of cloud service offering.

The remainder of this work is organized as follows: in section 2 we present the major initiatives in the field of information and cloud management, in section 3 we introduce a generic architectural concept that deals with the information management in cloud platforms in a holistic way. In section 4, we elaborate on each of the data models that we propose while in section 5 the mechanisms for retrieving and storing the information are presented. Finally, in section 6 we summarize and discuss our future steps.

2   Related Work

One of the biggest challenges in cloud computing is that there is no single standard or architectural method. The most common and widely adopted cloud model is based on the distinctive layers of Software as a Service (SaaS), Platform as a Service (PaaS) and Infrastructure as a Service (IaaS). Each cloud stack raises needs for information management and therefore several initiatives and solutions exist. To this end, there has been a lot of effort spent to the management of resources (IaaS). All the main providers (such as EC2[2], Rackspace[3], Azure [4], NewServers [5]) and technologies (such as OpenNebula [6] OCA, OCCI [7], etc.) offer APIs for the administration and control of the cloud infrastructure. In [8] an application centric management framework is presented that tries to integrate high level requirements throughout the application development process in the cloud. On the other hand, in [9] a hierarchical architecture model of cloud services resources management is presented. The architecture model achieves isolation between users and physical resources, however, from actual conditions, the architecture model is quite complex since a number of preparatory works need to be done, resulting in a certain degree of difficulty. In [10], a multi-cloud management platform that locates between cloud users and cloud sites is proposed. It brings valuable contribution for cloud federation and migration of services but it does not propose an information description scheme. Another interesting initiative is described in [11], where a self-organized cloud management model is presented. This concept is highly aligned with our work but it lacks in details regarding the information schemata as well as certain information flows that reside in the PaaS layer. Finally, an additional IaaS management solution is presented in [12], which uses abstractions for managing resources in a hybrid cloud environment for enterprise users.

In total, we have seen in the literature that most of the cloud management solutions are dealing mainly with the resource allocation or a combination of user requirements towards resource management. There is no holistic approach or modeling of the whole cloud platform lifecycle but individual abstractions of parts of it. In [13] we presented the baseline of the Unified Management model design. To this end, with our work in this paper, we are capturing all the information flows and define models that will manage those datasets in any cloud service situation. In addition, we identify the components responsible for each information flow and its relation with the corresponding model.

3   Management Architecture

The topic of management in cloud environments has several angles to be approached. As presented in the related work, there is the aspect of resource management that mainly lies on the IaaS cloud layer and interacts with the infrastructure middleware or hypervisor. On the other hand, the realization of the SaaS stack demands administration and management in terms of applications and high level requirements. The solution that we present in this section proposes a generic management architecture that is placed on the PaaS cloud layer covering the initial management steps of requirement specification and SLA management, to usage modelling and resource management.

The main focus of this paper is not to implement a management framework, but to identify the basic information flows within a cloud environment and propose a unified model that would be able to capture that information consistently. Therefore, in Figure 1 we present a generic architecture of the management layer.

The introduced generic service management architecture describes the following information flows:

- Initiation and SLA management: throughout this process a user is requesting a service and defines the high-level application requirements and QoS parameters described in an SLA.
- Service instantiation and resource allocation: The second conceptual procedure is the creation of the actual instance for the requested service. The internal analysis will map the high level requirements captured in the signed SLA to low level resource specification that will result in the resource allocation.

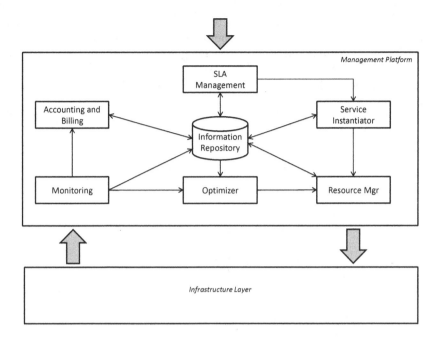

Fig. 1. Generic Management Architecture

– Feedback and optimization: An important feature of every cloud platform is the collection of information from the infrastructure layer and the utilization of that data for Billing & Accounting, SLA violation detection and optimization of the resource allocation with the aim to decrease Total Cost of Ownership (TCO).

4   Unified Management Model

Based on the previous generic architectural approach and the identified information flows, in this section we present several information models that capture the necessary data and create associations between all involved entities. All these models contribute to the overall proposed unified management model. The solution presented is focusing in a storage cloud situation but with minor modifications or additions into some of the defined models could facilitate the information representation of every cloud scenario. We should also note that apart from the basic storage service offered in this cloud, we have incorporated the offering named "storlet" which represents a computation service over a storage entity [14].

4.1   Requirements Model

In order for an application to run effectively over a cloud infrastructure the customer should be able to specify requirements, which will be used by the infrastructure to drive the data access operations of the application. To this end, a Requirements Model capturing the requirements emerging from application attributes modelling and the ones deriving directly from the user needs is necessary. In addition, the model defines structures to describe lower level requirements for the service offerings of the cloud as well as Resource requirements that are used for the resource provisioning.

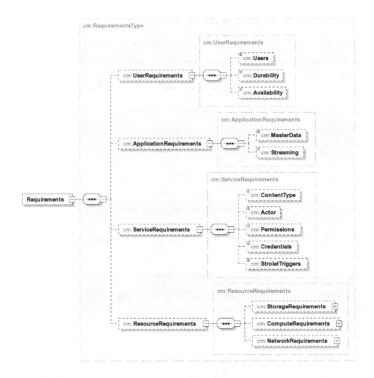

Fig. 2. Requirements Model

As presented in Figure 2 the proposed model covers the following entities:

- User requirements: this entity holds information that will be included in the SLA schema and are provided by the application user. Examples of parameters described are metrics like number of users, durability and availability requirements.
- Application requirements: those requirements are high-level characteristics that will be incorporated in the SLA and will be translated into low level, Storage (or Computational Storage) and Resource requirements. Those parameters will characterize the application to be deployed (Master or Transactional data to be stored, streaming etc.).
- Service requirements: those are the specific requirements that determine a cloud storage service that we have defined in our cloud scenario. This structured and formalized description will include information such as content

type information, data access permissions and other details that may affect the service deployment and operation. The requirements of a Computational Storage service (storlet) are also defined here, including parameters such as CPU speed and memory. This entity will be later incorporated in the Service Model.

- Resource requirements: this entity aims at specifying the resource requirements for the operation of a cloud service (storage as well as storlet). This structure will be utilized during resource provisioning and will keep the desired resources for meeting the constraints described in an SLA.

The transformation of the high level requirements, that are input for the SLA negotiation process, to the low level service and resource requirements is succeeded by the cloud platform throughout the mapping and resource provisioning operation. For example, attributes such as "Master Data" or "Transactional Data" are translated into requirements "low update rates, replicated with eventual consistency" and "high update rates, strong consistency" respectively.

4.2 SLA Model

This model contains the information related to the SLA, that is, the service level agreement between the customer and the service provider. It is separated into two groups:

- the context: which contains non-technical information of the agreement such as participants and dates and
- the terms: which contain the requirements, the conditions and the billing policies.

The requirements that are stated in the SLA utilize the requirement model defined earlier. The customer is able to provide high level requirements (user and application) that are specified for the usage of a specific service offering. Those requirements are being transformed to low level specifications by the platform's services. Moreover, the SLA is enhanced with terms that specify the actual content of the objects to be stored, therefore enabling the support of content-centric access to the cloud. More information can be found in [15].

4.3 Services Model

In this model we capture the information regarding the cloud offerings. The structure keeps general information (ID, name, status details) but also associates the service with a negotiated SLA. In addition, the model incorporates the Service Requirement model and the Resource Model for specifying the respective information. It is also worth noting that computational storage details are also incorporated in this model.

The role of the Service Model is three-fold: (1) to capture all the necessary details of an active service in the cloud, (2) associate each service with a signed

SLA instance and (3) to keep the technical requirements in terms of resources as well as service parameters needed for the instantiation. Through this model the cloud service orchestration is achieved and the component responsible for realizing that information structure is the Service Instantiator in the PaaS layer. Moreover, in case we want to apply our unified management model to another cloud situation, we need just to define an additional Service model according to the requirements of the new service offering.

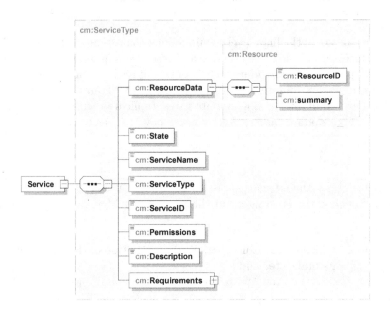

Fig. 3. Services Model

4.4   Resource Model

In every cloud environment the management of the resources is of major importance. Thus, our management model could not be missing this information entity. The model that we have defined has a hierarchical structure in order to facilitate cloud federation and in general a distributed cloud infrastructure management. Therefore, we propose three entities:

- Node: this entity describes the specification of a single node of the resources of a provider. Apart from the static information for each node, we associate each node with the cloud services deployed on this very resource ("service ID list").
- Cluster: the cluster resource model is the parent element of the previous, node entity. It defines characteristics of the whole cluster as well as lists the respective nodes.

– Data Center: hierarchically this structure is the parent element of the cluster entity. Each data center could include one or more clusters. This relationship is defined by the "Clusters" field of the structure. Apart from that, the Data Center model will also specify information such as location, capacity, energy consumption etc.

The existence of a resource model in the PaaS layer of a cloud environment serves the need of management in terms of resource allocation, services deployment and execution and finally optimization. The feedback collected from the Monitoring and processed by the Analyzer will be ingested in the Resource Manager which optimizes the cloud Service Situation (this could be a deployment of a storage service, migration of an active service offering, enabling an elasticity rule etc.) based on the resource model at the given time.

4.5   Usage Model

Usage characteristics (e.g. geographical access distribution or read / write access frequency) encode the knowledge on the typical application behavior. Usage models will be automatically harvested. They capture application access patterns with regard to storage. These characteristics are of major importance since they may be used afterwards for optimizing the mapping of cloud storage resources to application requirements. For example data and storlet placement may be optimized for both the application performance and low operational costs of cloud providers.

In addition to automatic harvesting of usage characteristics, applications may inject into the cloud storage infrastructure a priori knowledge on the application behavior with regard to storage. Self knowledge may be used to further optimize mapping of application requirements to cloud storage resources. Therefore, usage models will also include representations and descriptions to inject application self-knowledge. With regard to multi-tenant applications, the usage characteristics and the information injected by the application as self-knowledge may be encoded in a tenant template that will be used in the subsequent provisioning of data services for new tenants. This enables an optimized management of the new tenant's data and storlets right from the beginning. Figure 4 is an example representation of an application's behavioral characteristics (Usage Model) in the level of cluster that is deployed, cloud that the cluster is hosted and tenant that is authorized to consume that application.

5   Retrieving and Storing Information

The aforementioned models need to populated with real information in order to be used by the various consumers. To this end, within the context of the VISION cloud project, a novel monitoring and aggregation mechanism is being developed that is capable of retrieving the needed information.

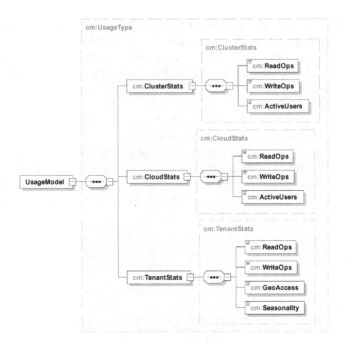

Fig. 4. Usage Model

5.1   Monitoring Architecture

A monitoring instance that runs on every node of the cloud is responsible for collecting local monitoring information and events. Consequently this information is aggregated and propagated to the interested recipients. from the node it resides before processing and storing it, in order for all the information to be available to the decision making modules of the platform. The communication is achieved through the use of 0MQ [16].

Hardware metrics are collected through probes that are configured to pass the relevant information to the local representative of the monitoring subsystem. The modularity of the implementation also allows for other metering systems to be deployed and to be used as sources of information, as long as the specified event format is followed. Services residing on the same host can also utilize the interfaces the monitoring system exposes to propagate events to it using the same format.

5.2   Storing of Information

The information collected need to be stored efficiently and be available to all management modules that require an up to date view of the system. Due to the distributed nature of the cloud, as well as its size, which contains multiple data-centers and clusters, geographically distributed, a NoSQL distributed database is used. Due to the CAP theorem [17] we have chosen to provide availability and eventual consistency. The aforementioned models are transformed into the appropriate structures and the monitoring mechanism is responsible for populating these during run-time. Any module needing to use the information stored is able to query the database and retrieve the needed information.

6   Conclusions and Future Steps

Information management of resources and services in cloud is a challenging task mainly due to the lack of standards and the flexibility of the infrastructure. In this paper we presented a unified management model designed for a storage cloud situation, extendable though for any kind of cloud service offerings. By analyzing the information flows of the cloud service framework we captured the requirements for the management and therefore we defined the core models (requirements, SLAs, services, resources and usage model). In addition, we identified the responsible components for the realization of the models within the service framework of the cloud architecture. The efficient management of the cloud platform is based on the consistency of the models and the ability to associate information of one model to another. In that context, the whole status of the cloud platform can be captured effectively as a single unified model and not separate information structures. That capability allows us to store "snapshots" of the system and in order to migrate it or re-enable it in the future. The future step regarding this work is the investigation of ontologies specifications and the possibility of transforming this unified model into a cloud ontology which could form the management core of a cloud environment. We are also working on validating the model against several cloud scenarios such us cloud federation and hybrid cloud. Finally, we enforce the work on this topic by participating in the Common Cloud Ontologies Working Group [18] where we promote and discuss our design with the research community.

Acknowledgements. This work has been supported by the VISION Cloud project [19] and has been partly funded by the European Commission's ICT activity of the 7th Framework Program under contract number 257019. This work expresses the opinions of the authors and not necessarily those of the European Commission. The European Commission is not liable for any use that may be made of the information contained in this work.

References

1. Buyya, R.: Market-oriented cloud computing: Vision, hype, and reality of delivering computing as the 5th utility. In: 9th IEEE/ACM International Symposium on Cluster Computing and the Grid, CCGRID 2009 (May 2009)
2. Garfinkel, S.L.: An evaluation of amazons grid computing services: Ec2, s3 and sqs. Technical report, Center for (2007)
3. Rackspace Cloud (2009), http://www.rackspacecloud.com

4. Microsoft Azure (2010), http://www.microsoft.com/windowsazure
5. NewServers Inc. (2008), http://www.newservers.com
6. Milojic, D., Llorente, I.M., Montero, R.S.: Opennebula: A cloud management tool. IEEE Internet Computing 15(2), 11–14 (2011)
7. OCCI Working Group (2009), http://occi-wg.org
8. Harmer, T., Wright, P., Cunningham, C., Hawkins, J., Perrott, R.: An application-centric model for cloud management. In: 2010 6th World Congress on Services (SERVICES-1), pp. 439–446 (July 2010)
9. Sun, Y., Xiao, Z., Bao, D., Zhao, J.: An architecture model of management and monitoring on cloud services resources. In: 2010 3rd International Conference on Advanced Computer Theory and Engineering (ICACTE), vol. 3, V3-207–V3-211 (August 2010)
10. Liu, T., Katsuno, Y., Sun, K., Li, Y., Kushida, T., Chen, Y., Itakura, M.: Multi cloud management for unified cloud services across cloud sites. In: 2011 IEEE International Conference on Cloud Computing and Intelligence Systems (CCIS), pp. 164–169 (September 2011)
11. Liu, Z., Tong, W., Gong, Z., Liu, J., Hu, Y., Guo, S.: Cloud computing model without resource management center. In: International Conference on Cyber-Enabled Distributed Computing and Knowledge Discovery, pp. 442–446 (2011)
12. Yan, S., Lee, B.S., Zhao, G., Ma, D., Mohamed, P.: Infrastructure management of hybrid cloud for enterprise users. In: 2011 5th International DMTF Academic Alliance Workshop on Systems and Virtualization Management (SVM), pp. 1–6 (October 2011)
13. Voulodimos, A., Gogouvitis, S., Mavrogeorgi, N., Talyansky, R., Kyriazis, D., Koutsoutos, S., Alexandrou, V., Kolodner, E., Brand, P., Varvarigou, T.: A unified management model for data intensive storage clouds. In: 2011 First International Symposium on Network Cloud Computing and Applications (NCCA), pp. 69–72 (November 2011)
14. Kolodner, E., Tal, S., Kyriazis, D., Naor, D., Allalouf, M., Bonelli, L., Brand, P., Eckert, A., Elmroth, E., Gogouvitis, S., Harnik, D., Hernandez, F., Jaeger, M., Lakew, E., Lopez, J., Lorenz, M., Messina, A., Shulman-Peleg, A., Talyansky, R., Voulodimos, A., Wolfsthal, Y.: A cloud environment for data-intensive storage services. In: 2011 IEEE Third International Conference on Cloud Computing Technology and Science (CloudCom), November 29-December 1, pp. 357–366 (2011)
15. Mavrogeorgi, N., Gogouvitis, S., Voulodimos, A., Katsaros, G., Koutsoutos, S., Kiriazis, D., Varvarigou, T., Kolodner, E.K.: Content based slas in cloud computing environments. In: 2012 IEEE Fifth International Conference on Cloud Computing, pp. 977–978 (2012)
16. Zeromq, http://www.zeromq.org/
17. Brewer, E.A.: Towards robust distributed systems (abstract). In: Proceedings of the Nineteenth Annual ACM Symposium on Principles of Distributed Computing, PODC 2000, p. 7. ACM, New York (2000)
18. Common Cloud Ontologies WG,
http://www.holaportal.eu/content/abdo-ymo-neo-ut-os-facilisis-abbas
19. VISION Cloud, http://www.visioncloud.eu/

On Local Separation of Processing and Storage in Infrastructure-as-a-Service

Jörn Künsemöller[1] and Holger Karl[2]

[1] University of Paderborn, Graduate Program Automatisms,
Warburger Str. 100, 33098 Paderborn, Germany
[2] University of Paderborn, Computer Networks Group, EIM-I,
Warburger Str. 100, 33098 Paderborn, Germany

Abstract. When processing and storage are obtained as internet services, the actual location of the providing facility is undetermined. Factors like a robust and cheap power supply, cooling-relevant climate conditions as well as legal and risk-related considerations are important for selecting a facility's site. As storage and processing facilities feature different economies of scale and location, their local separation is an alternative to combining them in one location. This paper contributes a game-theoretic model to investigate the market success of separate processing and storage facilities compared to a combined approach. It can be shown that stable market constellations with separate service specific facilities are possible.

Keywords: Cloud Computing, Markets, Game Theory.

1 Introduction

With cloud computing, a huge variety of IT applications become available as on-demand services that are accessible over the network. All services are based on processing and storage. These can in turn be obtained in form of a service. These hardware-bound services are referred to as *Infrastructure-as-a-Service (IaaS)*. In addition to an abstraction of the actual hardware that is running underneath, transparency of IaaS also means an undetermined location of this hardware. IaaS providers are free to place data centers at any place with network access.

Clustering the provision of services is interesting for providers due to economies of scale. Local conditions like cheap power or a cool climate can lower operating costs even further. In practice, these possibilities are limited by technical restrictions, risk awareness and law.

Restrictions and savings potential are not necessarily the same for all service types. This paper explores the possibility of separate processing and storage centers and their ability to compete with centers that combine those resources in one location. It takes into account that storage and processing, though different service types, affect each other: Both might handle the same data. Market dynamics in our model are not determined by different service qualities as in related work (Section 2) but by scale and location of provider facilities. This work contributes a new perspective on the infrastructure cloud's future market and

K. Vanmechelen, J. Altmann, and O.F. Rana (Eds.): GECON 2012, LNCS 7714, pp. 125–138, 2012.

geographical development. The question is whether and under what conditions several facility types can coexist in a stable market situation.

Considerations for storage and data center placement regarding relative as well as geographical location are discussed in Section 3. A game-theoretic market model that combines these factors is given and analyzed in Section 4. Section 5 states implications on the actual cloud that can be derived from these theoretic observations. A discussion of further aspects of the model and perspectives for future work are presented in Section 6.

2   Related Work

Cloud provider competition is the subject of some game-theoretic work regarding service quality and pricing. The existence of stable market shares in a duopoly [1] and recently also for n competitors [2] has already been shown. Our work proposes a model for different but dependent service markets (different service types instead of service qualities) and analyses stable states in this set of markets.

Optimal placement of data centers is extensively discussed in [3]. Climate as a factor is specifically addressed in [4], but there seems to be a lack of scientific material that evaluates the effects of climate on data center economics. We discuss possible economies of location with a focus on their different impact on storage and processing facilities and provide an analytical perspective on the question whether separately located facilities can exist in a stable market situation.

When focusing on data center location, data protection directives are important as storage of personal data might be regulated. The European data protection supervisor talks about the role of cloud providers and EU law implications [5]; US law is discussed in [6]. Apart from legal reasons, widely discussed privacy and security concerns (e.g. [7,8]) might make customers more sensitive to storage location. While these factors can motivate a separation of storage and processing, they are hard to assess. Our model explores the existence of stable markets with separate facilities with a focus on economic factors.

Effects of cloud virtualization and remote data access on I/O performance are explored in [9,10]. These practical findings are important when storage and processing are separated in different services and locations as is discussed in this paper.

3   Placing Storage and Processing Infrastructure Sites

3.1   Separating Storage and Processing as Products

Local separation of storage and processing might appear impractical at first glance: Both services are associated with each other as processing generally involves data. While separate storage services make sense for archival purposes, exclusive processing usually cannot be utilized on its own. Combining both resources in one product thus appears to be a more sensible choice. Accordingly, processing usually is provided together with a certain amount of *processing instance storage* in today's infrastructure cloud market. Stand-alone storage is common practice, though.

Whenever data has to be shared between several processing instances, using instance storage is problematic as it is inaccessible from other instances. When instances are booted and shut down to flexibly adapt to actual processing demand, a lot of data management becomes necessary as the temporary instance storage is abandoned together with the instance. A separate shared storage like a distributed file system on block storage instances is far more handy. It can be accessed by independent processing instances which do not have to provide any disk storage. Such a setup is a lot more flexible for clients, who can scale the amounts of utilized storage and processing independently and also can combine services of different providers. It thus makes sense to provide storage and processing resources in separate products. Providers gain the possibility of separate facilities for resource types and can specialize on just storage or processing services.

Separating processing and storage in different products does not imply that corresponding hardware is placed in different locations. As a lot of traffic between the services can be expected, latency and traffic cost rather suggest to keep both resources close together. Providing both resources from the same facility can offer performance similar to that of instance storage and does not cause internet traffic. There are some reasons in favor of a separation of both resources in different locations, though.

3.2 Separating Storage and Processing Locations

Most data center operating costs are caused by administration and energy. Automatization can reduce average administration cost in larger data centers, which usually also have a better power usage effectiveness. Energy cost is not only affected by size, but also a lot by a data center's location. From a worldwide perspective, energy prices vary a lot. Cooler climate in some areas allows free-air cooling, which keeps both energy consumption and investments in cooling equipment down. From an economic point of view, combining economies of scale and locational advantage by operating huge data centers in cool areas with cheap power supply is the only sensible choice.

Loss of data can be considered a lot worse than failure of processing as the latter should only be a temporary effect in most cases. As a consequence, safety from natural disasters might have more weight than e.g. climate during the selection of storage center locations. By building two separate facilities, both can gain from better locality.

Regulation of private data is another issue that can drive storage and processing facilities apart. Imposed by European privacy law, such data has to be kept on European territory or areas of comparable protection [5]. These legal boundaries fragment the internet in several zones that limit the technical freedom of storage deployment. Personal data might be processed in other zones, though, in an anonymized or pseudonymized form.

Data stored in the cloud is beyond clients' control as internal activities of the provider are hidden. Data recovery is doubtful when the service shuts down e.g. due to legal issues or bankruptcy. It also might be deleted in case a client cannot pay for the service. In consequence, clients may refrain from cloud storage

options and keep vital data in their own storage facilities while benefiting from
cheap and flexible cloud processing services at the same time.

4   Game-Theoretic Model

4.1   Setup

A simple evolutionary game-theoretic model (evolutionary game theory was first
introduced in [11]) is hereby proposed to identify stable market shares of separate
facilities for storage and processing services. Required conditions are determined
regarding economic factors. Risk and law is considered in Section 5.2.

The model distinguishes the two service types *storage* and *processing* and the
three different facility strategies p (process), s (store) and c (combine). While
c means operation of storage and processing in one facility, strategies p and s
stand for an exclusive operation of one service type in that facility. The strategy
to exclusively provide the service type of market x (s in the storage market and
p in the processing market) is called *exclusive provisioning strategy* of x in the
following. Any parameter or function that is defined specifically for a service
type is indexed accordingly while facility strategies are specified as a function
parameter.

An IaaS provider has to decide for a facility strategy and passes on data
center operation and investment costs to the service charges. Constant R_x stands
for reference amortization costs of a single unit of service type x. Some cost-
determining factors are influenced by data center size, others by its location. For
the moment, these factors are merged into and addressed as *EoS* (economies
of scale) and *EoL* (economies of location). EoS and EoL express the influence
of size and location on production costs. Both depend on the facility's strategy.
They are zero when neither size nor location have any effect. EoL$(y) = 0.2$
means that costs of a facility with strategy y are reduced by 20% due to local
effects (e.g. cheaper energy) in comparison to R_x. EoS is also increasing with
facility size. Only one facility per strategy is assumed for now and a facility can
only follow one strategy. EoS(y) hence increases over market share of strategy
y. Production costs of service type x in the facility with strategy y are defined
as follows:

$$C_x(y) = R_x \cdot (1 - \mathrm{EoS}(y)) \cdot (1 - \mathrm{EoL}(y)) \tag{1}$$

Different service types x are reckoned as different markets that are modeled as
individual games (dependencies between them are explained in Section 4.2). The
market share of a facility strategy y in the market of service type x is defined as
$S_x(y)$. A market share cannot be negative. For each market applies:

$$\begin{aligned} S_x(y) + S_x(c) &= 1 \\ S_x(z) &= 0 \end{aligned} \tag{2}$$

where y is exclusive provisioning strategy of x and $z \notin \{y, c\}$. For our two markets (storage and processing) it hence holds:

$$S_{\text{processing}}(p) + S_{\text{processing}}(c) = 1$$
$$S_{\text{storage}}(s) + S_{\text{storage}}(c) = 1$$
$$S_{\text{processing}}(s) = 0$$
$$S_{\text{storage}}(p) = 0$$

Demand is modeled accordingly to market shares:

$$D_x(y) + D_x(c) = 1$$
$$D_x(z) = 0 \tag{3}$$

where y is exclusive provisioning strategy of x and $z \notin \{y, c\}$.

Although demand types match the modeled strategy types, the demand of a certain type does not necessarily have to be met by a facility of the same type: Combined processing and storage demand can be met by independent p and s while c might also meet independent processing and storage demand (Figure 1). Accordingly, $D_s(c)$ is the share of storage demand that is used together with $D_p(c)$, regardless of where this demand is actually met. $S_s(c)$ on the other hand gives the storage market share of combined facilities, no matter how it is used.

The whole provisioning is not completely arbitrary, though, as facility competitiveness differs: While separate locations might feature better EoS or EoL, remote data access when combining p and s means additional transfer charges and also affects performance. We define combined demand for each market in order to be able to differentiate between demand that is affected by these disadvantages and demand that is not. Client B in Figure 1 for example can choose to meet its storage and processing demand in different facilities. If the demand is combined demand, though, it can benefit from choosing c over s and p.

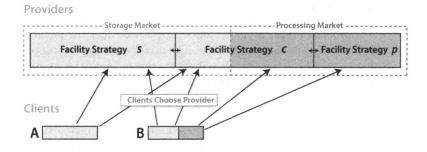

Fig. 1. Clients are free to choose a provider for their storage and processing demand

4.2   Fitness Functions

The fitness of each facility strategy reflects its relative commercial success in this context. As $C_x(y)$ give relative production costs of service x in a facility following strategy y, the fitness function for s and p in the market of service x can simply be defined as:

$$F_x(y) = \frac{1}{C_x(y)}$$

$$F_x(z) = 0$$

(4)

where y is exclusive provisioning strategy of x and $z \notin \{y, c\}$.

Unlike the strategies s and p, the fitness of strategy c is potentially raised by the savings of transfer costs or performance gains in comparison to the other strategies. This only affects demand that benefits from colocated services but is not met by c:

$$F_x(c) = \begin{cases} \frac{1}{C_x(c) - G_x} & \text{when} \quad S_x(c) < D_x(c) \\ \frac{1}{C_x(c)} & \text{else} \end{cases}$$

(5)

where constant G_x (gain) is the amount a user saves by using one unit of service x in a combined center over combining separate services.

The overall gain G is split up between all G_x. Each is between zero and G but cannot be reckoned individually. As this gain only applies when a user obtains all services from c, an equal (or higher) fraction $\frac{S_x(c)}{D_x(c)}$ is required in all other markets for the first case in Equation 5 to apply. If $S_x(c)$ is too low in another market, shares have to be raised in that market as well in order to gain from colocation. Client B in Figure 1 for example has to choose c for both, storage and processing, or it does not gain from colocation. Hence, the individual markets are dependent on each other.

4.3   Analysis Results

Following the approach of replicator dynamics [12], we consider the facility population as the player of an evolutionary game. The mixed strategy this player pursues corresponds to the strategy distribution throughout the population (e.g. facility size). The fitness of each facility strategy depends on the current strategy distribution. The fitness of a mixed strategy is the weighted average of these facility strategy fitnesses.

A mixed strategy m that has a higher fitness than any other mixed strategy n has under m's market shares is an *evolutionarily stable strategy (ESS)*. A mixed strategy is *dynamically stable*, when all similar strategies n feature a lower fitness than m under n's market shares. An ESS is also dynamically stable.

For each market, the game features up to two ESSs and up to one other dynamically stable strategy that is not an ESS:

ESS 1 All demand is met by colocated data centers $(S_x(c) = 1)$.

ESS 2 All demand is met by locally separated facilities $(S_x(y) = 1$, y is exclusive provisioning strategy of x).

DSS Combined demand is met by colocated facilities and independent demand is met by locally separated facilities $(S_x(c) = D_x(c))$.

Which dynamically stable strategies actually exist depends on the magnitudes of scale/location economies and colocation gain. A mixed strategy's fitness improves with a higher share of a strategy with better fitness. It hence is sufficient to compare the fitnesses of pure strategies in order to determine whether there is a mixed strategy that features a higher fitness. When the market share of the strategy with the highest fitness is 1, there is no mixed strategy with a better fitness.

ESS 1 exists when the following condition is true for $S_x(c) = 1$. This is the case when the condition is true for some $S_x(c) > D_x(c)$:

$$F_x(c) > F_x(y)$$
$$\Rightarrow C_x(c) < C_x(y) \tag{6}$$

ESS 2 exists when the following condition is true for some $S_x(c) < D_x(c)$:

$$F_x(c) < F_x(y)$$
$$\Rightarrow \quad G_x < (C_x(c) - C_x(y)) \tag{7}$$

where y is exclusive provisioning strategy of x.

As stated in Section 4.1, the colocation gain cannot be split up on service type specific gains (G_x) in a reasonable way. Hence, a more general condition for ESS 2 has to be formulated:

$$G < \sum_{x=1}^{n} (C_x(c) - C_x(y)) \tag{8}$$

where y is exclusive provisioning strategy of x.

Although dynamical stability is a similar concept, DSS is not an evolutionarily stable strategy. The higher fitness of facility strategy c at a $S_x(c) < D_x(c)$ can cause a mixed strategy with a $S_x(c) > D_x(c)$ to have a higher fitness than DSS as DSS's market shares. This incentive to increase $S_x(c)$ above $D_x(c)$ violates the conditions for an ESS. The new situation with the reduced $F_x(c)$, though, may give incentive to switch back and decrease $S_x(c)$ again. This is further explained in Section 4.4. A dynamically stable strategy m has a neighborhood of strategies that give incentive to switch to m.

DSS exists when the following condition is true for some $S_x(c) > D_x(c)$:

$$F_x(c) < F_x(y)$$
$$\Rightarrow C_x(c) > C_x(y) \tag{9}$$

and the following condition is true for some $S_x(c) < D_x(c)$:

$$F_x(c) > F_x(y)$$
$$\Rightarrow \quad G > \sum_{x=1}^{n} (C_x(c) - C_x(y)) \tag{10}$$

where y is exclusive provisioning strategy of x.

As EoS(c) depends on $S_x(c)$ in other markets, the whole IaaS market is only stable when all individual markets are in a stable state. Next to all markets being in ESS 1, ESS 2 or DSS at the same time, the IaaS market can also be in a state where the storage respectively processing market is in ESS 1 and the other one is in ESS 2. A market can only be in DSS when $S_x(c) \geq D_x(c)$ is true for all markets (Section 4.1). Thus, ESS 1 and DSS might coexist in different markets, while ESS 2 and DSS cannot.

4.4   Development Over Time

A modification of strategy shares does not necessarily require rational choice. In a growing market, a facility with a more successful strategy features faster growth than its competitors and thus also a growing market share. Although the mixed strategy of the population changes, this does not have to be considered an intentional move. Such dynamics can be simulated by consistently changing strategy shares based on their relative fitness. Doing so, different initial market shares can lead to different stable states. The market in Figure 2 for example converges to DSS when a separate storage facility meets a relatively low share of storage demand (left). It converges to ESS 2 when the separate storage facility has a higher initial market share (right).

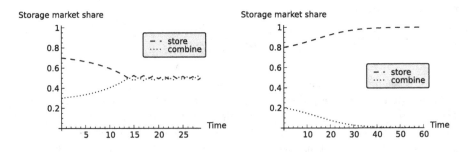

Fig. 2. Different initial market shares result in different stable states

EoS grows with a facility's market share, which again raises the facility's fitness. A strategy with initially better fitness enters a positive feedback loop that ultimately ends in either ESS 1 or 2 in most cases. A higher fitness of strategy s respectively p results in exclusively separated facilities and a higher fitness of strategy c results in all facilities being colocated.

There might be the case, though, that initially better fitness of an exclusive provisioning strategy of type x reduces with growing market share despite this feedback loop. When s respectively p feature lower production costs than c, but users demanding combined services have a gain over separate services that is larger than the fitness difference caused by production costs, the fitness of c is raised and outperforms competition as soon as $S_x(c)$ drops below $D_x(c)$. As the fitness of c shrinks again when its share outgrows combined demand, the market is stuck in DSS or oscillates around it.

As costs depend on EoS and thus on market share, the cost advantage of s/p might exceed the colocation gain at very low market shares of c. The market converges to ESS 2 despite of the existence of DSS in that case.

Mixed strategies where $F_x(y) = F_x(c)$ (y is exclusive provisioning strategy of x) create thresholds between market shares that result in different ESS:

$$C_x(c) = C_x(y) \quad \text{when} \quad S_x(c) \leq D_x(c) \tag{11}$$

$$G = \sum_{x=1}^{n} (C_x(c) - C_x(y)) \tag{12}$$

where y is exclusive provisioning strategy of x. The equations can be solved to either $S_x(y)$ or $S_x(c)$ to calculate the threshold for market x.

If all three dynamically stable states exist for the market, both thresholds exist. Shares resulting in ESS 1 and DSS are separated by the threshold defined by Equation 11, Equation 12 separates shares leading to ESS 2 and DSS. If DSS does not exist, Equation 11 is never true and the second threshold separates shares that result in ESS 1 or 2. As the markets are linked, the thresholds in one market depend on the shares in the other markets.

All possible IaaS market shares can be represented in an 2-dimensional space (n-dimensional for n markets). Each dimension states the market share of the exclusive providing strategy, which leaves the rest of both markets to the colocated strategy. The stated thresholds divide the space in fragments that end up in a specific ESS over time (Figure 3). The threshold by Equation 11 is market-specific while the threshold by Equation 12 is the same for both markets. Figure 3 only shows the thresholds for the storage market; for the processing market, the dashed threshold would be vertical. Threshold market shares are in an equilibrium but not dynamically stable and thus very prone to disturbance, which makes them unlikely to exist long.

The higher the colocation gain is compared to maximum economies of scale and location, the smaller becomes the area of shares resulting in ESS 2. The area regarding ESS 1 grows with shrinking EoL(s) as the colocation strategy needs lower EoS to compensate. When the threshold would exceed $D_s(c)$ (identical with the dotted line marking DSS) there is no DSS.

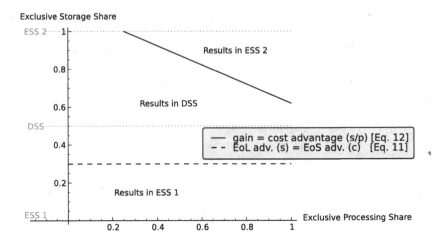

Fig. 3. Mapping of IaaS market shares and resulting stable state in the storage market. The dotted lines indicate the market share of s after the market reaches a specific stable state.

5   Implications on IaaS Clouds

5.1   Possible Economies of Scale and Location

As discussed in earlier work [13], economies of scale of almost 20 % are realistic for a processing facility by scaling up from 1 000 servers to over 50 000. This can be achieved by major reductions of administration effort and better power usage effectiveness. Those savings get close to optimality and only marginal further improvements can be expected. Scale economies of storage seem to be a lot better with large-scale commodity storage solutions being about six times cheaper (per GB) than storage area networks in small facilities [14]. This means possible storage EoS of over 80 %.

Potential economies of location are less complex infrastructure (e.g. cooling, uninterrupted power supply) and cheaper operating costs regarding energy consumption (infrastructure) and price in the first place. In the total cost of ownership example in [13], infrastructure cost is about 7.5 %, electricity cost about 15 % (€0.1 per kWh) of yearly costs of a processing facility. In a place with a free and reliable power supply and a climate that allows passive cooling (no infrastructure and energy costs), location economies of a little over 20 % would be possible. This means that the theoretic maximum of EoL is about the same as EoS. Contrary to the latter, EoLs close to optimality are unrealistic. International industry energy pricing suggests that cutting costs in half is possible, so processing EoL of about 10 % might be realistic for a cool country with cheap energy. Storage EoL are negligible due to the small impact of energy and cooling on storage costs.

5.2   Stable Markets in IaaS

The existence of the potential stable market situations presented in Section 4.3 is discussed with respect to the estimations from Section 5.1 in the following.

As the data center location is important for the costs of processing but not for storage, only facilities following strategy p or c have an incentive to choose an economically interesting location. Due to legal circumstances and clients' risk awareness, s might prefer a location close to the client instead. Strategy c either chooses the location of p with high EoL for processing (scenario 1) or the location of s e.g. to meet legal demands of potential customers (scenario 2). When leaving out any synergetic scale economies, EoS and EoL of strategy c can be defined market independent.

In scenario 1, c features the same EoS and EoL for service x as the exclusive provisioning strategies do at the same market share. At a higher share of c, Equation 6 is true and hence ESS 1 exists. In scenario 2, there are no EoL(c) in the processing market. ESS 1 exists nevertheless, as the possible EoS-difference of 20 % is larger than EoL(p) of 10 %.

An existence of ESS 2 requires the colocation gain to be smaller than all possible savings (Equation 8). These savings can be quite significant at very low shares of c with up to 30 % for processing and 80 % for storage in both scenarios. A client's gain due to better performance of colocated services has two major reasons: Better performance and no traffic charges. Data rates between Amazon S3 and EC2 within the same region are about 10 MB/s [15], whereas moving data from one S3 region to another is reported to be a mere 1 MB/s. Although this is more of an example than a proper evaluation and not all applications need a lot of bandwidth, it shows how massive the colocation gain can be. Latencies can also be expected to be a lot higher over some distance than in a facility's local network. Thus, ESS 2 is only a possible outcome for very small shares of c, but even its existence is quite unlikely.

In contrast, the DSS condition in Equation 10 is very likely met. DSS also requires scale and location economies of c to be lower than those of the exclusive provisioning strategy when all combined demand is met by c (Equation 9). Like in the case of ESS 1, the strategy with the larger share features lower costs in scenario 1, thus DSS can only exist in a market when $D_x(c) < 0.5$. In scenario 2, the worse location economies of c make the existence of DSS a lot more likely for processing: It exists when $D_p(c) < 0.75$ (assuming linear growing scale economies).

If DSS exists, the market reaches it at initial shares of $S_x(c) < 0.5$ (respectively $S_p(c) < 0.75$ in scenario 2). If shares are higher or DSS does not exist, the market reaches ESS 1. At very low shares of c, a potentially existing ESS 2 could also be reached.

5.3   Conclusions

A market where all demand is met by colocated facilities (ESS 1) is in a stable constellation and there are no circumstances to challenge this stability.

Demand of $D_x(c) < 0.5$ might be realistic for storage, where lots of data just sits around, but processing of more than half of the available quantities without data I/O can hardly be expected. When combined facilities consider risk-aware customers or those with legal restrictions in their site selection (scenario 2), the share of processing without much data access that is necessary for DSS to exist is lower but remains unlikely. Hence, the coexistence of storage centers and combined facilities (DSS) is a possibility while the persistence of exclusive processing centers is unrealistic (but could become an option in a very large market, see Section 6).

Separate storage services exist in today's market with object storage like S3, which is reported to store over a trillion objects [16]. It is difficult to obtain the amount of actual storage demand, but assuming an average size of 100 kilobytes per object, this sums up to 100 petabytes. Each of the suspected 450 000 blade servers in use for EC2 [17] would require an average of 240 GB of disk space to generate the same amount of combined storage demand. This means that separate storage demand appears to be high enough in order that corresponding storage facilities are large enough to be competitive in separate locations. It depends on the amount of separate storage which actually takes place in separate facilities today, whether the market converges to a situation where these separate facilities (still) exist.

With respect to the large shares of combined services like Amazon EC2 in the current market, the possibility of a market where processing and storage takes place in completely separate facilities (ESS 2) is a rather academic option. It also requires massive improvements of latencies and bandwidth for data access over the internet for such a stable market situation to exist.

6   Discussion and Outlook

This section discusses further aspects of the presented model for clarification and also gives a scope for future research.

6.1   Discussion of the Model

Preference of Combined Demand. The fitness function of colocated facilities suggests that any demand such a facility provides is preferably combined demand. In theory, it could provide clients with independent storage and processing demands while some combined demand is still met in separate facilities. Limiting the influence of a colocation gain to $D_x(c) > S_x(c)$ underestimates the fitness of strategy c in such a case. But separated facilities feature better EoL and can offer lower charges whenever the colocated strategy does not feature better EoS of the same magnitude. As clients with independent demand do not benefit from a colocation of services, they are expected to generally prefer separated facilities if they can offer lower prices. If the EoS advantage of colocated facilities is higher than the competitor's EoL advantage, this results in higher fitness of c anyways.

Segmentation of Facility Strategies. As described in Section 4, the mixed strategy of the player reflects market shares of the pure facility strategies. Those shares can be formed by either providers exclusively following one pure strategy as modeled previously or by providers following a mixed strategy. For instance, there might be one provider operating both facility types s and p and another provider running type c. This hardly affects the model presented so far. Another option, though, is the existence of several facilities of the same type that provide the share of a strategy together. Such a segmentation of a strategy results in smaller EoS for each facility and less average fitness of this strategy. This affects the constraints that lead to specific stable state and especially reduces the likelihood that higher segmented strategies are successful. The model currently does not include unbalanced scattering of the strategies' market shares. Such scattering would affect the gradient of EoS over market share and thus alter the thresholds in Section 4.4. Possible EoS (Section 5.1) might not be reached when many facilities follow the same strategy as the market is of limited size. This could also affect the existence of the stable states.

Very Large Facilites. Economies of scale appear to reach a maximum at today's facility sizes (Amazon's EC2 facilities appear to exceed 50000 servers in the US and Europe [17]). In an even larger market, this results in an initial strong increase of EoS that more and more flats out over facility size (market share): The larger the market gets, the less important do scale economies become compared to locational gains. This means for the processing market that DSS exists for even higher $D_p(c)$ and is reached at accordingly low shares of p. Assuming the initial market entry barrier of reaching this share can be taken, locally separate processing becomes more likely in the future.

6.2   Outlook

The model assumes that all clients have the same gain of colocation or no gain at all. Although this keeps down the model's complexity for an initial discussion, it might make sense to work with a distribution instead in future work. Generally, assessing the colocation gain turns out to be a difficult experience.

While the proposed market model is applied to IaaS in this paper, it approaches specialized vs. diversified product strategies in general. Its adaptation to similar problems, which also may involve more than two service types, should be possible without much difficulty.

References

1. Dube, P., Jain, R., Touati, C.: An Analysis of Pricing Competition for Queued Services with Multiple Providers. In: ITA Workshop (2008)
2. Pal, R., Hui, P.: Economic Models for Cloud Service Markets. In: Bononi, L., Datta, A.K., Devismes, S., Misra, A. (eds.) ICDCN 2012. LNCS, vol. 7129, pp. 382–396. Springer, Heidelberg (2012)

3. Alger, D.: Choosing an Optimal Location for Your Data Center. In: Build the Best Data Center Facility for Your Business. Cisco Press (2005)
4. Galbraith, K.: Using the Weather to Cool Data Centers, http://green.blogs.nytimes.com/2009/10/05/using-the-weather-to-cool-data-centers/
5. Hustinx, P.: Data Protection and Cloud Computing under EU law. In: Third European Cyber Security Awareness Day BSA, European Parliament (2010)
6. Gellman, R.: Privacy in the Clouds: Risks to Privacy and Confidentiality from Cloud Computing. In: World Privacy Forum (2009)
7. Kaufman, L.M.: Data Security in the World of Cloud Computing. IEEE Security & Privacy 7, 61–64 (2009)
8. Pearson, S.: Taking Account of Privacy when Designing Cloud Computing Services. In: Proceedings of the 2009 ICSE Workshop on Software Engineering Challenges of Cloud Computing, CLOUD 2009, pp. 44–52. IEEE Computer Society, Washington, DC (2009)
9. Shafer, J.: I/O Virtualization Bottlenecks in Cloud Computing Today. In: Proceedings of the 2nd Conference on I/O Virtualization, WIOV 2010, p. 5 (2010)
10. Baun, C.: Untersuchung und Entwicklung von Cloud Computing-Diensten als Grundlage zur Schaffung eines Marktplatzes. Dissertation, Hamburg (2011)
11. Smith, J.M., Price, G.R.: The Logic of Animal Conflict. Nature 246(5427), 15–18 (1973)
12. Taylor, P.D., Jonker, L.B.: Evolutionary Stable Strategies and Game Dynamics. Mathematical Biosciences 40, 145–156 (1978)
13. Künsemöller, J., Karl, H.: A Game-Theoretical Approach to the Benefits of Cloud Computing. In: Vanmechelen, K., Altmann, J., Rana, O.F. (eds.) GECON 2011. LNCS, vol. 7150, pp. 148–160. Springer, Heidelberg (2012)
14. Hamilton, J.: Cloud Computing Economies of Scale, MIX 2010 talk (2010), viewable at http://channel9.msdn.com/events/MIX/MIX10/EX01/
15. HostedFTP.com: Amazon S3 and EC2 Performance Report How fast is S3?, http://hostedftp.wordpress.com/2009/03/02/
16. Amazon Web Services Blog: Amazon S3 - The First Trillion Objects, http://aws.typepad.com/aws/2012/06/amazon-s3-the-first-trillion-objects.html
17. Liu, H.: Amazon Data Center Size, http://huanliu.wordpress.com/2012/03/13/amazon-data-center-size/

Value Creation in IT Service Platforms through Two-Sided Network Effects

Netsanet Haile and Jörn Altmann

Technology Management, Economics, and Policy Program (TEMEP)
College of Engineering, Seoul National University
151-744 Seoul, South-Korea
netsanet@temep.snu.ac.kr, jorn.altmann@acm.org

Abstract. IT service businesses can achieve economies of scale and scope faster than in traditional product businesses. In particular, as IT service platforms will become the founding infrastructure of our economies, the analysis and understanding of the value that a service platform can generate is of great importance. IT service platforms provide all involved market participants with different values. For this paper, we consider application service users, service developers and service platform providers as market participants and analyze the interrelationship between the value creations of these market participants. The basis for the description of the values and their interrelationship is the identification of parameters. Based on these parameters, a simulation model has been developed. It helps inferring the relative impact of these parameters on the evolution of the IT service platform stakeholder values. The results imply that there is a two-sided network effect. All stakeholders of a service platform mainly benefit from a growing installed base of application users. The benefit of a large service variety, however, mainly benefits the service platform provider. Therefore, we can state that a large fraction of the value from two-sided network effects goes to the platform provider.

Keywords: IT service platform, value creation, system dynamics, two-sided network effect, business modeling, IT business, SaaS, cloud computing.

1 Introduction

IT service platforms provide an enabling technology for the development and provision of application services in service-oriented environments. Examples of those service platforms are Software-as-a-Service (SaaS) platforms, Platform-as-a-Service (PaaS), and Infrastructure-as-a-Service (IaaS) platforms. As economies of scale and scope can be achieved very quickly with IT service platforms, some IT service platforms will become the founding infrastructure of our economies. Therefore, an understanding of their value creation and value distribution becomes important. In this context, one of the major challenges that business managers face is to determine the value of services and to measure the value they obtain from services they offer [1], [25].

K. Vanmechelen, J. Altmann, and O.F. Rana (Eds.): GECON 2012, LNCS 7714, pp. 139–153, 2012.
© Springer-Verlag Berlin Heidelberg 2012

In determining the economic values of networked services, such as IT platform services, the role of network effects is important. Direct network effects, a value generated from the number of existing users of a service, and indirect network effect, a value built by the availability and interoperability of complimentary products, are well-developed concepts in network economics. The double impact of both effects is explained through two-sided network effects. Two-sided network effects have been considered a source of value in traditional software markets. Users and providers experience value growth due to such effects. It has been argued that two-sided network effects give rise to demand-side economies-of-scale and that consumers form expectations regarding the size of competing networks. Its impact on competition, market equilibrium, and compatibility decisions among firms and adoption pace of new technologies have been widely recognized in literature [2], [3], [4], [5], [6], [7], [8], [9], [10]. A recent study also addressed the presence of direct and indirect utilities in the context of services, in particular the role of mobile app stores in application delivery environments [11]. Another study discusses the openness of services [25].

In the traditional software industry, Microsoft Windows is a very good example of the significance of two-sided network effects. Microsoft built a platform business model that utilized indirect network effects. The more windows applications are available, the more reasons for a user to choose Windows, the more reasons for developers to build applications for windows. However, for IT service platforms, interconnecting users and service integrations are more important factors than in traditional software markets. Service platforms can reach a large number of users and developers much faster. An example of that is the raise of the social network platform Facebook. A few studies have also been performed in this area [12], [13], [14], [15]. However, a comprehensive system model showing the stakeholders as well as the interdependence of their utilities has not been developed so far.

Developments in service technologies, specifically the change in the mode of delivery and the ways of use, reinforce a new way of thinking about business values [12]. For example, IT service platforms can target different user groups by designing specific pricing models, fitting the usage scenarios preferred by those different user groups.

In terms of capabilities for value creation, the characteristics of service markets are also different to those of traditional IT markets. In today's service business environments, service providers can no longer rely on simple comparisons of features, functions, and prices of their products with those of competitors, to determine their competitive advantage in the market. As values created through service integration, user content, and user networks have a significant impact, those need to be considered for the value creation analysis as well.

The main distinguishing feature of service platforms from traditional two-sided software markets is, in addition to delivering end user services, the provisioning of an environment for service developers to build functionalities and deliver them as services to end-users.

Summarizing, these unique characteristics result in new ways of value creations. Consequently, evaluation approaches need to consider these new value creations, in order to identify the competitive advantages of providers.

Theoretical value creation frameworks for e-businesses and, in particular, for service platforms have been proposed in recent literature [13], [14], [15], [16], [17], [26],

[27]. A study of value creations in the general context of e-business has been conducted by Amit and Zott [13], which identified dimensions of value creations and evaluations of different business models of service platforms. User-created values have been discussed by Lee et al. [14], and a research on the value transformation in the mobile service ecosystems by Smedlund [15]. However, an evaluation of the effect of the platform value for its stakeholders, which is important for any business decision, has not been achieved with these frameworks. Hence, more sophisticated definitions of value factors and their measurable parameters are required.

Conclusively, we can state that the research works mentioned above do not fully explain the value system of IT service platforms in terms of all relevant parameters, the stakeholders involved, and the value exchange between the stakeholders. This paper aims at addressing this gap by introducing a new value creation framework for IT service platforms, which can provide a useful tool to service providers and policy makers. As the framework helps explaining the value of service offerings to application service users, service developers, and platform providers, it can also be used as decision support on investments in service offerings, investments in platforms, design of business models, service bundling policies, and market structure evolutions.

In the course of achieving its objective, this paper identifies four parameters, explaining the net value of a service to a stakeholder of an IT service platform. The four service parameters, which are quality of service (QoS), service variety, installed base (i.e., number of users), and cost, are integrated into additive utility functions for application users, service developers, and platform providers. The utility functions enable the evaluation of the value creations of a service platform. For the analysis of the relative changes of values of platform stakeholders, a simulation technique (system dynamics) was used. The analysis result implies that the value obtained by service developer is quite low in comparison to platform provider. In a mature market, the major beneficiary is the platform provider, while the application users and the service developers benefit only little. This indicates a risk that developers withdraw from the platform market, causing a market failure.

The outline of the remainder of this paper is as follows: Section 2 presents the description of the proposed model, followed by the simulation settings and results in Section 3. Section 4 concludes the paper with a brief discussion and summary.

2   Proposed Value Creation Model for IT Platforms

Our value creation model comprises three parts: stakeholder specification, value parameters, their effect on stakeholders, and the quantification of the values generated.

2.1   Stakeholders

In the IT service platform ecosystem, the major stakeholders, who contribute to the value creation, are application users, service developers, and platform service providers [28]. Even if there are other stakeholders such as brokers, service integrators, and content creators, their main role ultimately falls under one of the above-mentioned three stakeholders, who we have selected to study in this paper.

A service provider takes on the role of producing and publishing services, which are ready to be executed. In the context of this paper, both service developers and platform service providers qualify as service providers, since they own their respective services and are responsible for implementing and maintaining them. Nevertheless, they will be treated as two different stakeholders as they are at different positions in the IT platform ecosystem.

A platform provider offers an environment, in which different types of third-party services (e.g., social network services, communication services, search engine services, entertainment services, market place services, computing services, and storage services) can be executed. A platform provider also plays a role of an intermediary between a service developer and service consumers, it enables service discovery by potential customers and potential integration with other services.

Service developers, who are software vendors or individual programmers, use development kits provided by the platform service providers to create applications (e.g., social network services, communication services, search engine services, entertainment services, market place services, computing services, storage services), to be deployed on platform services.

Application service users are users of services offered by application service developers and platform service providers. Application service users aim at accomplishing a certain task through the use of an application, which match their requirements.

The value exchange between these stakeholders can be direct (i.e., direct payments for services offered and used) or indirect (i.e., revenue through advertisement), resulting in net utility for users, profit/loss for the IT platform provider, and profit/loss for service developers. The relationships among these stakeholders, which are based on a literature study, are depicted in Figure 1.

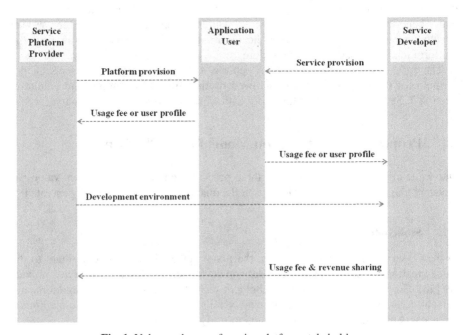

Fig. 1. Value exchange of service platform stakeholders

The value exchanged between a platform service provider and service developers comprises the provisioning of deployment and service provisioning environments in exchange for cash fees or a share of the developers' revenue obtained from their respective users. Service developers provide their services to application users for a subscription fee or free of charge but with advertisements. To both platform providers and service developers, the application service users are the major source of revenue; the revenue here comes from subscription and usage based charges or from using customer profiles for selling advertisement services.

2.2   Value Parameters and Their Effect on Stakeholders

Service value parameters determine the value obtained by participants. They indicate the source of the values that have been generated from using the service platform. Understanding the impact of these parameters is important for platform providers for formulating their business policies. Existing theoretical frameworks have compared single factors and identified their interdependence [13], [14].

Based on those theoretical frameworks and concepts, this paper presents a consolidated set of measurable parameters. In detail, for building the value creation model proposed in this paper, we consider quality of service (QoS), service variety, installed base, and cost. They are used for quantifying stakeholder values and to construct the value creation model proposed in this paper (Figure 2).

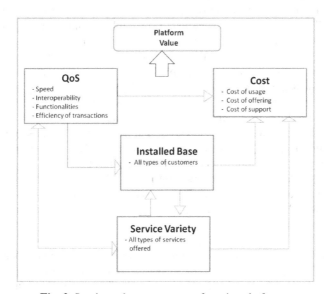

Fig. 2. Service value parameters of service platforms

As shown in Figure 2, QoS impacts the number of customers and the number of services that a service platform can attract [3], [19]. QoS is also a major factor of the cost of service development and provision for service developers and platform providers. The installed base impacts the number of service varieties to be provided through attracting more developers [23]. However, the installed base also causes cost of supporting customers. The service variety also changes the cost of offering, the cost of support, and the QoS offered, ultimately influencing the number of customers attracted.

Besides describing the value parameters in detail in the following subsections, we also explain how they impact each of the three stakeholders (Figure 3).

Quality of Service. QoS measures functional capabilities of services. It indicates whether the functionality, interoperability, and performance of a service are up to the requirements of the users and meet the intended service level objectives. With respect to software, it is to be noted that QoS also considers the quality of data that is returned by an application [18]. Quality of service is an important factor in driving the value of products. There are cases where late entrants managed to take the market leadership from incumbents by offering a better QoS [3, 19]. Similarly, the value obtained by IT service platform customers is also determined by the QoS they are offered (Figure 3). The QoS offered by a platform provider can be constant or dynamic. If platform providers invest in new functionalities to meet user requirements, they improve the quality of the development environment for service developers and service offering environment for end users.

Installed Base. Installed base represents the number of active users of a platform. The installed base affects the value of all stakeholders as a source of revenue (Figure 3). The effect of the installed base on the stakeholders' values is explained through network effects. The network effect benefits all stakeholders and attracts even more customers [10], [13], [20], [21]. Platforms with a larger number of users can leverage their user network to gain competitive advantage. Considering the time and effort a user needs to adapt to services on a new platform (e.g., social networking platforms), many users are less likely to switch platforms [13].

Specifically, network effect has been identified as an IT platform business strategy [14], [22]. For platform providers, the idea behind network effects is that customers pay more to get access to a bigger network and, as the installed base grows, so will the platform providers' revenues. Therefore, platforms with a critical mass have the advantage to stay in lead among equally innovative platforms.

The network effects that come into play in a platform environment are: The increase in the number of users is reinforced by the installed base as well as the increase in service variety due to the increase in the number of users, which, in turn, makes more users join the platform.

Service Variety. Service variety represents the availability of complementary services that users of the platform can access. Service variety is one of the value sources in platforms. If platform providers offer services, which are complimentary to services offered by the same platform, they generate a network effect, increasing the value of the platform to their potential customers as the platform's customer size increases. Availability of complementary services makes the offerings of a platform provider more valuable to their customers [13], [23]. Therefore, in order to create more value, cooperation between complementary service providers is a likely successful strategy in the service industry [24]. In sum, the idea of increasing variety of services in the context of platform services as a value driver is well supported. Therefore, we consider service variety as a value parameter in our model. Service variety impacts the platform provider's revenue and the application users' benefit positively (Figure 3).

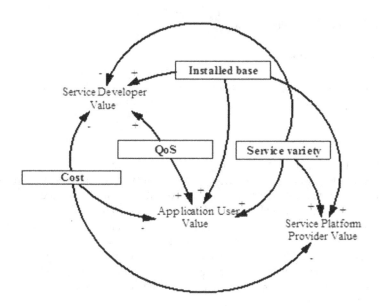

Fig. 3. Effect of service value parameters on value obtained by stakeholders

Cost. Cost is used in this model to represent all types of costs incurred by all stakeholders. Cost incurred by stakeholders negatively affects their value (Figure 3).

The usage cost of application users in the context of platform services includes the subscription and periodical fees paid by users to both of the providers.

The platform provider and service developers face costs for offering services (e.g., service maintenance) and supporting their customers in case of problems with services.

Reducing the cost of offering services (e.g., through improved efficiency) for service providers results in an increase of their net value [13]. However, in the overall platform ecosystem; the increase in the cost of one stakeholder might result in the increase in value of another. For example, if the price of an application is set high, the users' value will be affected negatively, while the service provider's revenue gain increases up to a certain threshold.

2.3   Stakeholder Value Representations

Based on the variables identified and their relationships, we construct functions quantifying the value that the three stakeholders obtain from an IT service platform.

The decision problem studied here involves one IT service platform, a fixed number of potential users and developers. The application users and service developers continuously have to decide on the adoption of the IT service platform based on the four value-determining parameters mentioned in the previous section. At each time period, new users may join the platform and subscribe to services offered. Similarly, new developers may join the platform, buy development kits, develop services, and sell their applications to the installed base of users. The value functions, representing the utility of the application user, the platform provider, the service developer, use the value determining parameters as input.

Application User Value. Based on the value creation model, we define an application user's net utility U_{ja}. It is determined by the functional benefits that they obtain from using services offered by the platform. The net utility is defined as follows:

$$U_{ja}(t) \quad = \quad u_{1ja}(Q_j(t)) \quad + \quad u_{2ja}(S_j(t)) \quad + \quad u_{3ja}(N_j(t)) \quad - \quad C_{ja} \tag{1}$$

where $U_{ja}(t)$ is the total utility that an application user a gets from adopting the service platform j at a given time t. It is the sum of all positive benefits minus the respective cost. $u_{1ja}(Q_j(t))$ represents the user's utility from the quality of service Q_j offered at time t, which is the functional benefit of the service. $u_{2ja}(S_j(t))$ denotes the user's utility from the number of services S_j that are available to the users of the service platform at time t. It determines the user's value from adopting a service platform of a certain level of service availability. $u_{3ja}(N_j(t))$ is the utility of the user generated from the level of installed base of users on the service platform j. It represents the additional benefits obtained from the number of users of the platform service. Each utility is normalized between [0,1], indicating the level. The value 1 means that the maximum level has been reached, while a value of 0 represents the lowest level. C_{ja} specifies the application usage cost a user faces for using one or more services. The net utility that a customer gets from adopting the platform service is obtained by deducting this total cost from the benefits.

Service Developer Value. Considering the overall structure of the value creation model, the value of a service developer U_{js} can be detailed as follows:

$$U_{js}(t) \quad = \quad u_{js}(Q_j(t)) \quad + \quad RS_{js} * C_{ja} * N_j(t) / S_j(t) \quad - \quad C_{js} \tag{2}$$

where $U_{js}(t)$ is the total value that a service developer s gets from adopting the service platform j at a given time t. A service developer's revenue comes from the average fee a user pays for a service C_{ja} multiplied with the fraction of the number of users $N_j(t)$, who are using service s. In this model, the fraction of the number of users of the platform is calculated as the total number of users $N_j(t)$ divided by the number of services $S_j(t)$. It represents the average number of users per service. The total revenue obtained is reduced by the revenue share RS_{js} that the platform provider gets. The cost types are either fixed subscription fees or variable usage costs that have to be paid to the platform service provider.

Service Platform Provider Value. In our value creation model, the value of the service platform provider U_{jp} is defined as:

$$U_{jp}(t) = C_{js}*S_j(t) + (1 - RS_{js})*C_{ja}*Nj(t) - C_{jpa}(Nj(t)) - C_{jps}(S_j(t)) \tag{3}$$

where $U_{jp}(t)$ is the value (profit) of a platform provider p from offering service platform j at a given time t. The profit is calculated as the difference between the revenue that the platform generates from all service developers, $C_{js} * S_j(t)$, and all application users (i.e., the revenue that is shared with the service developer, (equation 2)) and the cost of supporting users C_{jpa} and maintaining services C_{jps}. Service platforms provide maintenance, data storage, and security to the application services they host. It constitutes their cost for services and users, which increases as the number of services $(S_j(t))$ and users $(N_j(t))$ increases.

3   Simulation

3.1   Value Creation Dynamics

The simulation model used here (Figure 4) helps evaluating the dynamics of the value creation. The values, which are created by the service platform for the three stakeholders in a certain time period, are based on equations 1, 2, and 3.

As illustrated in Figure 4, the service variety increases by a certain number of new services in every time period. A service developer, who subscribes to the service platform, requires a development environment to offer an application service. The number of the new services or service developers is denoted by $s_j(t)$. The installed base increases by a certain number of new adopters in every time period. This number of new adopters is represented by $n_j(t)$. Note, we do not consider an outflow of customers here. Consequently, the installed base $N_j(t)$ and the number of services $S_j(t)$ are cumulative values increased though new adoptions over time.

Interactions between the stakeholders occur through the value-determining parameters (Figure 4). The QoS offered to the service developers and application users is positively affected by the utility of the platform provider. The higher the platform provider's utility, the more the incentive of the platform provider to improve its services to meet the requirements and expectations of its customers. This, in turn, attracts more customers, increasing the platform's value. The number of service developers is positively impacted by the utility of existing service developers, as a high utility motivates more developers to join. The number of application users increases as more services are offered and QoS is improved. This increase in the number of users motivates more users to join the platform and positively impacts the value of the platform provider and the service developers.

In an effort to improve the actual value created, platform providers can make business decisions to improve the QoS offered and to reduce the cost incurred through deploying a better infrastructure. Service developers make choices about joining a platform or develop more services to increase the number of services offered. They also make similar decisions as the platform service providers with respect to cost and QoS. Application users simply decide on adopting a platform and using a certain number of services.

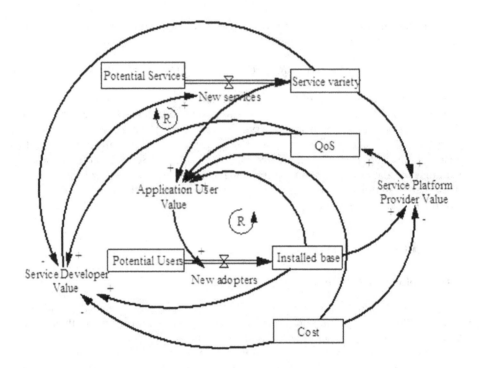

Fig. 4. A model of stakeholder value dynamics with feedback loops

3.2   Settings and Assumptions

For the implementation of the simulation, we use Vensim system dynamics software. The simulation duration was set to 47 months to see the dynamics over a longer period of time and to model the development of Apple iTunes since its launch in July 2008 [29].

The service scenario used here to observe the behavior of the value of stakeholders is based on real situations and practices observed in the market. The scenario considers one provider, 650000 service developers and 400 million application service users. The cost of offering services C_{js}, which incurred by service developers and is mainly due to development and hosting fees to service platform providers, varies based on the size of the application, the number of users supported, storage capacity, and the amount of back-end processing required. Monthly cost of offering services C_{js} is set to $2, monthly cost of use for application users C_{ja} is set to be $0.05, the cost of support for users C_{jap} as $0.01 per application user and the cost of support for services C_{jsp} to be $0.1 per service [29], [30], [31], [32].

The value of $Q_j(t)$ is considered to be an indicator of the level of QoS offered and represented by a range [0,1]. The value 1 represents the highest value. In our scenario, $Q_j(t)$ was modeled to dynamically show a slight increase as the utility of the platform provider increases. It indicates that the growth of the platform results also in additional functionality and performance, benefiting the customers. Revenue share of the platform provider $(1 - RS_{js})$ is set to be 30% and the revenue share of service developers RS_{js} is consequently 70% of the total revenue obtained from application users. Those are settings that are practiced by major service platforms (e.g., Apple iTunes and Google Apps Marketplace [29], [30], [32]).

Regarding the behavior of stakeholders and the market environment, it is assumed that an application user subscribes to one or more services at a time and a service developer supplies one service. Even in cases where the application users and service developers are using free services, they generate a certain value for the providers; therefore in order to simplify the model, all customers are considered paying for the services they consume. This means that they either pay a monthly service fee or with advertisement placement on their services.

With respect to the adoption of users, it is assumed that, if the value of application users $U_{ja}(t)$ remains greater than 0, a certain number of new users $n_j(t)$ decides to join the installed base $N_j(t)$ until the point of market saturation. In this model, market saturation occurs when $N_j(t)=1$. Applying the same principles to service variety $S_j(t)$ and assuming that the value of the service developers $U_{js}(t)$ is positive, new services $s_j(t)$ will also join the platform. In our experiment, the number of new users $n_j(t)$ and the number of new services $s_j(t)$ can also be variable in each time period. In this case, the adoption rate of users per month increases (decreases) as the value of the existing users increases (decreases). To calculate the actual number of new users, the adoption rate is multiplied by the number of potential users (i.e., users that have not adopted the platform yet). In the same way, the actual number of new services can be calculated. As the next sections shows, this adoption scheme is simulated for cases of high and low two-sided network effects. The constant adoption scheme represents low variations over time (i.e., a low network effect of installed base and services on adoption). The dynamic rate of adoption increases along with the installed base and services and, therefore, represents a high network effect.

3.3   Results

In case of a high two-sided network effect (Figure 5), there is a large increase in the stakeholder values. The installed base grows faster due to faster changes in all of the three values $U_{ja}(t), U_{js}(t),$ and $U_{jp}(t)$. In case of low two-sided network effects (Figure 6), the value of stakeholders are mainly generated from the level of QoS ($Q_j(t)$). Thus, the change in value remains low.

The two cases are used to show the level of dependence of growth of the service platform on the value of the application users $U_{ja}(t)$, service developers value $U_{js}(t)$, and the value of the platform provider $U_{jp}(t)$. If the level of QoS $Q_j(t)$ and the cost of usage C_{ja} and C_{js} are assumed to be fixed, the difference in the value of application users, the value of service developers, and value of platform providers is caused by the level of installed base $N_j(t)$ and the level of service variety $S_j(t)$ only.

The simulation results that are presented in Figure 5 and Figure 6 show the effect of high and low two-sided network effects.

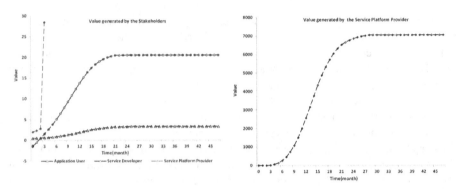

Fig. 5. Dynamics of value generated by the stakeholders in cases of a high network effect

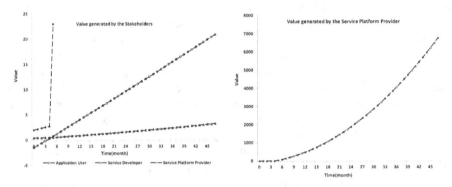

Fig. 6. Dynamics of value generated by the stakeholders in cases of a low network effect

Looking at the application user values of Figure 5 and Figure 6, application users subscribe to a service, which performs a certain task, from their service developers at the beginning of period $t=0$, which outweighs their user cost C_{ja}. This value that the user obtains at the time of joining the platform is indicated by $Q_j(t)$ in equation 1. Consequently, they receive a value $U_{ja}(t) > 0$ at period $t=0$. Maintaining a positive utility of application users is a condition, which has to be fulfilled in order to success-fully launch any application service or a service platform.

Service developers also need to subscribe to a service platform and utilize its offer-ings to build their services (equation 2). However, the values of service developers show a different behavior in the beginning. This is because their initial cost is higher than the cost faced by application users. They cannot recover their costs of offering C_{js} until they acquire a sufficiently large number of customers and generate revenues. Therefore, they take more time until they receive a value $U_{js}(t) > 0$, as it is shown in Figure 5 and 6, at the time period $t=3$.

Figures 5 and 6 show that, unlike service developers and application service users, which share a common behavior as customers of platform providers, platform provid-ers behave as service providers only. Consequently, their value received $U_{jp}(t)$ at the beginning of the period $t=0$ remains 0 until they start obtaining customers and generate revenue through development kits and hosting fee from service developers C_{js} and application usage fee from application users C_{ja}. The only cost that has to be covered are the cost of supporting application users C_{jap} and the cost of managing services C_{jsp}.

The value of service platform providers $U_{jp}(t)$ grows faster than the value of service developers $U_{js}(t)$ and application users $U_{ja}(t)$, as the size of both stakeholder groups grows (Figure 5 and Figure 6). The platform provider obtains benefit from both sides of the market. The value of application users shows a slow growth compared to the other two stakeholders, since they benefit the least from the growing number of customers. However, the value of the service developers is only slightly larger than the value of the application service user.

All stakeholder values are interdependent and changes in one of them affect the values of the other stakeholders. An evaluation of the relative impact of all value parameters indicates that the installed base $N_j(t)$ is a common positive determinant of value for all stakeholders. Although the value of the application users is important as the basis for value creation, a sufficiently large value obtained by service developers is necessary to sustain the service platform market. Currently, the value of service developers is quite low, having the risk of developers withdrawing from the service platform.

The implications of these results to the service platform market and to the stakeholders considered in this study is that both service developers and service platform providers need to focus on finding a way of sharing the value such that it allows developers to sustain their services over a longer time period. Otherwise, as the number of services still increases in the real world, the average return on developing an application service will reduce even further and, therefore, increase the risk of developers withdrawing from the market, causing a market failure.

4   Conclusions

This paper has presented a value creation model for stakeholders of an IT service platform, using additive value functions. The model can be used as a tool for evaluating values created for application users, service developers and platform providers. It allowed the integration of value-determining parameters to calculate the value (i.e., utility, profit) of stakeholders. Quality of service, service variety, installed base, and user cost are the parameters considered. The value creation model was evaluated using simulation software, in order to examine the value creation dynamics.

The simulation results indicate that the installed base of application users benefits all stakeholders and the service platform provider benefits largely from the two-side network effect. As a strategy for platform providers, it is not only important to focus on building the network of application users but also to maintain attractive returns for developers. This is important for sustaining the value of all stakeholders and growth of the service platform.

Our future studies may explore additions to the model by incorporating more factors such as pricing policies and market structures. We could investigate how the competition between multiple IT service platform providers impacts the values of platform providers and service developers.

Acknowledgments. This work has been funded by the Korea Institute for Advancement of Technology (KIAT) within the ITEA 2 project 10014 EASI-CLOUDS.

References

1. Demirkan, H., et al.: Service-oriented technology and management: perspectives on research and practice for the coming decade. Electronic Commerce Research and Applications 7, 356–376 (2008)
2. Katz, M.L., Shapiro, C.: Network externalities, competition, and compatibility. The American Economic Review 75(3), 424–440 (1985)
3. Liebowitz, S.J., Margolis, S.E.: Network externality: An uncommon tragedy. The Journal of Economic Perspectives 8(2), 133–150 (1994)
4. Farrell, J., Saloner, G.: Standardization, compatibility, and innovation. Rand Journal 16, 70–83 (1985)
5. Farrell, J., Saloner, G.: Installed base and compatibility: Innovation, product preannouncements, and predation. The American Economic Review, 940–955 (1986)
6. Farrell, J., Saloner, G.: Coordination through committees and markets. The RAND Journal of Economics, 235–252 (1988)
7. Farrell, J., Saloner, G.: Converters, compatibility, and the control of interfaces. The Journal of Industrial Economics, 9–35 (1992)
8. Clements, M.T.: Direct and indirect network effects: are they equivalent? International Journal of Industrial Organization 22(5), 633–645 (2004)
9. Economides, N., Flyer, F.: Compatibility and Market Structure for Network Goods. Stern School of Business. Department of Economics Working Paper Series (1997)
10. Katz, M.L., Shapiro, C.: Technology adoption in the presence of network externalities. Journal of Political Economy 94, 822–841 (1986)
11. Basole, R.C., Karla, J.: Value transformation in the mobile service ecosystem: A Study of App Store Emergence and Growth. Service Science 4(1), 24–41 (2012)
12. Bieberstein, N., Bose, S., Fiammante, M., Jones, K., Shah, R.: Service-oriented architecture(SOA) compass: business value, planning, and enterprise roadmap. FT Press, Upper Saddle River (2005)
13. Amit, R., Zott, C.: Value creation in e-business. Strategic Management Journal 22, 493–520 (2001)
14. Lee, S., Kim, T., Noh, Y., Lee, B.: Success factors of platform leadership in web 2.0 service business. Service Business 4(2), 89–103 (2010)
15. Smedlund, A.: Value co-creation in service platform business models. Service Science 4(1), 79–88 (2012)
16. Iansiti, M., Levien, R.: Strategy as ecology. Harvard Business Review 82(3), 68–81 (2004)
17. Gawer, A., Cusumano, M.A.: How companies become platform leaders. MIT Sloan Management Review 49(2), 28–35 (2008)
18. Agarwala, S., Yuan, C., Milojicic, D., Schwan, K.: QoS and utility aware monitoring in Enterprise Systems, pp. 124–133. IEEE (2006)
19. Evans, D.S.: Some Empirical aspects of multi-sided platform industries. SSRN Electronic Journal (2003)
20. Katz, M.L., Shapiro, C.: Product introduction with network externalities. Journal of Industrial Economics 40(1), 55–84 (1992)
21. Katz, M.L., Shapiro, C.: Systems competition and network effects. Journal of Economic Perspectives 8(2), 93–115 (1994)
22. Eisenmann, T., Parker, G., VanAlstyne, M.W.: Strategies for two-sided markets. Harvard Business Review 84(10), 92 (2006)
23. Zhu, F., Iansiti, M.: Entry into platform-based markets. Strategic Management Journal 33, 88–106 (2012)

24. Nalebuff, B.J., Brandenburger, A.M.: Co-opetition: competitive and cooperative business strategies for the digital economy. Strategy & Leadership 25, 28–35 (1997)
25. Gebregiorgis, S.A., Altmann, J.: IT service platforms: Their value creation model and the impact of their level of openness on their adoption. In: Annual SRII Global Conference, SRII 2012, San Jose, California, USA (2012)
26. Kim, K., Altmann, J., Hwang, J.: An analysis of the openness of the Web2.0 service network using two sets of indices for measuring the impact of service ownership. In: Hawaii International Conference on Systems Science, HICSS44, Koloa, Hawaii, USA (2011)
27. Kim, K., Altmann, J., Hwang, J.: Measuring and analyzing the openness of the Web2.0 service network for improving the innovation capacity of the Web2.0 system through collective intelligence. In: Symposium on Collective Intelligence, COLLIN 2010. Springer Advances in Intelligent and Soft Computing, Hagen, Germany (2010)
28. Altmann, J., Ion, M., Bany Mohammed, A.A.: Taxonomy of Grid Business Models. In: Veit, D.J., Altmann, J. (eds.) GECON 2007. LNCS, vol. 4685, pp. 29–43. Springer, Heidelberg (2007)
29. Apple iTunes (2012), http://www.apple.com/itunes
30. Apple Development Kits (2012), https://developer.apple.com/programs/ios/
31. Amazon Appstore for Android (2012), http://www.amazon.com/mobile-apps/b/ref=sa_menu_mas2?ie=UTF8&node=2350149011
32. Google Apps Marketplace (2012), http://www.google.com/enterprise/marketplace/

Cheat-Proof Trust Model for Cloud Computing Markets

Mario Macías and Jordi Guitart

Barcelona Supercomputing Center (BSC) and
Universitat Politecnica de Catalunya - Barcelona Tech (UPC)
Jordi Girona 29, 08034 Barcelona, Spain
{mario.macias,jordi.guitart}@bsc.es

Abstract. Online Reputation Systems would help mitigate the information asymmetry between clients and providers in Cloud Computing Markets. However, those systems raise two main drawbacks: the disagreement for assuming the cost of ownership of such services and their vulnerability to reputation attacks from dishonest parties that want to increase their reputation. This paper faces both problems by describing a decentralized model that would not need from the intervention of a central entity for managing it. This model includes mechanisms for allowing participants to avoid such dishonest behaviour from other peers: each client statistically analyses the external reports about providers and accordingly weights them in the overall trust calculation. The validity of the model is demonstrated through experiments for several use cases.

Keywords: Trust, reputation, cloud computing, dishonest behaviour.

1 Introduction

Online reputation systems help mitigate the information asymmetry between clients and providers in commerce markets. With the popularization of the World Wide Web, sites such as eBay [2] allow their users to submit and consult information about quality of products or the trustworthiness of both buyers and sellers. Such reputation systems enforce the confidence between parties and boost the number of commercial transactions.

This model has been also ported to Utility Computing Markets [14]. In Utility Computing Markets, both resource users and providers are autonomous agents that negotiate the terms of the Quality of Service (QoS) and the price that the client will pay to the provider for hosting their tasks or services in the resources. When the negotiation is finished, the terms of the contract are established in a Service Level Agreement (SLA). The most successful implementation of the Utility Computing paradigm is Cloud Computing, thanks to features of virtualization such as isolation of Virtual Machines (VMs), secure access to VMs with administrative privileges, or on-demand variation of the allocated resources.

Cloud Providers could not fulfil always the agreed QoS by several reasons, such as high load of resources, poor admission control, or dishonest behaviour.

K. Vanmechelen, J. Altmann, and O.F. Rana (Eds.): GECON 2012, LNCS 7714, pp. 154–168, 2012.

We suggest a reputation system to help clients choosing a provider and allow avoiding the providers with low QoS.

Traditional web reputation systems are based on reports from humans. This service can be part of a site (e.g. eBay reputation) or an independent site. They have clear business models: they increase the trust level to boost the economic transactions; also the service provider may get paid by advertisement. The incomes from the business model will amortize the cost of providing the service.

However, the aforementioned business model is not directly portable to Cloud Computing markets because the users and the providers of the resources are autonomous agents that are not able neither to communicate nor understand the human language; in addition, they are not a target for advertising campaigns and the Reputation Service Provider cannot make business from advertising. This raises two issues: (i) opinions about Cloud providers must be modelled for allowing their automatic processing; (ii) if there is no business model for a reputation service, nobody will provide it. There is many related work about modelling a reputation service (see section 2), but the need of making it economically feasible must be faced.

Reputation systems are vulnerable to reputation attacks [6]: dishonest companies can send biased opinions to increase their reputation or to decrease the reputation of their competitors. Such behaviour can be mitigated in traditional reputation systems by moderating the opinions. In addition, most users would be smart enough for discarding the dishonest reports. None of these methods can be applied to a decentralised, automatised agent-based reputation system.

Considering the aforementioned, these are our contributions:

- Description of a reputation model that applies to Cloud Computing business model and is easily implementable in a decentralized Peer-to-Peer (P2P) network. The cost of providing such service is not assumed by any central organisation; it is proportionally assumed by all the actors in the system.
- Statistical analysis for allowing market participants to detect dishonest behaviours from other peers that want to bias the true reputation of a provider.
- Validation of the model through experiments for several use cases.
- Discussion about the implementability of Reputation Systems in real Cloud Computing Markets.

The rest of the paper is structured as follows: after the presentation of the related work, section 3 describes the mathematical model created for describing the reputation of Cloud Computing providers. After the experimental validation of the model (section 4), section 5 discusses the requirements for implementing such system in a real Cloud market. At the end, we expose the conclusions and our future research lines.

2   Related Work

Our previous work [9] showed the importance of the reputation for a provider. To maintain a high reputation is a key factor for maximizing the revenue of providers in Utility Computing Markets. We introduced a centralised proof-of-concept reputation architecture that relied in simple reputation models and ideal market conditions. This paper intends to be a step beyond: we add multiple reputation terms and a decentralized architecture which is robust to dishonest market actors.

This paper adopts some ideas from Azzedin et al. [4] and Alnemr et al. [3]: we differentiate between *direct* and *reputation* trust; we consider multiple provider facets to evaluate our trust methods; we also consider the trust factor to a recommender. Despite Azzedin et al. provide a reputation model, they do not detail how that would be implemented. This paper provides a pure mathematical model that is easily implementable for its computation. We detail and discuss some practical issues for implementing it in real platforms.

Rana et al. [15] monitor reputation from three points of view: Trusted Third Party, Trusted Module at Service Provider, and Model at Client Site. They introduce the figure of a trusted mediator to solve conflicts between parties. Our main objection is the difficulty to find some company or institution that is willing to host and maintain the trusted mediator, because the business model is not clear. In consequence, our paper suggest a purely P2P reputation mechanism.

This paper adopts various facets from the model of Xiong et al. [18] for ensuring the credibility of a feedback from a peer: number of transactions and transaction context. We agree with the necessity of a community-context factor for incentive peers for reporting true feedbacks. This paper differs from the work of Xiong et al. because we are focusing the particularities of current Cloud Computing markets: multiple SLOs, providers that are not integrated with the reputation system, and trust relations that are classified two types: trust on peers (for consultancy) and trust on providers (for commercial exchange).

Yu et al. [19] define a model in which reputation propagates through networks. They define a trust propagation operator that defines how trust propagates from a source peer (who reports the trust) to a destination peer in multiple steps. Unlike our paper, their model assumes the same trust both for service provision and trust report, and they do not update the trust on peers in function of the honesty of their reports.

The need of avoiding dishonest opinions in reputation systems is firstly raised by Kerr et al. [6]. In their work, the show several reputation attacks to allow dishonest peers to increase their revenue. They argue that the notion of 'security by obscurity' does not prevent attackers from cheating successfully. Our paper shows a method for protecting honest clients from dishonest peers that is complementary to other existing security mechanisms.

3   Description of the Reputation Model

3.1   Previous Definitions

Let $\vec{U} = (u_1, u_2, \ldots, u_n)$ and $\vec{V} = (v_1, v_2, \ldots, v_n)$ be two vectors that contain n elements. The Element-wise Product is defined as $\vec{U} \odot \vec{V} = (u_1 v_1, \ldots, u_n v_n)$ and the Element-wise Division is defined as $\vec{U} \oslash \vec{V} = (u_1/v_1, u_2/v_2, \ldots, u_n/v_n)$.

Let $CP = \{cp_1, cp_2, \ldots, cp_m\}$ be the set of m Cloud Providers that are competing in a market to sell their resources to the clients.

Let $C = \{c_1, c_2, \ldots, c_n\}$ be the set of n clients that want to host their services or tasks in the set CP of Cloud providers. Each client c_x is communicated to a set of peers, represented by the set $P_x = \{p_1^x, p_2^x, \ldots, p_r^x\}$, formed by r peers of client c_x. Each peer is also a client ($P_x \subseteq C$). The peer-direct communication between clients is established by means of Peer-to-Peer (P2P) networks [5].

When clients try to buy resources to host their services or applications, they send offers to the providers for starting a negotiation. Each provider owns a set of N physical machines. Each physical machine can host several VMs that execute single tasks, such as Web Services or Batch Jobs. The SLA of a task is described as $SLA = \{\overrightarrow{S}, \Delta t, Price\}$, in which $\overrightarrow{S} = (s_1, \ldots, s_k)$ are the Service Level Objectives (SLOs) that describe the amount of resources or the QoS terms to be purchased by the client. Each s_* term represents the number of CPUs, Memory, Disk, network bandwidth, and so on. Δt is the time period during which the task will be allocated in the VM. $Price$ is the amount of money that the client will pay to the provider for provisioning $\overrightarrow{S}$ at Δt.

Because this paper is about trust and not about revenue management, for simplification purposes this paper does not consider the direct economic penalties derived from the violation of the SLA terms. The details of revenue management by considering revenue and penalty functions can be referred in our previous work [10,8,11,13].

Both Cloud clients and providers are entities that have a degree of trust between them as individuals. The degree of trust can be expressed in multiple terms, represented as a Trust Vector: a client trusts a provider in multiple facets, related to the different terms of $\overrightarrow{S}$ (e.g. a Cloud provider could provide resources that are suitable for CPU-intensive applications but unstable in terms of network connection). Let $\overrightarrow{T}(A, B) = (t_1, \ldots, t_k)$ be the Trust Vector from the entity A to the entity B. This is, how much A trusts B. Both A and B belong to CP or C.

$\overrightarrow{T}(A, B) = \omega_1 \overrightarrow{D}(A, B) + \omega_2 \overrightarrow{R}(B)$; this is, the overall trust from A to B has two components: $\overrightarrow{D}(A, B)$ is the direct trust from A to B, which is built based on previous experiences between A and B; $\overrightarrow{R}(B)$ is the reputation trust, which is calculated by asking the set of peers of entity A about their experiences with B (see section 3.2, equation 2) . In plain words, the direct trust is *what A directly knows about B* and the reputation trust is *what the others say about B*. ω_1 and ω_2 are used to weight how much importance the client assign to each of the terms, and may vary in function of each particular client. All the terms of $\overrightarrow{T}$, $\overrightarrow{D}$ and $\overrightarrow{R}$ are real numbers between 0 (no trust) and 1 (maximum trust).

Because trust and reputation have many terms, a provider could deserve high trust when considering some SLOs and low trust when considering others. This does not have to be detrimental to a given client. For example, a provider that deserves high trust only in terms of CPU could not be suitable for many applications such as web services or databases, but could be suitable for some

CPU-intensive scientific applications. Some types of workloads can be allocated in such providers with a high degree of trustworthiness. This raises a question: which incentive would clients have for allocating their workloads in such providers? Would it not be better to allocate them in providers whose trust level is high in all the terms of $\overrightarrow{T}(A, B)$? The response would be affirmative if there were not economic incentives at client side. Previous work from the authors [10,8,11] shown the economic benefit for both clients and providers of dynamically negotiating the prices in function of many factors, such as offer/demand ratio, allocated resources or QoS, and how those prices could vary in function of the reputation of the provider [9]. If a provider is able to guarantee the QoS requirements of a client at lower prices, the client will have incentive to allocate there its workloads; even if the provider has low reputation in factors that are not important for the client.

Considering the aforementioned, each client c_x has its own Trust Ponder Vector $\overrightarrow{I}(c_x)$, which weights each of the SLOs of $\overrightarrow{T}(A, B)$ in function of the importance the client assigns to each of them. The Element-Wise product $\overrightarrow{T}(c_x, cp_y) \odot \overrightarrow{I}(c_x)$ returns a vector that scores how trustworthy is the provider p_y in function of three facets: the reputation of cp_y, the direct trust from c_x to cp_y and the QoS needs of c_x. All the terms of $\overrightarrow{I}$ are real numbers between 0 and 1.

Let $Score(SLA, c_x, cp_y)$ be a function that scores the suitability of the provider cp_y in function of the SLA and the trust from client c_x to provider cp_y. For each SLA negotiation, the client will choose the provider whose $Score$ is the highest.

The definition of $Score_y^x$ may vary depending on the client policies and negotiation strategies. For evaluating the validity of the model, the clients evaluated in this paper score the providers according to equation 1. In this equation, the scores are always negative. The nearer to 0 the better score. The client divides the calculated trust from c_x to cp_y by the Trust Ponder Vector (element-wise division), and the negative of the magnitude of the resulting vector gives a scoring that shows how trustworthy is a provider for the preferences of c_x (in positive it would be the lower the better, that is why the result is multiplied by -1). This score is divided by the price: the client would accept sending tasks to providers to which the trust is lower if the price they establish is low enough.

$$Score(SLA, c_x, cp_y) = -\frac{\left\| \overrightarrow{T}(c_x, cp_y) \oslash \overrightarrow{I}(c_x) \right\|}{Price} \tag{1}$$

The scoring function in equation 1 will incentive providers to keep its maximum trust level and, if not possible, to lower prices.

3.2   Dishonest Behaviour towards the Reputation Model

A Cloud Provider could not provide the amount of resources that previously agreed with a given client. This fact can be caused by technical failures [17], errors in the calculation of the number of resources to provide [8,11], or dishonest behaviour. The reputation model described in this section is intended to alert the market participants when a provider is not fulfilling its agreed SLAs.

However, dishonest providers could enable fake clients to perform collusion: to report false or dishonest feedback for (1) increasing artificially the reputation of a provider; or (2) decreasing artificially the reputation of other providers from the competition. Since our reputation model is decentralized and unmanaged, the clients need a model for preventing false reports from dishonest peers.

Let $T(c_x, p_y)$ be a single-term trust relation from a client $c_x \in C$ to one of its peers $p_y \in P_x$. Let $P_x^z = \{p_1^z, \ldots, p_s^z\} \subseteq P_x$ the subset of s peers of c_x that have any direct trust relation to provider cp_z (this is, they can report previous experiences to cp_z), the Reputation Trust from c_x to cp_z is calculated as:

$$\overrightarrow{R}(c_x, cp_z) = \sum_{y=1}^{S} \left(T(c_x, p_y^z) \cdot \overrightarrow{D}(p_y^z, cp_z) \right) \oslash \sum_{y=1}^{S} \overrightarrow{T}(c_x, p_y^z) \tag{2}$$

Equation 2 is calculated by asking the peers that have any direct relation with cp_z and pondering their reports by the direct trust from the client to its peers. The report of a client to which there is high trust has more weight than the report of a client to which there is low trust. The key issue is to establish this trust relation between a client and its peers to avoid dishonest behaviours and give more consideration to the accurate reports.

The trust relation between a client and its peers is continuously updated in base to the next assumption: most peers are honest and, when asked, they report their true validation to the provider. Related work considers many incentives to peers for reporting honestly [20,7]. Our contribution is complimentary to them, since we deal with the minimization of the impact of the dishonest reports.

Assuming the aforementioned, the trust from a client to each of its peers is calculated according to algorithm 1:

begin
    The average values and the variances of all the reports from the peers of the P_x^z set are stored, respectively, in $\overrightarrow{A}$ and $\overrightarrow{\Sigma^2} = (\sigma_1^2, \ldots, \sigma_s^2)$;
    foreach p_y^z *in* P_x^z **do**
        $\overrightarrow{F} \leftarrow \overrightarrow{A} - \overrightarrow{D}(p_y^z, cp_z) = (a_1 - d_1, \ldots, a_s - d_s)$;
        foreach $|a_n - d_n|$ *in* $\overrightarrow{F}$ **do**
            if $|a_n - d_n| > \alpha \cdot \sigma_n^2$ **then**
                Decrease $T(c_x, p_y)$;
            else
                Increase $T(c_x, p_y)$;
        end
    end
end
end
        Algorithm 1. Updating trust from c_x to all its peers

To detect *potentially* bad reputations, algorithm 1 checks which peers reported a trust which is far from the other reports for the same provider. We stress *potentially* because, by any reason, a honest peer could have been provided with bad QoS while the others do not: because a punctual failure, or because the provider starts to underprovision QoS by an outage or because it starts to behave dishonestly when its reputation is high enough. These cases must not penalise too much the client that starts reporting different than the others. Only repetitive reports that are different would decrease considerably the reputation of a client.

There are two parts of algorithm 1 that will depend on the client policies. α multiplies the variance of the trust reports, and indicates how tolerant is the client with the concrete reports that are far from the average. The lower α, the lower tolerance. The other part that depends on the client policy is the function to increase or decrease the trust on a peer. In this paper we have used a piecewise-defined function that multiplies $T(c_x, p_y)$ in function of how far the trust report from the average. If there is no difference from a report to the average of all the other reports, the trust relation is multiplied by $MAX\_REWARD > 1$. The trust relation is not affected when $|a_n - d_n| = \alpha \cdot \sigma_n^2$, and if $|a_n - d_n| > \alpha \cdot \sigma_n^2$, the trust relation is multiplied to a minimum of $MAX\_PENALTY < 1$. Instead of the simplicity of $f(x)$, it is proven as effective in the evaluation (section 4).

Figure 1 shows that the slope of the linear function that penalizes the trust is less pronounced than the slope of the linear function that rewards the trust. In addition, $\frac{MAX\_PENALTY + MAX\_REWARD}{2} < 1$. The reasons are two: (1) the imbalance between $MAX\_PENALTY$ and MAX_REWARD will difficult that dishonest peers recover easily their trust; and (2) honest peers that, by any reason, punctually report values near $\alpha \cdot \sigma_n^2$ are not penalized with severity. Previous experimentations demonstrated that not dividing the function in pieces with different slopes would entail too much instability in the trust updating, and honest peers would lose their trust without solid reasons.

When the trust to a peer reaches 0, it is definitely expelled from the trust ring of the client, and its trust cannot be recovered any more.

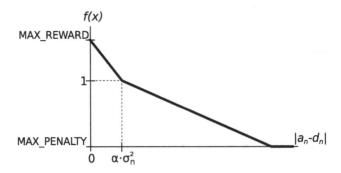

Fig. 1. Function to multiply the trust to a given peer, based on its previous report

3.3   Considering Reputation at SLA Negotiation Stage

As proven in previous work [9], low reputation lead to decrease the revenue of a Grid Provider: the lower trust the less currency will the clients pay for a service. In other words, if two providers offer the same QoS at equal prices, the client will choose the provider whose reputation is the highest. By this reason, a provider needs to adjust its price to its real reputation due to the effects of market competition. Our previous work showed how prices may be dynamically decided in function of many facets, such as number of resources, QoS, client relationship and market status [8,10,11,12,13]. This paper also defends the need of considering reputation as an additional facet when the provider negotiates a SLA with the client. There are two reasons: adjusting the revenue to the reputation will allow providers to maximize their benefit when reputation is high and sell its resources when reputation is low; the other reason is that selling the resources when reputation is low will allow provider recover its reputation.

Pricing in function of the trust involves two key issues that must be solved:

Calculating the trust from a given client. As seen in section 3.1, the trust from a client to a provider depends on three factors: the direct trust, the reputation as reported by all peers, the Trust Ponder Vector, and the weights that a particular client assigns to both direct trust and reputation. Direct Trust and Reputation can be approximated statistically, but the Trust Ponder Vector and the weights are completely private parameters that depend on the preferences of the client.

Defining a pricing function. Each provider must decide what are the proportion and distribution that trust would influence the prices. It is difficult to model because it depends on the emergent behaviour of all the market clients. Our previous work demonstrated that Genetic Algorithms [12] are suitable for this type of problems, because they rapidly adapt the pricing function to a changing/unknown environment. However, for simplification purposes, this simulation in this paper uses linear correlations between reputation and price [9].

4   Experiments

This section validates the model in section 3 by means of a custom Market Reputation Simulator [1]. In the simulation, clients look for resources for allocating their tasks in the providers that fit their QoS requirements. The experiments consider three SLOs: CPU, disk and network bandwidth. Therefore the Trust Vector and the Trust Ponder Vector is formed by 3 terms. Each experiment is a succession of market iterations. Each market iteration performs the next steps for all the clients in the market:

1. The client sends an offer to the providers. The offer specifies the QoS requirements and the time slot. The providers that have enough resources to handle it return a price.
2. The client asks its peers for the reputation of the providers that returned a price.

3. The client scores all the providers according to equation 1. It reaches an agreement with the provider whose score is the highest.
4. The client updates its trust to its peers according to equation 2. When the task is executed, it also updated its direct trust relation to the provider in function of the actual QoS.

The simulations rely on some constant values of which functionality is not to reflect real market data, but to evaluate the model in terms of relative results and tendencies: the honest providers whose resources work normally provide around 97% of the agreed QoS; at the beginning of the experiments, all providers and clients have an initial direct trust of 0.5. Other constant values are described in their respective experiments.

4.1   Basic Provider-Side Reputation

In the first experiment, five providers are competing in a market during 100 simulation steps. Four providers are honest and a provider is behaving dishonestly: it only provides the 60% of the QoS that it has previously agreed with the client. In addition, one of the honest providers suffers an outage [17] in its network at step 33. In consequence, it is providing the 50% of its network capacity until step 67.

Figure 2 shows the average trust from the clients to the providers. All the elements of the trust vectors are shown separately, but grouped the next way: the trust terms corresponding to the SLOs of the dishonest provider are shown as crosses; the trust element corresponding to the network of the provider that suffers the outage is a continuous line; the trusts for the rest of SLOs are shown as points. Figure 2 shows that the dishonest provider has a reputation proportional to the percentage of agreed QoS that is providing. The market also quickly notices that one of the providers is starting to provide a bad QoS in network and, after a quick decrease of the reputation, it slowly converges to 0.5, which corresponds to the percentage of QoS that is providing due to the outage. When the provider solves its network problems, its reputation increases fast, until it converges to the average reputation of the other SLOs.

4.2   Client-Side Reputation

This section evaluates the trust relations between peers in the scenario of the previous section. In that experiment, the market demand is formed by 24 clients that negotiate with the providers for allocating the workloads in the cloud resources. Before starting a negotiation with a provider, a client ask its peers for the reputation of the provider, then weight it with its direct trust (if any) and multiply it by the Trust Ponder Vector $\vec{I}(c_x)$. When the provider returns a price for a requested amount of resources, the client evaluates it in function of the price and the pondered trust.

When the client calculates the reputation of a provider, it tries to detect the dishonest peers as explained in section 1: it decreases or increases its trust to

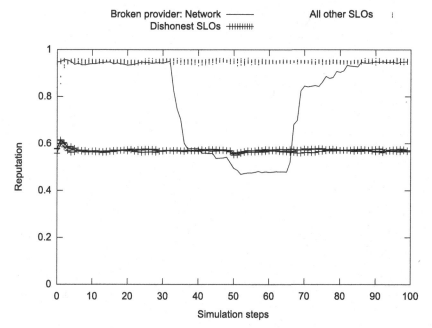

Fig. 2. Evaluation of reputation of providers

each peer in function of what they report. This paper does not intend to set the optimum values for MAX_REWARD and $MAX\_PENALTY$ constants (figure 1), so we have set $MAX\_REWARD = 1.05$ and $MAX\_PENALTY = 0.8$ as intuitive values for showing the tendencies. Different values would make the trust to peers evolve quicker or slower.

In the experiment, the dishonest provider infiltrated two peers that report trust values near 1 for the dishonest provider (while its real reputation is 0.5) and the 50% of the actual trust for the other providers. Figure 3 shows that, as initial state, all the peers of a given client have a trust of 0.5. The first dishonest client is reporting false trust values from the beginning, so it is quickly expelled from the list of peers (when it reaches trust 0). The trust to all the other providers is increased, including the second dishonest peer, whose strategy is to increase its reputation for increasing the influence of its false trust reports in the future. When the second dishonest client starts cheating at step 50, the client detects it and progressively decreases its reputation until reaching 0 value at step 59.

4.3   Effectiveness of Scoring Function for Allocating Tasks

To evaluate the effectiveness of equation 1 as rule for selecting a suitable provider while saving money, four providers are competing in a market for selling CPU, Disk and Network Bandwidth as SLOs: the first provider has the maximum reputation in all the SLOs; the second, third and fourth provider have the maximum reputation in all the SLOs but in CPU, Disk and Network, respectively. 32 clients want to submit their workloads to the providers, so they score them in

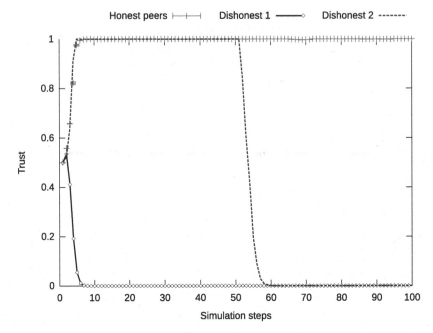

Fig. 3. Evaluation of trust to peers

Table 1. Values of the Trust Ponder Vector for each group of clients

Group	$\overrightarrow{I}(c_x) = (i_{cpu}, i_{disk}, i_{network})$
1	$(1, 1, 1)$
2	$(1, 0.3, 0.3)$
3	$(0.2, 0.8, 0.6)$
4	$(0.6, 0.3, 1)$

function of the trust, the Ponder Vector, and the price they ask. The 32 clients are divided in four groups depending on which necessities they have respecting the trust to each SLO (see table 1). Values of table would correspond to different types of workloads, for example: applications with a balanced resource usage (group 1), CPU-intensive applications that do neither intensively use disk nor network (group 2), Database applications with intensive disk and network usage (group 3) or some kind of web services that intensively use CPU and Network but not disk (group 4). The values of table 1 do not reflect any real measure of workloads. Their purpose is to be varied to see how the scoring function of equation 1 behaves.

In the first few iterations of the experiment, the tasks are allocated in the different providers pseudo-randomly. When the reputation of each provider is near to their true QoS, the next allocation of tasks is measured:

- All tasks from group 1 are placed in the provider with maximum QoS in all the SLOs. QoS is critical for this group and they are not willing to allocate their tasks in other providers despite the lower prices.

- All tasks from group 2 are placed at ~50% in provider with low network reputation and ~50% in provider with low disk reputation. Only CPU is critical for this group.
- All tasks from group 3 are placed in providers with low CPU reputation, because other SLOs have high importance.
- All tasks from group 4 are placed in provider with low disk reputation, because disk is the SLOs with the lowest importance.

The measured results tend to round numbers (e.g. 100% of tasks are allocated in the same provider when the system becomes stable) because of the experiment is repeated in a controlled simulation environment. A real market would add some statistical noise to the results.

5   Discussion: Implementing the Model in a Real Market

This paper demonstrates the validity of the reputation model from an experimental point of view. Since this paper is focused on the definition of the model, some implementation details are not considered from a formal view. This section wants to argue the implementability of the model, and what are the conditions for allowing the reputation model being feasible from the trust and economic side. Summarizing, we identify the next requirements:

- It is required to specify a communication protocol about trust information exchange for all the peers in the same network.
- A digitally-signed proof of purchase must be provided by peers that report their trust to a provider. The proof of purchase could be the agreed SLA, digitally signed by both client and provider. In consequence, a trustworthy Cloud Market requires certification authorities and identity management.
- Precisely quantify the SLAs to measure whether the provider is allocating all the resources to fulfil them. Some resources, such as CPU cycles, are difficult to measure accurately from a client side. We suggest negotiating in terms of high-level metrics (e.g. web-services throughput) and then translate such high-level metrics to low-level metrics by means of SLA decomposition [16].

The cost of implementing our trust model is not carried out by any centralised component, but it is shared by all the peers. The cost for each peer, in terms of memory space and extra calculations, is the next: let s the number of SLOs in a SLA; let r be the number of peers of a client; let m be the number of Cloud Providers. According to the model of section 3.1, the complexity of calculating the trust of all the providers is $O(s \cdot m \cdot r)$. According to algorithm 1, the complexity of updating the trust from a client to all its peers is $O(r \cdot s)$.

In terms of space complexity, a client needs to store a $O(m \cdot s)$ map with all the direct trust values to all the providers, and another $O(r)$ map with all the direct trust values to its peers.

The incentive-compatibility property of the mechanism must also be discussed. We suggest Cloud providers to penalize dishonest peers by increasing the price of their resources for such type of peers. This has two positive effects on the market: peers are encouraged to report the true valuation of the service providers, and providers get an economic compensation for possible reputation attacks, as if it were an assurance.

6   Conclusions and Future work

This paper describes a reputation model that faces some open issues in the state of the art. First, we propose a P2P architecture for dealing with the cost of provision of centralized reputation services, which may be a good architecture for other markets but not for Cloud Computing. Second, we define a mathematical model for calculating the trust relationship from a client to a provider. This model also defines trust relations between peers and updates them in function to statistical analysis for detecting the trustworthiness of their reports. The validity of the model is demonstrated through exhaustive experiments in three use cases: calculation of the trust in a scenario with a dishonest provider and a provider that suffers an outage; calculation of the trust between peers in a scenario with dishonest clients that report false data about providers; usage of the model for the economic benefit of the clients in function of their requirements.

This paper opens a wide range of future work lines: the model can be used also by providers to improve their business models. By evaluating trust, they can analyse the economic consequences of their resource management policies (for example, to calculate the impact in reputation of cancelling a task from a given client [11,13]). The trust information may also be used for allowing more accurate negotiations with clients. This requires opening another research line: how to statistically poll and evaluate the reputation of a provider in the market for reducing the uncertainty.

Another future work line is to improve the model at trust level for avoiding other types of reputation attacks, such as coordinated attacks or whitewashing (reporting well on small transactions for acquiring high reputation and then attack for high price contracts, and then disappear).

Acknowledgements. This work is supported by the Ministry of Science and Technology of Spain and the European Union (FEDER funds) under contract TIN2007-60625, by the Generalitat de Catalunya under contract 2009-SGR-980, and by the European Commission under FP7-ICT-2009-5 contract 257115 (OP-TIMIS).

References

1. Market Reputation Simulator, https://github.com/mariomac/reputation
2. eBay (2012), http://www.ebay.com/
3. Alnemr, R., Koenig, S., Eymann, T., Meinel, C.: Enabling usage control through reputation objects: A discussion on e-commerce and the internet of services environments. Journal of Theoretical and Applied Electronic Commerce Research 5(2), 59–76 (2010)

4. Azzedin, F., Maheswaran, M.: Evolving and managing trust in grid computing systems. In: Proceedings of the IEEE Canadian Conference on Electrical Computer Engineering CCECE 2002, Winnipeg, Manitoba, Canada, vol. 3, pp. 1424–1429 (2002)
5. Gupta, M., Judge, P., Ammar, M.: A reputation system for peer-to-peer networks. In: 13th International Workshop on Network and Operating Systems Support for Digital Audio and Video (NOSSDAV 2003), pp. 144–152. ACM, Monterey (2003)
6. Kerr, R., Cohen, R.: Smart cheaters do prosper: defeating trust and reputation systems. In: Proceedings of The 8th International Conference on Autonomous Agents and Multiagent Systems, International Foundation for Autonomous Agents and Multiagent Systems, AAMAS 2009, Richland, SC, vol. 2, pp. 993–1000 (2009), http://dl.acm.org/citation.cfm?id=1558109.1558151
7. Kerr, R., Cohen, R.: Trust as a tradable commodity: A foundation for safe electronic marketplaces. Computational Intelligence 26(2) (2010)
8. Macias, M., Fito, O., Guitart, J.: Rule-based SLA management for revenue maximisation in cloud computing markets. In: 2010 Intl. Conf. of Network and Service Management (CNSM 2010), Niagara Falls, Canada, pp. 354–357 (October 2010)
9. Macias, M., Guitart, J.: Influence of reputation in revenue of grid service providers. In: 2nd International Workshop on High Performance Grid Middleware (HiPer-GRID 2008), Bucharest, Romania (November 2008)
10. Macias, M., Guitart, J.: Using resource-level information into nonadditive negotiation models for cloud market environments. In: 12th IEEE/IFIP Network Operations and Management Symposium (NOMS 2010), Osaka, Japan, pp. 325–332 (April 2010)
11. Macías, M., Guitart, J.: Client Classification Policies for SLA Negotiation and Allocation in Shared Cloud Datacenters. In: Vanmechelen, K., Altmann, J., Rana, O.F. (eds.) GECON 2011. LNCS, vol. 7150, pp. 90–104. Springer, Heidelberg (2012)
12. Macías, M., Guitart, J.: A genetic model for pricing in cloud computing markets. In: Proceedings of the 2011 ACM Symposium on Applied Computing, SAC 2011, TaiChung, Taiwan, pp. 113–118 (2011), http://doi.acm.org/10.1145/1982185.1982216
13. Macias, M., Guitart, J.: Client classification policies for SLA enforcement in shared cloud datacenters. In: 12th IEEE/ACM International Symposium on Cluster, Cloud and Grid Computing (CCGrid 2012), Ottawa, Canada, pp. 156–163 (May 2012)
14. Neumann, D., Stoesser, J., Anandasivam, A., Borissov, N.: SORMA – Building an Open Grid Market for Grid Resource Allocation. In: Veit, D.J., Altmann, J. (eds.) GECON 2007. LNCS, vol. 4685, pp. 194–200. Springer, Heidelberg (2007)
15. Rana, O., Warnier, M., Quillinan, T.B., Brazier, F.: Monitoring and Reputation Mechanisms for Service Level Agreements. In: Altmann, J., Neumann, D., Fahringer, T. (eds.) GECON 2008. LNCS, vol. 5206, pp. 125–139. Springer, Heidelberg (2008)
16. Reig, G., Alonso, J., Guitart, J.: Prediction of job resource requirements for deadline schedulers to manage high-level SLAs on the cloud. In: 9th IEEE Intl. Symp. on Network Computing and Applications, Cambridge, MA, USA, pp. 162–167 (July 2010)
17. Tehrani, R.: Amazon EC2 outage: what the experts tell us. Customer Interaction Solutions 29(12), 1 (2011)
18. Xiong, L., Liu, L.: Peertrust: Supporting reputation-based trust for peer-to-peer electronic communities. IEEE Transactions on Knowledge and Data Engineering 16(7), 843–857 (2004)

19. Yu, B., Singh, M.P.: A Social Mechanism of Reputation Management in Electronic Communities. In: Klusch, M., Kerschberg, L. (eds.) CIA 2000. LNCS (LNAI), vol. 1860, pp. 154–165. Springer, Heidelberg (2000)
20. Zhang, J.: Promoting Honesty in Electronic Marketplaces: Combining Trust Modeling and Incentive Mechanism Design. Ph.D. thesis, School of Computer Science, University of Waterloo, Waterloo, Ontario, Canada (May 2009), http://hdl.handle.net/10012/4413

Trust Factors for the Usage of Cloud Computing in Small and Medium Sized Craft Enterprises

Holger Kett, Harriet Kasper, Jürgen Falkner, and Anette Weisbecker

Fraunhofer Institute for Industrial Engineering IAO, Stuttgart, Germany
{holger.kett,harriet.kasper,juergen.falkner,
anette.weisbecker}@iao.fraunhofer.de

Abstract. Although many benefits of cloud computing exist for SMEs, the development and usage of cloud computing solutions still face various challenges. The decision for applying cloud computing solutions, depend mainly on the length of time an enterprise exists, the degree of specialization, and finally the degree of need for security. Therefore, one of the key obstacles towards the adoption of cloud computing is among technical issues the establishment of trust into the performance, security, data protection and other features of cloud services and their providers. However, trust strongly depends on the target users and their characteristics. Over 16 percent of German SMEs apply cloud computing and realize its potentials. In the research project CLOUDwerker, funded by the German Federal Ministry of Economic and Technology, software as a service solutions for SMEs in the craft sector are examined and developed. In order to increase the usage of cloud computing at the target group of those SMEs, the paper focus on identifying and comparing the factors which influence trust into cloud computing solutions from the craft-specific view of small and medium sized craft enterprises and craft-specific cloud service providers who both have been addressed and questioned in two separate surveys. The results are considered to improve the development of trusted cloud computing applications which achieve a high user acceptance.

Keywords: Cloud Computing, Trust factors, SMEs.

1 Introduction

During the last years, cloud computing became a very popular topic from the view of IT-providers who started to offer cloud-based services as well as of users who aimed to benefit from their usage (see [1–3]). When addressing cloud computing in this paper, the term is understood as defined by NIST which considers cloud computing as a model for enabling ubiquitous, convenient, on-demand network access to a shared pool of configurable computing resources (e.g., networks, servers, storage, applications, and services) that can be rapidly provisioned and released with minimal management effort or service provider interaction [4].

[5] refines the cloud computing definition and states that cloud computing-based IT offerings must, in order to be counted as such, involve the abstraction from buyers

K. Vanmechelen, J. Altmann, and O.F. Rana (Eds.): GECON 2012, LNCS 7714, pp. 169–181, 2012.

of hardware ownership and control, buyers incurring infrastructure costs as variable operating expenditures on a pay-per-use basis with no contractual obligations and infrastructure capacity that can be scaled up or down dynamically and immediately.

In this context, the usage of cloud computing provides certain benefits for companies. [6], for example, mention the benefits of cost flexibility, business scalability, market adaptability, masked complexity, context-driven variability, and ecosystem connectivity. Whereas, [5] emphasizes that the most important benefits are reduced IT capital expenditure (CapEx) and reduced or re-deployed IT staff headcount, improved business scalability in response to client demands through elastic provisioning of IT, faster time-to-market for new goods and services, paying only for computing capabilities that are required and used, and lower barriers to entry to markets due to reduced fixed costs of entry.

If the risks of applying cloud computing are considered higher than the benefits which can be achieved, potential users are going to hesitate of using cloud-services. Information security, reliable service availability, and service performance are crucial success factors which are strongly valued by cloud users and affect their buying decision [7]. In Germany, only 16 percent of small and medium sized enterprises (SMEs) apply cloud computing. Many of them are not convinced by the currently available cloud-based services and their results. The high expectations have not been met. Security concerns as well as uncertainties of the future technological trends hinder the adoption of cloud computing in SMEs [8].

Among the technical factors, factors of trust into cloud-based services and their providers play an important role when convincing potential users for applying cloud computing [9]. In this context, trust is defined according to the definition of [10] as the willingness to depend, which "is both a belief about the other party and a behavioral intention". However, trust strongly depends on the target users and their characteristics as shown by [11] and [12]. Therefore, when examine factors which influence the trust in cloud-services, the consideration of the target users and their characteristics become important.

The objective of this paper is to identify the important factors which influence the users' trust into cloud computing applications and their providers. In this context, the paper focuses on small and medium sized craft enterprises in Germany as special target users. In Germany, more than 975.000 small and medium sized craft enterprises exit. With 4,75 million employees, these enterprises provide 9 percent of the German gross value and they are an important part of the German industry. Because of the business relationships and interaction with customers, business partners and public authorities cloud services become more and more crucial for them.

The paper introduces the methodology which was used, firstly, to generally identify the factors of trust which are published in the literature and, secondly, to examine their importance for craft-specific cloud-services from the view of providers and of small and medium sized craft enterprises as their users (section 2).

The trust aspects and are identified by applying a literature research and conducting a comparison of approaches and the addressed trust aspects (section 3). To the identified trust aspects relevant trust factors are assigned and examined. The examination is based on the results of two studies which focus on cloud-service providers on the one hand, and small and medium sized craft enterprises on the other hand. Here, the priorities of both groups are analyzed and insights into the prioritized trust factors from the view of the SMEs and their influence of the development of cloud-based services are derived (section 4). The paper ends with a conclusion of the findings and a description of the further activities (section 5).

2   Methodology

In order to identify the aspects which influence the trust of small and medium sized craft enterprises for cloud-services, the generally discussed trust aspects were collected by conducting a literature research in a first step. 12 publications have been identified which examine trust and introduce relevant aspects which influence trust.

In the second step, for each trust aspect concrete trust factors have been derived based on interviews with craftspeople. Afterwards, the target users of small and medium sized craft enterprises were questioned about their personal perceptions, opinions and practices in the context of cloud computing and related trust factors. Thus, an online questionnaire has been developed, published and promoted at the target users. In a six weeks period of time, over 350 replies were collected. [13] shows the methodology applied to conduct the survey and its results. The survey is not considered representative. However, a considerably large amount of feedback has been received to derive valuable trends.

In the third step, providers and their craft-specific cloud-service offers were identified. Here, information about their companies, their cloud-based services and their activities to build and increase trust in their offers by the target users of small and medium sized craft enterprises were gathered. The providers were questioned about their priority of trust factors when communicating with their target groups of crafts enterprises. In order to methodically collect the information, a structured online questionnaire had been developed and published. The main craft-specific IT-providers who had been mentioned by the participants of the users survey (see second step) had been examined and motivated to participate in our activities. 14 of them filled out the questionnaire. [14] documents the results of the survey in further details.

Finally, the gathered information from both groups were compared, examined and the findings are introduced in section 4. The results show the importance of factors which influence trust from the view of small and medium sized craft enterprises in Germany and providers of craft-specific cloud-service offers. The different priorities of both groups are made transparent and are discussed.

3   State of the Art

A review of selected papers on trust has been conducted to examine the addressed trust aspects which may be relevant for improving cloud computing for small and medium sized craft enterprises. [15] introduce the four disciplines, i.e. philosophy, psychology, management, and marketing which follow different objectives and address various issues, such as interpersonal trust and the morality of trust, trust in terms of social values and benefits, trust in organizational context, trust to reduce the cost of both intra- and inter-organizational transactions, trust in the context of distribution channels and long-term customer relationships etc.

However, at the beginning of this century, the discipline of online sales has emerged which focuses on the challenge to improve trust at online-users to increase their motivation for purchasing tangible and intangible goods over the Web (see [16, 17, 12, 18–20]). In this context, researchers discussed about online-trust especially with a strong focus on Web offers and online transactions which, lately, has been extended to social media and cloud computing (see [9, 21]). The latter aims to find solutions for the non-technical challenges which need to be solved to improve the usage of cloud computing by increasing the target users' trust.

Table 1 shows an overview of selected approaches which focus on online trust, either with a focus on CRM (Customer relationship management), Web, social media or cloud computing. Publications which focused on cloud computing security are not considered in this context due to their mostly technical orientation. This view has been examined already in many research papers. The analysis of the trust aspects which are considered within the selected approaches concern the main categories products/services, providers/vendors, users, and finally, trust.

Table 1. Selected trust approaches characterized by the relevant trust aspects

trust approaches	trust aspects — products/services				trust aspects — providers/vendors				trust aspects — users			characteristics of the approaches — focus area				characteristics of the approaches — focus areas			
	features of product/service	features of user interface	data aspects	operational aspects	customer relationship management	marketing and sales	vendor / provider characteristics	legal aspects	target users and their characteristics	interaction and advice	risks	CRM	Web	Social Media	Cloud	trust characteristics	phases of trust development	forms of online trust	trust model
SINUS-Instituts heidelburg 2012 [11]									•			•	•			•			
Khan and Malluhi 2010 [9]			•	•										•		•			
Shimba 2010 [21]	•		•		•		•	•	•						•				
Urbana et al. 2009 [22]		•		•		•			•			•				•			•
Büttner and Göritz 2008 [16]										•			•						
Heath et al. 2007 [23]									•			•							
Schulz 2006 [24]																			
Bart et al. 2005 [12]	•			•					•		•	•				•		•	•
Dzeyk 2005 [17]									•		•	•					•	•	•
Wang and Emurian 2005 [15]		•				•			•			•							•
Egger 2003 [18]		•		•							•	•							•
McKnight et al. 2002 [19]			•				•		•			•							•

The trust approaches which focus on Web sites, transactions and eCommerce consider the features of the user interface as one of the most consistent issues of trust. Most of the trust models are developed by those trust approaches. Since cloud computing technologies become more and more alternatives for license-based software and self-owned hardware, security and trust issues gain importance. However, only a few trust approaches which focus on cloud computing currently exist.

When examining the selected trust approaches, we identified 15 trust aspects which are assigned to the categories of products/services, providers/vendors, users, and trust. Each of the 11 trust aspects are described in Table 2. In order to analyze the importance of the trust aspects for craftspeople, relevant trust factors are assigned to the trust aspects, where applicable, within the conducted surveys. The trust factors for each of the trust aspects have been gathered from interviews with craftspeople prior to the surveys. The assigned trust factors (see Table 2) have been addressed in both of the surveys.

Table 2. Description of the derived trust aspects and the examined trust factors in the two surveys of small and medium sized craft enterprises and providers of craft-specific cloud-services

Trust aspects	Description	Potential craft-specific trust factors examined in the surveys
Features of product/service	This trust aspect includes all features of a product/service which influence the users' trust into the offering. Concrete factors are, for example, functions, availability, integration, administration, maintenance, costs, exclusion criteria, notice periods, suspension of services, and customer's involvement into a product/service.	• Functionality meets requirements • Availability/resilience • Comprehensible price model • Price
Features of user interface	The user interface is the contact point of the users with a cloud service. In this context, issues are usability, graphical/visual design (presentation), structural design (navigation), content design, design of social cues, up-to-date, trustworthy information, search for information, products or services [12, 17, 15, 18, 19].	• Ease of use • Easy to start with
Data aspects	Users of public cloud services store their data at a provider. In order for data not to get lost or diffuse outside the company, issues such as storage, ownership, security, data protection, deletion, and registration data need to be considered.	• Security (data storage, data transfer, data access) • Backup and security concept

Table 2. (*continued*)

Trust aspects	Description	Potential craft-specific trust factors examined in the surveys
Operational aspects	The provisioning of cloud services requires solving certain challenges in order to increase users' trust, e.g. scalability, multi-tenancy, service level agreements, service (level) monitoring, fulfillment of services performance, and privacy.	• Performance and speed • Availability / resilience
Customer relationship management	The communication between users and their providers are crucial aspects for creating trust. Here, issues are contact options, accessibility, quality of support, personal contact, fulfillment (of support), confirmation of order, availability of support, and dealing with complaints.	• Good support • Information about new functionalities, etc.
Marketing and sales	Trust aspects in this context are dedicated to foster the sales processes, e.g. selection of adequate communication channels, brand strength, well developed sales channels and sales partners.	• Clear presentation of the range of services • Professional marketing and Web page • Presence in media (magazines, TV, new, etc.)
Provider/vendor characteristics	Here, aspects which influence the positive judgment of cloud service users of the providers. Thus, the following elements play a major role: provider information, product/service information, information (security and data protection), risks, risk management, competence, integrity, and reputation.	• Provider experience with craft enterprises • Clear presentation of the range of services
Legal aspects	The legal context influences trust in cloud computing, e.g. transparency of sub-contractor and third party relations, legislation, and legal domicile.	• Provider's country of origin
Target users and their characteristics	There exist many user criteria which have an effect on their trust in cloud computing, e.g. autonomy, digital culture, diversity, hedonism, underdog culture, disorientation, social criticism, resistance, slow down, balance and harmony, sustainability, regrounding, adaptive navigation, age and income, online expertise, internet shopping experience, online entertainment or chat experience [11, 17].	Has not been applied in the surveys.

Table 2. *(continued)*

Trust aspects	Description	Potential craft-specific trust factors examined in the surveys
Interaction and advice	Friends, colleagues, and recognized experts support the decision making process and, thus, the development of trust in a cloud-service. Here, for example, communities, customer ratings, recommendations, certificates, and experts may be of importance.	• Awarded certificates and quality seals • Recommendation by chambers (crafts), guilds, etc. • Recommendation by friends and colleagues • User ratings on Internet-platforms and forums
Risks	The more uncertainty and risk, the less trust in a cloud service is put. Different kind of risks occur, such as financial risk, information risk, etc. However, aspects such as control/ checkability, transparency, prevention, and lock-in effects may also foster or hinder the usage of cloud services of the target users [9, 17].	Has not been applied in the surveys.

For a better understand of the effects of trust on cloud computing and ways how the discussed trust factors can be influenced by the providers, the next section documents the trust factors and their prioritization from the view of craftspeople and providers of Cloud-based services which are shown at Table 2. Since those trust factors strongly depend on the target users [11], we conduct the examination from the view of the target users of small and medium sized craft enterprises.

4 Craft-Specific Trust Factors of Cloud Computing

In order to identify the craft-specific factors which influence the trust of small and medium sized craft enterprises in cloud-services, the trust factors at Table 2 have been examined on the bases of the two surveys with craft enterprises and providers of craft-specific cloud-services. The trust factors which are mainly relevant during usage of the applications:

— **Performance and Speed.** It is often a major concern that cloud services are slow and less efficient due to not available bandwidth. For both craftspeople and providers this is a very important factor.
— **Availability and Resilience.** Being able to use the services is crucial for businesses and therefore very important. According issues are commonly regulated in service level agreements.
— **Ease of Use.** Usability is less important for providers than enabling an easy start with their product, since according problems often do not reveal until actual operation. Still for both craftspeople and providers this factor ranks very high, right after functionality that meets the requirements.

- **Backup and Security Concept.** Comprehensible backup and security measures are very important for customers, but not so much emphasized by providers.
- **Good Support.** During preparation of the craftspeople survey interviews showed that support is an important factor. Perceived importance between providers and craftspeople match.
- **Information about New Functionality etc.** Craftspeople like to be informed about improvements, providers do not really emphasize this point.
- **Price.** Last but not least price is always an essential business factor. In our surveys it's importance between customer- and provider view has the biggest difference: providers do consider price far less important than craftspeople.

The following trust factors are mainly concerned with the actual service or product:

- **Clear Representation of the Range of Services.** Especially in IT-distal sectors like crafts and for new cloud based services this is crucial and therefore rated as very important by the craftspeople.
- **Functionality Meets Requirements.** Specific demands must be met and overloaded applications must be avoided. After security and availability issues this is the most important point for craftspeople.
- **Comprehensible Pricing Model.** Flexible pay per use is often referred to as an advantage of cloud computing, but makes overall cost calculation difficult and therefore must be adequately explained.
- **Security (Data Transfer).** The submission of data over the internet is often subject to fraud and must be secured. Although it is often not possible for the target group to examine security transfer, storage and access of data is the most important factor for them.
- **Security (Data Storage).** In terms of storage facilities high standards must be fulfilled to provide better solutions than on premise applications.
- **Security (Data Access).** Preventing unauthorized people from accessing customer's data is especially important for cloud based services.
- **Easy to Start with.** Beginning to use a new application must be efficient. Although very important craftspeople might take into account some more effort at start and are more focused on ease of use in general. Providers on the other hand concentrate more on enabling an easy start and draw back on actual ease of use.
- **Recommendations by Friends and Colleagues.** Private references complement official product information but are not very often used by craftspeople. Providers see word of mouth as the most important recommendation possibility.
- **Recommendations by Chambers (Crafts), Guilds, etc.** Associations from the same industry sector help assessing actual business relevance and are important to some craftspeople.
- **Awarded Certificates and Quality Seals (e.g. EuroCloud Star Audit).** Unbiased references and also performance in tests are important towards the decision for any new application, especially if there is no previous experience available, which is often the case for cloud services. It is surprisingly the least important factor for providers, although somehow important for the target group.

- **Presence in Media (Magazines, TV, News, etc.).** According to craftspeople this factor is least important for them, but they are however influenced by media which makes it a more important factor for providers.
- **User Ratings in Internet Platforms and Forums.** To gather information through social media is not considered important by the majority of craftspeople, but providers see chances here.

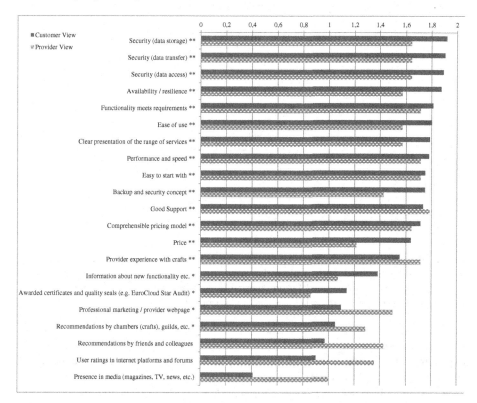

Fig. 1. Importance of online trust factors in crafts – a comparison between the views of customers and providers (0 = less important, 2 = very important; **= absolute ranking from user view >1.5, * = absolute ranking from user view between 1.0 and 1.5)

A comparison of the collected results shows very well that the perception of trust and the importance of the factors leading to trust differ between the two surveyed groups. Fig. 1 provides a comparison between the rankings of trust factors from the view of craftspeople with that of providers of craft-specific cloud services. It is outstanding that the implementation of security measures like secure storage, encrypted data exchange and secure ways to identify at and access cloud services range highest in the perception of users whereas providers believe more in the provision of good support, as well as their experience with and their understanding of the target group. The survey results furthermore show that the confidence in marketing measures is very high among providers whereas users do not seem to believe that much that they are influenced by marketing.

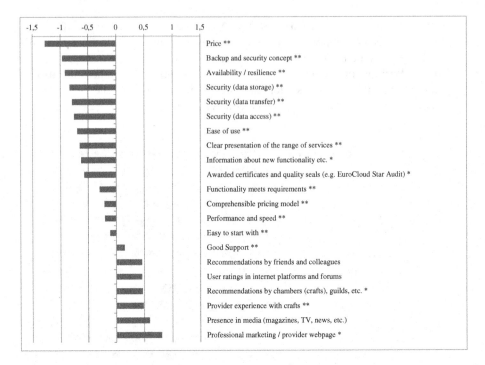

Fig. 2. Difference in perception of importance of trust factors between providers and their potential customers (negative values mean that factor is underrated by provider, positive values mean that the factor is overrated by providers; 0 = less important, 2 = very important; ** = highest ranking from user view >1.5, * = median user ranking between 1.0 and 1.5)

The results shown in Fig. 1 give some first information on how to bridge the gap between current offerings of cloud services and what their potential customers would expect them to provide in terms of trustability and reliability. In order to elaborate this further we took a look at the differences in perception between cloud providers and their potential customers as shown in Fig. 2. Negative values show that the factors are underestimated by cloud providers in comparison to what the surveyed craftspeople are looking at. Positive values on the other hand show factors overrated by cloud providers in comparison to the users' view. The sheer differences between the values had been weighted with the absolute importance of the different factors according to the user survey in order to obtain a list that shows the providers' fields of action with the highest urgency and therefore present a ranking of essential trust factors for crafts-specific cloud services. The factors marked with ** were highest in user ranking with values greater than 1.5 on a range from 0 (less important) to 2 (very important). The factors marked with * have median user ratings between 1.0 and 1.5. Those with no mark have values below 1.0.

Trust or acceptance factors like price, backup and security concepts, guaranteed service availability and security features seem to be neglected by providers whereas marketing efforts and their presence in media seem to be overrated. This could well explain why the customer numbers lag far behind the providers' expectations despite the current cloud hype [8].

Another factor that craftspeople rated as very important (values greater than 1.5) are the availability of free trial offerings. If this is available among the providers has not been surveyed. Also rated as important (values between 1.0 and 1.5) are the provider's reputation, service performance in tests and overall high profile concerning publicity and media presence.

For providers customer retention through personal contact is another very important factor. The compliance with technical and industry standards and reception of awards is also considered as important for their business.

Another provider related factor rated very important (values greater than 1.5) and examined in the craftspeople-survey only is the provider's country of origin. This is because internet privacy issues are very important in Germany [26]. This factor's high rating points towards a high information level and awareness of the polled craftspeople, which is also confirmed by their above-average use of IT-tools. In expert interviews the explicit wish to know at which physical place data is stored was expressed. Some cloud providers answer this demand by even offering guided tours of their data centers[1].

5   Conclusions and Further Activities

The adoption of cloud computing especially of SMEs lags behind the expectations. Some technical issues need to be solved which more or less hinder the usage of cloud computing (e.g. broad band access). However, soft factors of trust play in this stage of development an important role which shows the above introduced examination of the trust factors by SMEs in the craft sector (e.g. security issues).

For the target users of small and medium sized craft enterprises, the aspects of appropriate pricing, the availability of the cloud services, and security aspects, such as backup, security concept, data security, data transfer, etc. are crucial issues. When comparing the perceptions of the service providers, they are far away from evaluating those issues as important. They value more the marketing activities and building up some craft-specific experience.

In this situation, research needs to take up the challenge of identify adequate ways to introduce cloud computing to the addressed target groups and support providers in their effort to increase trust at their target users. Those aspects have to be integrated when conceptualizing the business model of cloud services [27, 28]. Trust aspects have to be considered during the design and development of cloud service. Furthermore, the trust model which are mainly focusing on Web sites, transactions and eCommerce need to be examined towards the requirements of trust in cloud computing and eventually new trust models for cloud computing may be developed.

---

[1] See http://www.skyway-datacenter.de/en
http://www.rackbase.de/infrastruktur/rechenzentrum/
telecitygroup_tour.html
http://www.telecitygroup.nl/uniserver-EN.htm
http://www.pironet-ndh.com/site/pndh-website-
site/get/22423/Flyer%20Datacenter%20A4.pdf

References

1. Kett, H.: Cloud Computing. Einsatz und Nutzen für kleine und mittlere Unternehmen. In: Prozeus, Prozesse und Standards, Erstaufl, pp. 23–24. Inst. der Dt. Wirtschaft Köln Medien GmbH, Köln (2011)
2. Weiner, N., Renner, T., Kett, H.: Geschäftsmodelle im "Internet der Dienste". Trends und Entwicklungen auf dem deutschen IT-Markt. Fraunhofer-Verlag, Stuttgart (2010)
3. Weiner, N., Renner, T., Kett, H.: Geschäftsmodelle im "Internet der Dienste". Aktueller Stand in Forschung und Praxis. Fraunhofer-Verlag, Stuttgart (2010)
4. Mell, P., Grance, T.: The NIST Definition of Cloud Computing. Recommendations of the National Institute of Standards and Technology. National Institute of Standards and Technology NIST, Gaithersburg (2011)
5. Hogan, O., Mohamed, S., McWilliams, D., et al.: The Cloud Dividend: Part One. The economic benefits of cloud computing to business and the wider EMEA economy, France, Germany, Italy, Spain, UK. Centre for Economics and Business Research Ltd., London (2010)
6. Berman, S., Kesterson-Townes, L., Marshall, A., et al.: The power of cloud. Driving business model innovation. IBM Institute for Business Value, New York (2012)
7. Vehlow, M., Golkowsky, C.: Cloud Computing. Navigation in der Wolke. PricewaterhouseCoopers, Frankfurt am Main (2011)
8. Heng, S., Neitzel, S.: Cloud Computing. Freundliche Aussichten für die Wolke. Deutsche Bank Research, Frankfurt am Main (2012)
9. Khan, K.M., Malluhi, Q.: Establishing Trust in Cloud Computing. IT Pro, pp. 20–26 (September/October 2010)
10. Moorman, C., Zaltman, G., Deshpande, R.: Relationships Between Providers and Users of Market Research: the Dynamics of Trust Within and Between Organizations. Journal of Marketing Research (29), 314–328 (1992)
11. SINUS-Instituts Heidelberg:Milieu-Studie zu Vertrauen und Sicherheit im Internet. Deutsches Institut für Vertrauen und Sicherheit im Internet (DIVSI), Hamburg (2012)
12. Bart, Y., Shankar, V., Sultan, F., et al.: Are the Drivers and Role of Online Trust the Same for All Web Sites and Consumers? A Large-Scale Exploratory Empirical Study. Journal of Marketing (69), 133–152 (2005)
13. Kasper, H., Kett, H., Weisbecker, A.: Anwenderstudie: Potenziale von Cloud Computing im Handwerk - Aktuelle IT-Unterstützung und Anforderungen an Internet-basierte IT-Lösungen. Fraunhofer-Verlag, Stuttgart (2012)
14. Christmann, C., Kett, H., Falkner, J., Weisbecker, A.: Marktstudie: Cloud-Lösungen für das Handwerk - Hintergrund, Anwendungsfelder und aktuelle Internet-basierte Angebote. Fraunhofer-Verlag, Stuttgart (2012)
15. Wang, Y.D., Emurian, H.H.: An Overview of Online Trust: Concepts, Elements, and Implications. Computers in Human Behavior (21), 105–125 (2005)
16. Büttner, O.B., Göritz, A.S.: Perceived trustworthiness of online shops. Journal of Consumer Behaviour 7, 35–50 (2008)
17. Dzeyk, W.: Vertrauen in Internetangebote. Universität zu Köln, Köln (2005)
18. Egger, F.N.: From Interactions to Transactions: Designing the Trust Experience for Business-to-Consumer Electronic Commerce. Eindhoven University of Technology, Eindhoven (2003)
19. McKnight, D.H., Choudhury, V., Kacmar, C.: Developing and Validating Trust Measures for e-Commerce. An Integrative Typology. Information Systems Research 13, 334–359 (2002)

20. Stanford, J., Tauber, E.R., Fogg, B., et al.: Experts vs. Online Consumers: A Comparative Credibility Study of Health and Finance Web Sites (2002)
21. Shimba, F.: Cloud Computing: Strategies for Cloud Computing Adoption. Dublin Institute of Technology, Dublin (2010)
22. Urbana, G., Amyxb, C., Lorenzonc, A.: Online Trust: State of the Art, New Frontiers, and Research Potential. Journal of Interactive Marketin 23, 179–190 (2009)
23. Heath, T., Motta, E., Petre, M.: Computing Word-of-Mouth Trust Relationships in Social Networks from Semantic Web and Web2.0 Data Sources (2007)
24. Schultz, C.D.: A Trust Framework Model for Situational Contexts. In: PST 2006 Proceedings of the 2006 International Conference on Privacy, Security and Trust: Bridge the Gap Between PST Technologies and Business Services, pp. 1–7. ACM Press, Markham (2006)
25. Fogg, B.J.: Prominence-Interpretation Theory: Explaining How People Assess Credibility Online. In: Proceedings of the Conference of Human Factors in Computing Systems (CHI), Ft. Lauderdale, Florida, USA, pp. 722–723 (2003)
26. Bundesministerium für Justiz Bundesdatenschutzgesetz (BDGS)
27. Spath, D., Raffler, H.: Integrated Service Engineering (ISE) Framework. Development of Business Services for Ecosystems in the Internet of Services. Fraunhofer-Verlag, Stuttgart (2011)
28. Kett, H.: A Business Model Approach for Service Engineering in the Internet of Services. International Journal of Service Science, Management, Engineering, and Technology 2(4), 1–8 (2011)

A Cost Analysis of Cloud Computing for Education

Fernando Koch, Marcos D. Assunção, and Marco A.S. Netto

IBM Research
Sao Paulo, Brazil

Abstract. Educational institutions have become highly dependent on information technology to support the delivery of personalised material, digital content, interactive classes, and others. These institutions are progressively transitioning into Cloud Computing technology to shift costs from locally-hosted services to a "renting model" often with higher availability, elasticity, and resilience. However, in order to properly explore the cost benefits of the pay-as-you-go business model, there is a need for processes for resource allocation, monitoring, and self-adjustment that take advantage of characteristics of the application domain. In this paper we perform a numerical analysis of three resource allocation methods that work by (i) pre-allocating resource capacity to handle peak demands; (ii) reactively allocating resource capacity based on current demand; and (iii) proactively allocating and releasing resources prior to load increases or decreases by exploring characteristics of the educational domain and more precise information about expected demand. The results show that there is an opportunity for both educational institutions and Cloud providers to collaborate in order to enhance the quality of services and reduce costs.

Keywords: Cloud computing, education systems, digital content, resource allocation, cost analysis, quality of service.

1 Introduction

Education has evolved in a way that institutions have become highly dependent on information technology to improve the delivery of personalised material, and to offer digital content and interactive classes. As mentioned in the 2010 UNESCO Report [23], "the economies of scale and other features of cloud computing are likely to mean an increasing shift way from institutionally-hosted services". We are heading towards a future where "the majority of educational services will be hosted in the cloud and institutions no longer host their own data centres with expensive hardware, power bills, staff salaries and computing resources which are rarely fully utilised".

In this context, the role of Cloud Computing is to assist educational organisations in reducing costs and focusing on their core business [2, 6, 14, 24]. For instance, by following the pay-as-you-go model, educational institutions are

K. Vanmechelen, J. Altmann, and O.F. Rana (Eds.): GECON 2012, LNCS 7714, pp. 182–196, 2012.

charged only for the services and resources they use (*e.g.* computing and storage resources, educational and specialised scientific software systems, and lecture material), whereas providers bear the costs of hardware and software provision. In this model, pricing may vary depending on factors such as the time of day when resources are used, peaks in demand, and electricity costs. Cloud computing users may therefore optimise the resource utilisation by executing tasks when the costs are lower.

To optimally exploit the cost-effectiveness of this business model, educational institutions require methods to estimate demand and promptly adjust the resource allocation in response to both pre-determined and fluctuating loads. This includes being able to allocate more resources just prior to the delivery of resource-demanding classes and releasing resources right after the classes end. Although educational institutions, specially small and mid-size schools, have limited understanding on their actual IT resource demand, they often have deep understanding of domain characteristics, such as class and teacher timetables and teacher and student profiles. Cloud computing resources can be provisioned and automatically managed by leveraging the understanding of the application domain for different schools' configurations. In this way, resource allocation is adjusted on-demand, depending on load fluctuations, on how students utilise the applications, timetables, and features of the educational material.

This paper evaluates the impact of more refined demand predictions when provisioning Cloud resources to educational institutions. We claim that if the proper method for dynamically allocating resources based on knowledge of the application is implemented, it can yield significant optimisation in capital and operational costs without compromising quality of service. Dynamic resource allocation has been highly investigated [4, 5, 10, 11, 18]. Therefore, we leverage existing work to study the effects of educational information published to Cloud providers in order to optimise resource allocation.

Our evaluation is based on a numerical analysis of three resource allocation methods that work by (i) pre-allocating resource capacity to handle peak demands; (ii) reactively allocating resource capacity based on current demand; and (iii) proactively allocating and releasing resources prior to load increases or decreases by exploring characteristics of the educational domain and more precise information about expected demand. The work assesses the impact of using specific domain information to assist resource allocation considering both IT costs and quality of service. The main contributions of this paper are the following:

– Impact evaluation of three resource allocation methods on monetary costs and quality of service. One of the methods explores domain understanding to provide better demand predictions on resource provisioning. This method considers specific features of this domain of application, such as when and how students utilise the applications, timetable, features of the educational material, and others.

- A system architecture containing the specialised elements and interactions to instrument the process of self-regulating resource allocation in Cloud computing for education.

- Analysis of the allocation methods based on the reservation of "safety margin" considering the cost/benefits of having more margin and how that can contribute to the overall QoS.

This project builds upon the business demands of the IBM Smarter Education project, which is part of the IBM Smarter Planet program. We envisage a collection of Cloud Computing based services ranging from operations, education tracking, delivery, and classroom instrumentation. In this environment, educational institutions will be able to contract services on-demand, reducing the time for and improving the cost-effectiveness of digitising the education system.

2   Background and Related Work

To meet business demands, educational institutions have become highly dependent on IT, thus constantly requiring substantial investments and skills to maintain and operate their IT systems. Keeping IT infrastructure up-to-date is important in delivering today's educational material, providing quality of service, and maintaining students' satisfaction [25].

Cloud Computing is being used by educational institutions as a platform for affordably offering modern and up-to-date IT resources to students [15, 16]. This is particularly important in developing countries [12, 17] and for meeting the limited budgets that institutions often have as a result of the current economic turmoil [20, 25]. Cloud computing offers opportunities for cost reduction due to the economies of scale, thus resulting in a shift away from locally-hosted services [23]. The 2010 UNESCO Report [23] on Cloud Computing in Education highlights the benefits of cloud computing for institutions and students. Apart from the claimed benefits of cost reduction, elasticity, and concentration on core business, the report mentions enhanced resource availability, better end-user satisfaction, and augmented learning process and collaboration.

Another study [26] has focused on the opportunities of cloud computing to increase collaboration among multiple institutions. In addition, as discussed by Sultan [25], there are several examples of educational institutions that have adopted cloud computing to not only rationalise the management of IT resources, but also to make the education process more efficient.

Cost reductions and quality of service are key factors for educational institutions. Such factors are impacted by how Cloud providers manage their resources, and having appropriate tools for doing so is an important differentiator. The following projects have investigated aspects related to Service Level Agreements (SLAs) and load prediction methods for optimising resource management. For instance, Emeakaroha et al. [8] investigated monitoring time intervals for detecting SLA violations wherein their proposed architecture can be used to determine whether an SLA is violated and then inform the resource allocation system. The solution is reactive and does not use service workload for proactively predicting resource consumption. Li et al. [18] introduced an approach to optimal virtual-machine placement for predictable and time-constrained load peaks. The solution, although focuses on a proactive resource allocation using prediction techniques, does not leverage specific information about the workload domain. Similar approaches were investigated by Ali-Eldin et al. [1].

Bodenstein et al. [5] have focused on resource allocation decisions, ignoring application information to predict when resource allocation should be adapted. Gong et al. [11] introduced a system called PRESS (PRedictive Elastic ReSource Scaling), which aims at avoiding resource waste and service level objective violations in the context of Cloud computing. Their goal is to avoid the use of application profiling, model calibration, and understanding of user applications. Our work takes another direction where Cloud customers provide information about their workloads in order to avoid SLA violations and reduce resource waste. Gmach et al. [10] also investigated capacity planning using historical data, but without considering the nature of the workload. Other projects [7, 9] have also explored the use of resource consumption prediction to better allocate resources. However they have not considered IT cost reductions and QoS in their studies. Adaptive resource allocation and demand prediction have also been explored in Grid and Cluster computing environments in the past [3, 4, 21, 27].

Furthermore, there are several projects on Cloud Computing and resource allocation. A key difference of our work is that it assesses the impact of using specific domain information of a workload to assist resource allocation considering both IT costs and Quality-of-Service for educational institutions.

3   Resource Allocation for Educational Institutions

This section presents three methods for resource allocation that educational institutions can use. The method described in Section 3.3 aims at enhancing allocation performance, thus reducing IT costs and increasing QoS, by exploring the understanding that education intuitions might have about their application domains.

3.1   Method to Pre-allocate Resources

The method is based on predetermined or off-line review of education environment requirements. For instance, estimate the amount of resources—e.g. cores, memory, disk space—required to execute a set of applications $\{a, b, \ldots, z\}$ for a school with X number of students, Y classrooms, among other requirements. This can be done by either simple calculation or based on historical resource demand.

This is the solution of choice by small- and mid-size schools being the simplest to implement. The drawback is that in order to guarantee quality of service the pre-allocation is done based on the demands during the peak hour plus a given margin. That is, outside the peak period, which depends on the school's timetable, the resources are largely idle, although the Cloud provider will still charge for their use. In this scenario, idle resources represent a waste of money for schools.

3.2   Method for Traditional Dynamic Resource Allocation

This method adjusts the resource allocation in reaction to fluctuations in demand but does not consider domain specific parameters, such as timetable, resource requirements for specific classes, student feedback, among others. For instance, the regulating method allocates more resources in response to a raise in demand. This method has clear advantages compared to pre-allocation, being more flexible and adaptable to load fluctuations. The drawbacks are: (i) resource allocation usually lags behind increases in demand, where resources are allocated a Δ_{start} amount of time after the raise in demand and remain allocated a Δ_{stop} amount of time after the demand decreases, and; (ii) this process does not perform very well under highly dynamic workloads with constant peaks and falls in demand. By using this method, a customer accepts the risks of not having the resources specified in the SLA [22].

3.3   Workload-Aware Dynamic Resource Allocation

This *workload-aware* method considers application domain specific parameters such as: (i) when and how students utilise their applications, (ii) class timetables, (iii) features of the education material, among others. This allows for assuming more "confidence" in the resource allocation adjusting process, leading to finer granularity. For example, by knowing that there is a resource demanding class about to start, the system can pre-allocate the estimated resources prior to the event. Reversely, resources can be released during blank periods in the timetable. Note that this method fits well into both physical and virtual lecture periods. The method would require adaptation when considering students accessing resources and services out of such periods.

Figure 1 depicts the proposed architecture. The core component of the architecture is the resource allocation assistant for education. This component is responsible for passing information to the resource allocation system which allocates and releases resources according to the school's demand. To do so, the allocation assistant relies on an analytics module that leverages the following information:

- **Class Schedule:** The times when classes start and finish;
- **Class Profile:** The expected set of applications and workloads to be used in the class, how many users are expected, and the profile of the users (*e.g.* how interactive they are in respect to the digital devices);
- **Interaction Patterns:** How students are interacting with their devices [13, 19].

Algorithm 1: Pseudo-code for dynamic resource allocation method using educational information

---

Input: Class Schedule, Class Profile, Device Interaction
Output: Updated Class Profile
1 class ← selectClass(classSchedule)
2 load ← getExpectedLoad(classProfile)
3 provisionDelay ← getExpectedProvisionDelay(classProfile)
4 provisionResources(class.startTime, provisionDelay, classProfile)
5 **while** *demand for resources* **do**
6 | monitor user interaction and resource consumption
7 | **if** *demand changed* **then**
8 | | adjust resources
9 | update(classProfile)
10 release resources
11 **return** classProfile

Additional information could be used to enhance the resource demand prediction. For instance, student interaction patterns collected from application interface can refine the class profile. Such information can determine how students are interacting with the application, and how much more content they are willing to consume from the Cloud. The pseudocode of the dynamic resource allocation method, which runs inside the analytics module, is described in Algorithm 1.

The algorithm starts by selecting a class according to the Class Schedule (Line 1). The second step collects the expected load (Line 2) and provision delay (Line 3) for the class. These two values are obtained from the class profile. The initial setup of the class profile can be done manually, and updated and refined during the class. Once the initial provisioning is performed (Line 4), the algorithm keeps monitoring the resources and user interaction (Lines 5-9) to determine whether resource allocation needs to be adjusted (Line 8). During this process, the class

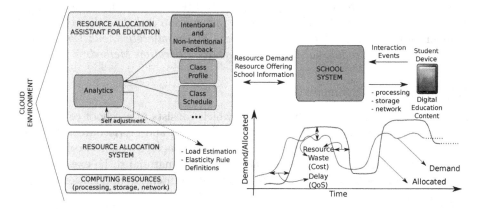

Fig. 1. Architecture for dynamic resource allocation using education information

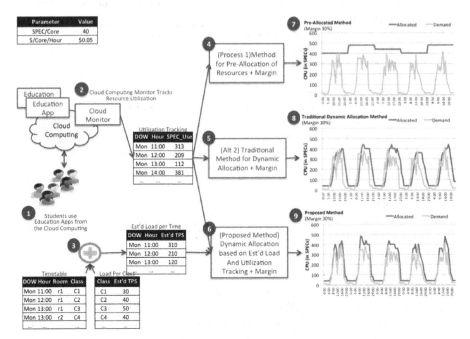

Fig. 2. Case study scenario

profile can be updated (Line 9). Once the class finishes, the resources are released (Line 10) and the updated class profile is stored (Line 11).

4 Case Study

In order to estimate the add-value of applying the three allocation methods described in the previous section, we elaborated a case study by comparing the opportunity cost in terms of resource utilisation between the dynamic allocation method that considers application domain information and the other two more common practices presented in Section 3 *viz* (1) *Pre-allocate Cloud Computing resources* and (2) *Traditional Dynamic Resource Allocation Method.*

4.1 Illustrative Scenario

Figure 2 depicts the case study scenario, which consists of a school contacting a Cloud provider that offers *Educational Applications* and IT Resources. For instance: *Collaboration Applications*, e.g. instant messenger, social network, email; *Digital Education Material*, e.g. interactive content material to be executed on tablet devices, and; *Remote execution* for resource intensive applications, such as CAD and planning systems.

In this environment, (1) students are equipped with tablet devices through which they access these resources. The Cloud provider has a (2) *Cloud Monitor* that tracks the resource utilisation per time. Here we consider that the school has a fixed timetable for classes and an estimate of required resources per class, based on historical information and/or any other evaluation. Thus, it is possible to (3) derive the estimate resource demand per time by cross-relating this information.

Let us also consider that the school contracts its Cloud Computing service based on allocated resources. That is, it pays for the allocated resources, such as CPU cores, network, and storage, regardless of their utilisation. In order to maximise the cost effectiveness of the Cloud Computing environment, the school must implement a solution to allocate resources just prior to foreseeable demand. Reversely, the solution must release resources when the system is expected to be idle.

The experiments presented in this section consider the three allocation methods described earlier and measure the following metrics:

- **Cost:** Money spent by the school to allocate a given number of resources;
- **QoS Violations:** Number of times the resource demand is higher than the allocated resources;
- **Allocated Resource:** Number of allocated resources.

CPU Cost: Regarding CPU allocation, utilisation, and price, we considered process utilisation in terms of "SPEC in use per time". One can calculate this metric based on the average CPU utilisation *versus* the provided SPEC performance for the CPU in use[1]. For the sake of calculation, we consider 40 SPEC per processor core at a cost of $0.05/core/hour. The absolute numbers are not relevant in this study, as they are directly related to the domain parameters. We provide absolute numbers for the sake of illustration. The argumentation builds upon the comparison between different scenarios.

Margin: Another variable considered in the evaluation is the cost margin, that is how much more from the estimated resources the school is willing to buy. The standard value for cost margin in the market is 30%, we therefore evaluated the margin of 10%, 30%, and 50%.

For the traditional dynamic allocation method, we configured the average utilisation of resources for the past 60 minutes, especially because some resource providers allocate virtual machines per hour basis.

4.2   Result Analysis

We first analyse the cost and quality of service considering the three methods. The results are summarised in Figure 3. We added a "safety margin" of 30% in this experiment.

---

[1] *SPEC performance*: this metric is provided by the Standard Performance Evaluation Corporation (SPEC); the benchmarks are available at http://www.spec.org/

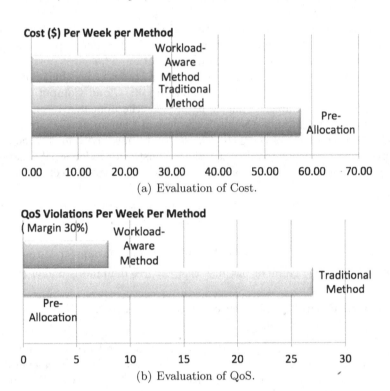

(a) Evaluation of Cost.

(b) Evaluation of QoS.

Fig. 3. Summary of results from applying different resource allocation methods

The *Method of Pre-Allocating Cloud Computing Resources* (see item 4 in Figure 2) is based on pre-determined or off-line review of education environment demand (Section 3). This method is *completely proactive* as it calculates the resource requirements to support the estimated demands of the peak hour (plus margin). In Figure 2 item (7), it is clear that there is an excess in allocation outside the peak hour period. As Cloud providers charge for allocated resources per time (*i.e.* regardless of utilisation), this excess translates into additional costs.

This is the method of choice by small- and mid-size schools and other corporations due to its simplicity to setup and maintain. As one can conclude from the summary in Figure 3, this approach:

– Implies higher costs due to the proactive allocation feature since resources are allocated considering the demands of the peak-hour plus margin for the whole day.
– Delivers the best quality of service, virtually zeroing the possibility of QoS violations. It happens as the pre-allocation based on the peak-hour demands results in plenty of resources available, even in the event of temporary utilisation peaks.

The *Method of Traditional Dynamic Resource Allocation* (see Figure 2 item (5))
works by adjusting the allocated resources in reaction to fluctuation in demand.
It implements a fine-granular model that adjusts the allocation by calculating
the average demand in the past minutes. That is, this method is *reactive* to
fluctuations of demand, adjusting the resource allocation. Figure 2 item (8) depicts the balance between past demand *versus* adjusted allocation. The major
highlights of Figure 3 for this method are that it:

- Delivers significantly better cost-effectiveness when compared to the Pre-
  Allocation method. This result is directly related to (i) the precision of the
  estimated allocation, (ii) the fine-granular reactiveness to fluctuations of demand, and (iii) the safety margin.
- Provides the worst quality of service due to the large number of QoS Violation. These events are clear in Figure 2 item (8), where the "demand line"
  surpasses the "allocated line". Again, this situation is directly related to the
  attributed safety margin.
- One can conclude that it is possible to mitigate the poor QoS issue by allocating more safety margin. This is definitively the case. Nonetheless allocating
  more margin implies increasing costs to a threshold where this method is no
  longer cost-effective.

The *Workload-Aware Dynamic Method* (see Figure 2 item (6)) considers domain
specific parameters such as: (i) when and how students utilise the applications,
(ii) timetable, (iii) features of the education material, and others. Hence, this
method combines both *reactive* adjustment to fluctuations of demand and *proactive* techniques by calculating the resource requirement to support the estimated
demand based on domain parameters. Moreover, it adds a safety margin. Figure
2 item (9) depicts the balance between fluctuating demand and self-adjusted
allocation. Compared to the *Traditional Method*, it is clear that the allocation
"follows closer" the fluctuations of demand. The results can be deducted from
the summary in Figure 3, as this method:

- Delivers cost-effectiveness similar to *reactive* methods (i.e. the *Traditional
  Dynamic Method*, thus significantly better than the Pre-Allocation method.
  The reasons are the same: (i) the precision of the estimated allocation, (ii)
  the fine-granular reactiveness to fluctuations of demand, and (iii) the safety
  margin.
- Provides significantly better quality of service when compared to the *Traditional Dynamic Method*, but not as good as the *Pre-allocation Method*.

Thus, the *Workload-Aware Dynamic Allocation Method* provides a clear add-
value solution leading to a better balance between costs and quality. As we
discuss below, the quality of service is directly influenced by the allocated safety
margin. The higher the margin, the better the quality of service. However, the
operational costs are higher as well. It is natural to ask: *"how to balance costs
and quality in the Workload-Aware Method?"*

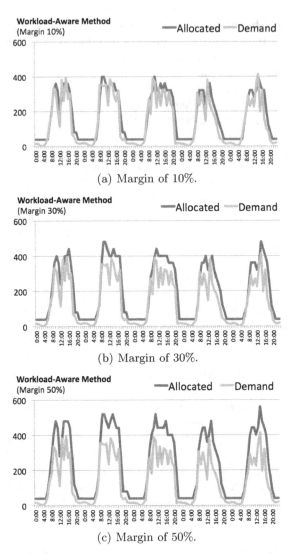

(a) Margin of 10%.

(b) Margin of 30%.

(c) Margin of 50%.

Fig. 4. Example of number of allocated and required resources for different safety margins

The Influence of Safety Margin. As mentioned, it is natural to think that allocating more safety margin to the calculations can mitigate the quality-of-service problem. Figure 4 depicts the allocated resources by applying three distinct safety margins in the *Workload-Aware Method*: (1) Margin 10%, (2) Margin 30%, and (3) Margin 50%. The visible difference is the "buffer" between the "allocated line" and the "demand line": the larger the margin, the larger the safety net, but with cost that needs to be considered.

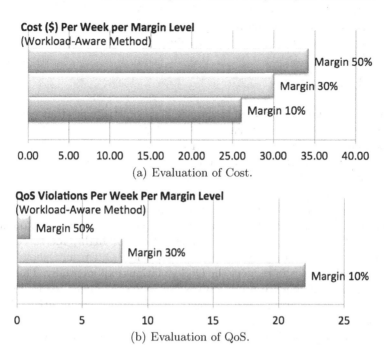

(a) Evaluation of Cost.

(b) Evaluation of QoS.

Fig. 5. Summary of results from applying different safety margins for the workload-aware method

The practical results can be deducted from the summary in Figure 5:

- Configuring more safety margin significantly improves the quality of service. As one can infer from Figure 5(b), increasing the safety margin reduces the QoS violations exponentially. This results in having more "manoeuvre room" in case of temporary peak loads, as one can see in the examples in Figure 4.
- Reversely, adding more safety margin increases costs. This is intuitive, as more resources are allocated. However, as one can infer from Figure 5(a), the cost increase is linear, whereas the QoS improvement is exponential. Again, the absolute values are domain dependent and the numbers being provided work for the sake of comparison. But with the parameters and workload information being provided, it shows that with an increase of around 23% in costs the system delivers an improvement of over 10 times fewer QoS violations. Multiple tests with different cost parameters yield to similar results, leading to conclude the "incremental more costs *versus* exponential better quality" trend.

Therefore, we conclude that the *Workload-Aware Method* provides an economically viable solution for delivering quality services to any-size schools. This is achieved by balancing proactive and reactive behaviour in estimating the demands for dynamic resource allocation. The side effect of poorer Quality-of-Service can be mitigated by adding more safety margin to the allocation.

We demonstrated that this approach yields significantly better quality without compromise the cost-effectiveness of the solution.

5   Final Remarks

This paper evaluated three Cloud resource allocation strategies that educational institutions can use to meet their IT demand. The strategies are: (i) resource pre-allocation based on peak demands; (ii) reactive resource allocation based on current demand; and (iii) proactive resource allocation that considers workload characteristics and parameters of the domain, in our case, education.

For the evaluation we considered two metrics: quality-of-service and resource costs. Our main finding is that the workload-aware proactive allocation method provides an economically viable solution for delivering quality services to schools. The quality-of-service provided by this method can be highly increased with a minor addition in the safety margin to the allocation. Our results show that increasing the safety margin reduces the QoS violations exponentially. This results in having more "manoeuvre room" in case of temporary peak loads. However, adding more safety margin increases costs. Although this is intuitive, the cost increase is linear, whereas the QoS improvement is exponential. In our experiments, we showed that increasing costs around 23% makes the system reduce QoS violations by over 10 times. Multiple tests with different cost parameters yield to similar results, leading to conclude the "incremental more costs *versus* exponential better quality" trend.

Therefore, the allocation method that explores domain specific information for better resource consumption predictions yields significantly better quality without compromising the cost-effectiveness of the solution. We find this result relevant and it serves as an incentive for educational institutions and Cloud providers to collaborate and understand better the schools demand in order to optimise the resource allocation strategies.

Acknowledgments. This material is based upon work supported by the FINEP under Contract 03.11.0371.00, MCT/FINEP/FNDCT 2010, related to the project "Platform for the Development of Accessible Vocational Training". Any opinions, findings, and conclusions or recommendations expressed in this material are those of the author(s) and do not necessarily reflect the views of FINEP or any other related institution.

References

1. Ali-Eldin, A., Tordsson, J., Elmroth, E.: An adaptive hybrid elasticity controller for cloud infrastructures. In: Proceedings of the IEEE Network Operations and Management Symposium, NOMS 2012 (2012)
2. Armbrust, M., Fox, A., Griffith, R., Joseph, A.D., Katz, R.H., Konwinski, A., Lee, G., Patterson, D.A., Rabkin, A., Stoica, I., Zaharia, M.: A view of cloud computing. Communications of the ACM 53(4), 50–58 (2010)

3. Berman, F., Wolski, R., Figueira, S., Schopf, J., Shao, G.: Application-level scheduling on distributed heterogeneous networks. In: Proceedings of the 1996 ACM/IEEE Conference on Supercomputing. IEEE (1996)
4. Berman, F., Wolski, R., Casanova, H., Cirne, W., Dail, H., Faerman, M., Figueira, S.M., Hayes, J., Obertelli, G., Schopf, J.M., Shao, G., Smallen, S., Spring, N.T., Su, A., Zagorodnov, D.: Adaptive computing on the grid using apples. IEEE Transactions on Parallel Distributed Systems 14(4), 369–382 (2003)
5. Bodenstein, C., Hedwig, M., Neumann, D.: Strategic decision support for smart-leasing infrastructure-as-a-service. In: Proceedings of the International Conference on Information Systems, ICIS 2011 (2011)
6. Buyya, R., Yeo, C.S., Venugopal, S., Broberg, J., Brandic, I.: Cloud computing and emerging it platforms: Vision, hype, and reality for delivering computing as the 5th utility. Future Generation Computer System 25(6), 599–616 (2009)
7. Chandra, A., Gong, W., Shenoy, P.D.: Dynamic Resource Allocation for Shared Data Centers Using Online Measurements. In: Jeffay, K., Stoica, I., Wehrle, K. (eds.) IWQoS 2003. LNCS, vol. 2707, pp. 381–400. Springer, Heidelberg (2003)
8. Emeakaroha, V.C., Netto, M.A.S., Calheiros, R.N., Brandic, I., Buyya, R., Rose, C.A.F.D.: Towards autonomic detection of sla violations in cloud infrastructures. Future Generation Computer Systems 28(7), 1017–1029 (2012)
9. Ganapathi, A., Chen, Y., Fox, A., Katz, R.H., Patterson, D.A.: Statistics-driven workload modeling for the cloud. In: Proceedings of the 26th International Conference on Data Engineering, ICDE 2010 (2010)
10. Gmach, D., Rolia, J., Cherkasova, L., Kemper, A.: Capacity management and demand prediction for next generation data centers. In: Proceedings of the IEEE International Conference on Web Services, ICWS 2007 (2007)
11. Gong, Z., Gu, X., Wilkes, J.: Press: Predictive elastic resource scaling for cloud systems. In: Proceedings of the 6th International Conference on Network and Service Management, CNSM 2010 (2010)
12. Greengard, S.: Cloud computing and developing nations. Communications of the ACM 53(5), 18–20 (2010)
13. Joung, H.Y., Do, E.Y.L.: Tactile hand gesture recognition through haptic feedback for affective online communication. In: Proceedings of International Conference on HCI (2011)
14. Kashef, M.M., Altmann, J.: A Cost Model for Hybrid Clouds. In: Vanmechelen, K., Altmann, J., Rana, O.F. (eds.) GECON 2011. LNCS, vol. 7150, pp. 46–60. Springer, Heidelberg (2012)
15. Katz, R.: The tower and the cloud: Higher education in the age of cloud computing. Educause (2010)
16. Katzan Jr., H., et al.: The education value of cloud computing. Contemporary Issues in Education Research (CIER) 3(7), 37–42 (2010)
17. Kshetri, N.: Cloud computing in developing economies. Computer 43(10), 47–55 (2010)
18. Li, W., Tordsson, J., Elmroth, E.: Virtual Machine Placement for Predictable and Time-Constrained Peak Loads. In: Vanmechelen, K., Altmann, J., Rana, O.F. (eds.) GECON 2011. LNCS, vol. 7150, pp. 120–134. Springer, Heidelberg (2012)
19. MacLean, K.E.: Designing with haptic feedback. In: Proceedings of the IEEE International Conference on Robotics and Automation, ICRA 2000 (2000)
20. Mircea, M., Andreescu, A.: Using cloud computing in higher education: A strategy to improve agility in the current financial crisis. Communications of the IBIMA 53(5) (2010)

21. Netto, M.A.S., Vecchiola, C., Kirley, M., Varela, C.A., Buyya, R.: Use of run time predictions for automatic co-allocation of multi-cluster resources for iterative parallel applications. Journal of Parallel and Distributed Computing 71(10), 1388–1399 (2011)
22. Petri, I., Rana, O.F., Regzui, Y., Silaghi, G.C.: Risk Assessment in Service Provider Communities. In: Vanmechelen, K., Altmann, J., Rana, O.F. (eds.) GECON 2011. LNCS, vol. 7150, pp. 135–147. Springer, Heidelberg (2012)
23. Sclater, N.: Cloud computing in education. Iite policy brief, UNESCO Institute for Information Technologies in Education (September 2010)
24. Stefanov, H., Jansen, S., Batenburg, R., van Heusden, E., Khadka, R.: How to Do Successful Chargeback for Cloud Services. In: Vanmechelen, K., Altmann, J., Rana, O.F. (eds.) GECON 2011. LNCS, vol. 7150, pp. 61–75. Springer, Heidelberg (2012)
25. Sultan, N.: Cloud computing for education: A new dawn? International Journal of Information Management 30(2), 109–116 (2010)
26. Wheeler, B., Waggener, S.: Above-campus services: shaping the promise of cloud computing for higher education. Educause Review 44(6), 52–67 (2009)
27. Yang, L.T., Ma, X., Mueller, F.: Cross-platform performance prediction of parallel applications using partial execution. In: Proceedings of the ACM/IEEE Conference on High Performance Networking and Computing (SC 2005) (2005)

Delivering Cloud Services with QoS Requirements: An Opportunity for ICT SMEs

Alfonso Quarati[1], Daniele D'Agostino[1], Antonella Galizia[1],
Matteo Mangini[2], and Andrea Clematis[1]

[1] Institute of Applied Mathematics and Information Technologies
National Research Council of Italy, Genoa, Italy
{quarati,dago,galizia,clematis}@ge.imati.cnr.it
[2] Network Integration and Solutions
matteo.mangini@nispro.it

Abstract. The acknowledged success and diffusion of Cloud computing is due to its great potential in terms of improving companies' business model. Notwithstanding this opportunity, two main issues arise: the need of brokers supporting users in the selection of the most suitable offers, and the provisioning of dedicated services with higher levels of quality different from mere availability. This paper discusses the expected performance in a real-case scenario of a Cloud brokering tool delivering two services: e-Learning courses in virtual classroom and Risk Assessment evaluation, each with a specific set of non-functional requirements. The broker relies on the resources supplied by a hybrid Cloud infrastructure, allocated following different scheduling strategies, which dynamically select the proposals better satisfying the QoS requested by users. The objective is the execution of the highest amount of user requests along with the maximization of the profit of the private Cloud provider, in a context of posted price economic model.

Keywords: Cloud computing, QoS in Cloud, Cloud Scheduling.

1 Introduction

Cloud computing is a paradigm that is having a huge success due to the potential of improving enterprises' business model. Now users can exploit a wide range of services and Cloud options but, on the other hand, a rich variety in the offer may somehow generate confusion [1]. In this scenario, important analysts such as Gartner[1] have predicted an exciting opportunity for the figure of the broker. According to Gartner, a broker is any service company who, acting as an intermediary between users and providers of Cloud services, offers its expertise in the evaluation of the proposals that are best suited to user needs and in the subsequent adoption or development of new products based on them [2]. A further business opportunity in the Cloud environment

---

[1] http://www.gartner.com/it/page.jsp?id=1064712

K. Vanmechelen, J. Altmann, and O.F. Rana (Eds.): GECON 2012, LNCS 7714, pp. 197–211, 2012.

derives from an important limitation present in most Cloud infrastructure and concerns the poor offer in terms of Quality of Service (QoS) supplied. In fact the availability of a service is generally the only QoS feature offered by service providers [3]. This represents a considerable effort made by a data center, but it is not sufficient for many business applications, which require features that are more specific. Such gap gives the opportunity for new players such as Small Medium Enterprises (SMEs) in the ICT sector to enter the market by offering both the brokering services and also specific high quality services with different QoS levels on their private Clouds.

In the context of an Italian research framework aimed to transfer ICT advancements from research centers towards ICT SMEs, CNR-IMATI and Network Integration and Solutions[2] (NIS) collaborated to establish a shared understanding of the technological and business perspectives brought about by Cloud technology. The project focuses on the design of a brokering tool for hybrid Clouds capable to adequately respond to QoS constraints raised by two use cases, respectively in the field of risk analysis and e-Learning. First of all the two applications have been analyzed in order to map the claim of a certain level of Quality of Service, for each one, into a request of a well-defined set of resources both from the quantitative and qualitative point of view. Consequently, a customer could require one of the two services with different characteristics in terms of non-functional requirements (e.g. security and privacy constraints, or high bandwidth video-throughput) and price, and these are mapped to suitable system capabilities. The brokering tool will transparently manage the allocation of the requested service to the public or to the private Cloud infrastructures, depending on the QoS expectations and the workload of the private Cloud resources, in order to try to satisfy the higher number of user requests and maximizing the profit of the private provider. Such maximization does not focus on the prices exposed to the user, which are fixed and non-negotiable for each service and QoS provided, but it will leverage on efficient use of the hybrid Cloud. To this aim, the presented scheduling strategy is able to adopt different allocation policies, based on the reservation of a quota of private resources for high-level QoS applications. To validate the different proposed strategies, we carried out a simulation-based testing, varying some parameters to highlight the possible advantages of different configurations scenarios as well as with alternative services prices applied.

The paper is structured as follows: in the next section related works are briefly reviewed. In Section 3 the applicative scenario and defining service requirements are explained. Section 4 introduces the proposed allocation policies. Section 5 details the peculiar aspects affecting the simulated scenarios, while Section 6 presents and discusses results. In Section 7 conclusions are drawn.

2   Related Works

Several economic models can be applied to the Grid and Cloud environments [4], [5], [6], [7]. The most important ones in our scenario are the Commodity market model

---

[2] http://www.nispro.it/

and the Posted price models. According to the Commodity market model, the resource providers define the price and conditions for the use of their services in terms of the amount of resources users intend to consume. Prices may be fixed for long periods, with possible variations due to the fluctuation of demand/supply ratio. The Posted price model is similar to the previous one except for the fact that providers may expose special offers. The aim is mainly to attract (new) consumers or motivate users to consider using cheaper deals. In these models, brokers typically do not negotiate any price with suppliers. Negotiation is instead a key aspect in other models such as the Bargaining, Tender/Contract-Net and Auction ones, which are not effectively applicable to our scenario. In fact, at present, only a Private Cloud may be capable of satisfying requests with high QoS. Moreover, being the number of resources of a private Cloud generally limited, many low-level quality requests will be assigned to a Public Cloud. Most of the public Clouds adopt one of the two aforementioned models. In particular, the Amazon EC2 is considered as the reference IaaS Cloud infrastructure, and can be viewed as an example of the Posted price model, because it offers the Spot instances[3]. From the point of view of a private Cloud that provides specific services without any direct competitor, as in the case of PP, there is little or no benefit to negotiate prices that can be established almost autonomously. For this reason, we considered the Posted price as the economic model of our scenario.

Most of the related works in the field of the Grid and Cloud scheduling aim at the design of efficient algorithm for the negotiation of the resources, as [8], at the minimization of energy consumption or, in reverse, to maximize the efficiency of resources, as [9,10]. While the first scheduling proposal is not applicable to our scenario, the second ones may be interesting, because their aim is to minimize the energy costs thus to increase profit margins of the providers. In our work, the focus is mainly on the study of a suitable allocation of the resources between the two Clouds, and energy-savings aspects, although valuable, will be considered as a quite immediate extension of our scheduling algorithm, as they do not imply substantial changes to the proposed approach. An example of a scheduler for the Cloud environment oriented to a set of specific applications is given in [11], which describes a system for analyzing data produced by the BaBar experiment for high-energy physics[4]. The scheduler interacts with the Condor Job Scheduler, which has the responsibility of managing priorities and applying the effective scheduling. That system aims to execute the requests as soon as possible, disregarding economic aspects, while our approach is focused on achieving a satisfactory trade-off between profit and user satisfaction.

3   The Applicative Scenario

We considered two distinct use cases: an e-Learning service, with the provision of classroom courses, and a Risk Assessment evaluation service, centered on a tool for

---

[3] Amazon Spot Instances: http://aws.amazon.com/ec2/spot-instances/
[4] The BaBar project: http://www-public.slac.stanford.edu/babar/

the security risk assessment. These services are provided through Virtual Machines (VMs), equipped with the necessary software, each supplied in three configurations, corresponding to six QoS classes namely R_1, R_2, R_3, E_1, E_2, E_3. Based on the non-functional requirements of the services delivered (e.g. security and privacy constraints, or high bandwidth video-throughput) and the hardware capabilities available in our testbed, we derived six Service Level Agreements (SLA) patterns, related to six VM templates, where for any non-functional requirement (QoS) is associated a SLA parameter, used to address the broker allocation mechanism (Table 1 and Table 2).

3.1   Courses in Virtual Classrooms

Traditional e-learning approaches propose some modular training offers on topics included into a catalogue of on-line courses. The use of the Cloud aims to meet the customers' needs to reduce logistics costs, to improve the flexibility, but also to be able to provide a larger number of courses at a time. For example, an E1 request related to the offering of a 1-week on-line course involving at least 25 participants, imply that at least a 2 cores VM has to be deploy to grant a satisfactory response to students activities (e.g. videoconferences, up/download of assignments,...). A less demanding VM (e.g. fewer cores and storage space) is adequate to respond to a 1-day course with less than 10 participants as in the case of an E3 request.

Table 1. Classes of eLearning services requests

Non-functional requirement/SLA	Class E1		Class E2		Class E3	
	QoS	SLA	QoS	SLA	QoS	SLA
N°Participants/CPU	>25	≥2cores	10-25	≥1core	<10	≥1core
Duration/Execution	1-5days	≤120h	1-2days	≤48h	1day	8h
Storage	≥45GB		≥15GB		≥5GB	

3.2   Risk Assessment Evaluation

As to risk assessment, the usual approach is to provide a software tool for the analysis, evaluation and management of risks of enterprises' assets, to be installed on dedicated resources. The use of the Cloud represents a good opportunity to enlarge the provider's business, because it allows reducing the customers' efforts in installing and maintaining the software, assuring at the same time the high level of security required by many companies for their data. Depending on the enterprise' asset dimension the capacity (i.e. CPU, HD, RAM) of the VMs is established thus to execute the risk analysis tool with the necessary response time required Furthermore due to their strict security constraints (i.e. "High" and "Medium") services of classes R_1 and R_2 (from now on R_{12}) have to be executed on the private Cloud zone, while R_3 requests can be executed also on the Public cloud.

Table 2. Classes of risk assessment services requests

Non-functional requirement/SLA	Class R1		Class R2		Class R3	
	QoS	SLA	QoS	SLA	QoS	SLA
Duration/ execution	≤1month	≤672h	≤2weeks	≤336h	≤1week	≤168h
N°assets/ CPU, HD, RAM	Not limited	≥2cores ≥50 GB 4 GB	≥1000	≥1core ≥20 GB 2 GB	≥500	≥1core ≥10 GB 1 GB
Security/ Cloud zone	High	Private	Medium	Private	Low	Public

4   The Scheduling Strategies

The scenario considered in the project is the following: a customer requires one of the private provider (PP)' services, and he/she would exploit it with specific characteristics and QoS. The request is sent to a brokering tool that transparently manages the allocation of the VM corresponding to the SLA specification in a hybrid Cloud composed by the resources of a Public Cloud provider (as the Amazon Elastic Cloud Computing EC2)[5] and the private ones. The purpose is to maximize both the number of satisfied users and the PP's profit. The profit is function of three prices: the access to the services, the brokering service and the actual provisioning. The first price corresponds to the license of the software usage: it is paid only once and for the purpose of this work is not relevant, therefore we will disregard it. The brokering service is the price to fulfill the request, and it is constant for all service classes. The third price depends on the capabilities required by each specific class and it is proportional to the execution time. In the case the service is executed on the private Cloud, the PP profit is the sum of these two prices. Otherwise, the Public Cloud provider will require the execution price, thus the PP profit just corresponds to the brokering service price.

The aim of the brokering tool has to deal with two main issues: it represents an NP-hard problem, and the maximization of each objective could be in contrast with the other. Therefore, the solution will be based on heuristics considerations on the efficient use of the Private Cloud resources. Actually, the services E and R_3 can be executed everywhere, while R_{12} have to be executed only on the private Cloud. Since R_{12} are the most profitable for PP, the brokering tool should preserve private resources to run R_{12}, allocating the other requests on the public Cloud. However, this strategy lowers the PP profit, while a greedy approach may results in a large number of refused R_{12} requests: this is the point where the objective functions conflict. A solution is represented by the use of part of the private resources to run E and R_3 services (thus to increase the profit) when the R_{12} requests do not saturate them, keeping however a reasonable amount of them to satisfy possible future R_{12} requests.

---

[5] http://aws.amazon.com/ec2/

Let us indicate with N the number of Private resources (res_{Priv}) and with $R \le N$ the portion reserved for the execution of requests for type R_{12}. Each request *req* of service execution is characterized by specific HW requirements through the tuple *<num_core, amount_RAM, amount_HD>*, by a deadline and belongs to one of the six classes of services presented in Section 3, i.e. *class(req)* $\in \{ R_1, R_2, R_3, E_1, E_2, E_3 \}$. Each resource r_i of the Private cloud (i.e. $r_i \in res_{Priv}$), has a given (fixed) number of devices (*maxcapability(r_i)* = *<tot_num_core, tot_amount_RAM, tot_amount_HD>*) of which, at any moment, only a subset is available for further execution (depending the requests currently executed). According to these definitions, the scheduling algorithm allows depicting three different allocation strategies strictly related to the value assigned to R:

- Feasible (FE): R = 100%, all resources are reserved for performing R_{12};
- Max Occupation (MO): R = 0, no resource is used exclusively to perform R_{12};
- Static Reservation (SR): R = 50%, the 50% of the resources reserved for R_{12}.

```
1. For each received req
2. if (class(req)=R₁₂)
3.   if ( ∃ rⱼ ∈ resPriv | requirement(req) ≤ availablecapability(rⱼ) ) se-
     lect rⱼ
4.   else if (execution_deadline(req)<current_time) resub-
     mit(req,current_time+1)
5.   else refuse
6. if (R == 100) select resPub
7. else
   if ( Σrⱼ∈resPriv availablecapability(rⱼ) > R * Σrⱼ∈resPriv maxcapability(rⱼ)
   AND (∃ rⱼ ∈ resPriv | requirement(req) ≤ availablecapability( rⱼ)) se-
   lect rⱼ
8.   else if (execution_deadline(req)<current_time) resub-
     mit(req,current_time+1)
9.   else select resPub
1C End for
```

5   Simulation Set-Up

We carried out an analysis of the behavior of the brokering tool under the three scheduling allocation strategies introduced in Section 4. To this end, we developed a discrete event simulator, taking into account the following description of the parameters affecting the simulated scenarios.

5.1   Workload

At the best of our knowledge, for Cloud infrastructures there is no availability of workloads repositories, as for the case of Grid environments[6]. Consulting people from NIS, we agreed the use of synthetic workloads generated by statistical functions.

---

[6] http://gwa.ewi.tudelft.nl/pmwiki/pmwiki.php?n=Main.Home

It was decided to model the frequency of arrivals during the day, with a uniform distribution, not privileging particular time ranges (e.g. daytime/night-time) and month (e.g. weekdays/weekends). This choice is in contrast to more sophisticated solutions adopted in other scenarios [12]. Our decision is justified by the fact that we are facing long execution times over (on average) by at least an order of magnitude (days vs. hours) the arrival times, see Section 2. Thus, it seems not particularly relevant to distinguish if a request that lasts three weeks arrives day or night. We adopted a uniform distribution of the classes of requests, as well as a uniform distributed execution time for each request, as defined in Table 1 and 2 (e.g. E_1 between 24 and 120 hours).

5.2   Private Cloud System Configuration

Based on characteristics of the cluster of the technology district of Liguria on Integrated Intelligent Systems[7] used to run scientific and industrial applications, the simulated system has been configured with 30 blades (two quad-core Intel processors, 8 GB Ram), and a 20Tb shared external storage. According to the application requirements expressed in Section 3, for simplicity we assumed that the capabilities of the VM for the classes with corresponding QoS levels are the same; they are listed in Table 3. From this configuration each blade may alternatively execute two R_1 or E_1 requests, four R_2 or E_2, eight R_3 or E_3 or any other feasible combination.

Table 3. Hardware requirements of the different classes of VMs

Request Classes	Virtual machine configuration
R_1 and E_1	MV1 = 4 cores, 4 GB Ram, 50 GB HD
R_2 and E_2	MV2 = 2 cores, 2 GB Ram, 20 GB HD
R_3 and E_3	MV3 = 1 core, 1 GB Ram, 10 GB HD

5.3   Definition of Prices

For the definition of the costs of the PP services, we have used the definition that Amazon EC2 offers to its customers, both for the classification of instances in terms of computational time[8] and cost prices[9]. However, R_1 and R_2 requests are not comparable with these instances, as they have very strong requirements of security, whereby the same hardware demands will cost more (i.e. 0.8€ and 0.5€ per hour respectively).

R_3 is equivalent to a Small Instance (0.1€ per hour) and it represent the only requests with potential flexible executions: for this reason they could be run as Spot instances. A customer can select this option (the use of spot instances for an R_3 -hereafter called R_{3Spot}), to save money. R_{3Spot} has a variable cost, whose detail is not interesting for the purposes of simulation because it does not modify the PP profit, being executed on the public Cloud. E_1 can be considered equivalent to a Large Instance (0.4€ per hour),

---

[7] http://www.siitscpa.it/index.php

[8] http://aws.amazon.com/ec2/instance-types/

[9] http://aws.amazon.com/ec2/pricing/

while E_2 lies halfway between the Large and the Small Instance (therefore we considered 0.2€ per hour). E_3 has the same requirements of R_3 (0.1€ per hour). The brokering service price, hereafter called C_S , is constant and set initially to 1€.

6   Simulation Results and Discussion

In the following, we compare the three proposed scheduling strategies, FE, SR and MO, in relation to two metrics: the number of user requests satisfied and the profit gained by the PP. To provide a more exhaustive picture about the ability of our algorithm to respond to different operating conditions, the results of hypothetical alternative scenarios will be presented. For this purpose, the impact on expected results caused by variations of the configuration of the private Cloud resources and the price of the brokering service C_S will be considered.

In order to ensure meaningfulness of simulated measurements, for each scenario a large number of iterations has carried out, thus to lead to stable values. In the present case, for more than 50 iterations, we have not got appreciable differences in the results obtained. The same has been done for the warm up of the system, tested for the different configurations; in the present case, we collected results for simulation longer than 6 months. All simulations have considered five different values of frequency of daily arrival requests λ, uniformly distributed, with $\lambda \in \{6, 12, 24, 48, 96\}$.

6.1   Evaluating Profit and User Satisfaction

Figure 1 shows the expected monthly average profit according to different values of the percentage R of the Private Cloud resources reserved for R_{12} requests at varying the frequency of daily requests (λ). For values of λ less than 24 we can notice a consistent profit rising proportionally to λ increases for all values of R. Profit curves start to low (especially for R=0) for a number of daily requests greater than 24. We can observe from Figure 1 that the Max Occupation (MO) scheduling policy allows higher profit than the other two for $6 \leq \lambda \leq 12$. In fact, if the number of R_{12} requests do not diminish, in-house execution of type E (plus R_3) requests allow PP to pocket an extra gain instead of merely the brokering service price C_s. For such a low workloads, MO grants major profits than Static Reservation (SR) because it allows for all private resources to be allocated to E or R_3 requests, instead of just a percentage of them. Similarly, SR is better than Feasible (FE) that leaves resources idle instead of assigning them to the other requests. From Figure 1, we can observe that the SR graph (the dashed one) lies beneath the other two until the MO curve begins to flex and is over or superimposed the FE curve. This fact testifies the advantages of SR above the other two policies, for $\lambda > 12$, as long as the profit metric is concerned.

Let us look at the other metric: the number of accepted requests. To clearly appreciate the variation of that measure, each histogram in Figure 2 depicts, for each λ/strategy pair, the total of R_{12} requests refused due to cluster saturation. Indeed these are the only possible refused requests as all other requests can always be addressed to the public Cloud. On the right y-axis (Expected Losses), we also report in a logarithmic scale the missing incomes (in Euros) due to the system inability in satisfying demand. By examining the main y-axis (the left one), we can see that for an arrival frequency around 1 hour, the system starts to refuse requests, and for higher load rates, the total number of rejected request further increases. This fact holds for all strategies but is particularly relevant for MO, which may "steal" up to all system resources to R_{12}, for allocating other requests, thus greatly suffering by load increases. For this reason, as we previously observed, MO profit curve begins to flex for $\lambda > 12$. The histograms in Figure 2 point out that the refused requests are mainly of type R_1 even if the R_2/R_1 ratio tends to increase with higher loads. Indeed R_1 requests are more consuming than R_2 in terms of time and resources. R_1 have a double average makespan with respect to R_2, i.e. 15 vs. 7 days, and require twice the cluster resources that are needed by R_2 (see Table 2). It is, therefore, clear that the system refuses more R_1 than R_2 requests: for any R_1 rejected request it is possible, at the same time, to accept in average four R_2 requests. When λ increases and the system is near saturation even many R_2 requests are refused. We want also point out that, at higher rates, the worst total amount of refused requests (i.e. R=0) increases from a 25% (λ=24) to a 72%, when 693 out of 960 R_{12} requests (λ=96) are rejected.

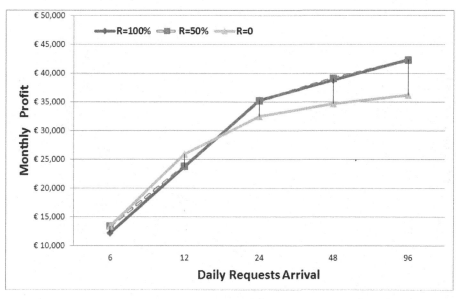

Fig. 1. Monthly PP profit

The dot above each histogram accounts for the missing gain that PP may expected due to the refused requests. For high loads ($\lambda \geq 24$) this is not the only (virtual) loss but, more important even if more difficult to measure, is the degree of frustration felt by R_{12} customers that see their requests rejected or delayed. A disappointed customer may easily turn into a disappearing one. To cope with this, a detailed cost/benefit analysis should be carried out aimed at the acquisition of new resources. It is interesting to note, by examining the Expected Losses graph, that for λ=6 and λ=12 notwithstanding no request is refused a missing gain is reported by all strategies. This fictitious loss accounts for the quota of E and R_3 requests that have not been executed in-house, even if the cluster was almost free. Particular remarkable is the case of the FE strategy: up to €850 and €2325 incomes has been lost. Due to its partial reservation policy, SR also suffers from an expected loss of circa €2270 when $\lambda=12$. A negligible loss of €96 is also visible for MO at $\lambda=12$, probably due to some E requests that have been assigned to the public Cloud instead of the private, arguably near to saturation. At higher load rates, when the number of refused requests rises, we observe an exponential (note the logarithmic scale) increase of missing gains. If this fact is not surprising, it is also essentially theoretic (especially at maximum load rates). Indeed may be not much sensitive to anticipate a gain if the system is not capable to sustain heavy loads. However, in our opinion, this kind of analysis is worthwhile as it allows highlighting the urgency or the opportunity to scale-up the enterprise hardware asset.

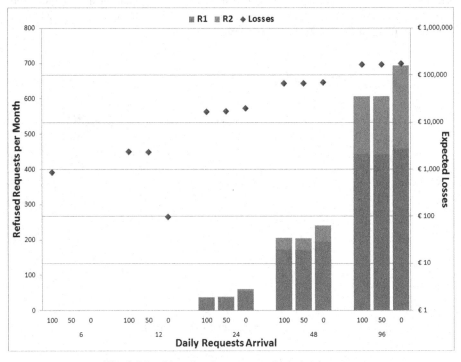

Fig. 2. Monthly refused requests and missing incomes

6.2   Varying System Capacity

From the last section, the usefulness of an analysis of the behaviour at varying capacity levels of the private Cloud is clear. We simulated a system with two different numbers of blades with respect the original one corresponding to half the capacity (N=15) and the double capacity (N=60). Figure 3 shows the profit curves for the three strategies at varying system capacity. The expected profits are directly proportional to the number of resources. We observe that at low arrival rates ($\lambda<12$) the greatest configuration (i.e. N=60) does not achieve remarkable higher profits with respect the other two. The difference is almost negligible with respect the 30 blades case, and only partly appreciable with respect to the 15 blades configuration. In the latter case, at λ=12, a quadruple number of resources achieved just a 25% major profit (R=100) up to a 44% for MO (R=0). As a first conclusion, we can affirm that if the expected arrival rate is under a request every two hours a system upgrade would likely be not advisable, but it is recommended to adequately cope with high arrival rates. In Figure 3, we see that at higher loads the greatest configuration achieved almost twice the incomes, for each value of R. Furthermore, we see that MO strategy outperforms the other until value of λ in the [24,48] interval. This outcome is essentially due to the fact that the double capacity of the cluster can be allocated to E and R_3 requests without penalizing R_{12}, for load rates twice the reference case. The decision to upgrade the resources of the private Cloud should be motivated, first and foremost, by the need to safeguard the user's satisfaction.

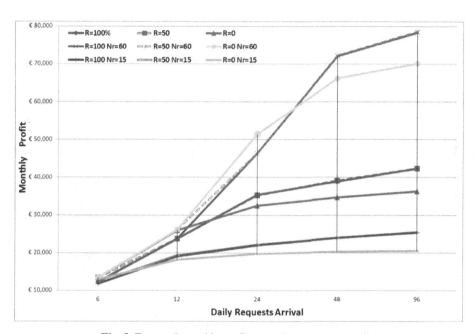

Fig. 3. Expected monthly profit at varying system capacity

In Figure 4 we show the pattern of rejected requests that is superimposed to the possible missing profits. The result of doubling the number of blades is readily visible from the histograms, where it is possible to appreciate that no request is rejected at least until the load values on the order of one request per hour. The system seems to be able to ensure a satisfactory response to the majority, approximately 75% of requests when λ = 48: we have a rejection of about 120 requests out of 480, in the worst case (R = 0), but with very few requests R_2 rejected. The situation tends to deteriorate for λ = 96, resulting in a refusal to more than 50% (R = 0).An examination of the alleged losses graph shows, as in the previous case, that the adoption of conservative strategies (i.e. FE and SR), at low workloads, penalizes the profits without improving the response. Up to values of $\lambda = 24$, the monthly loss of two strategies with respect to MO is almost the same and estimated at around €5000. When the system starts to saturate ($\lambda = 48$), the gap amongst strategies invert its sign, accounting for approximately €6000 of minor alleged profit of MO with respect to FE and SR, essentially due to the greater number of requests rejected by MO. At first sight, the algorithm seems reasonable scaling for both metrics at doubling system size. We notice however, that due the characteristics of the two kind of services delivered, in particular their long duration (Section 5.1), as well as the average customer "size" of a SME (as the PP envisioned one), it is perhaps not realistic to attend a number of (daily) requests greater than the ones considered.

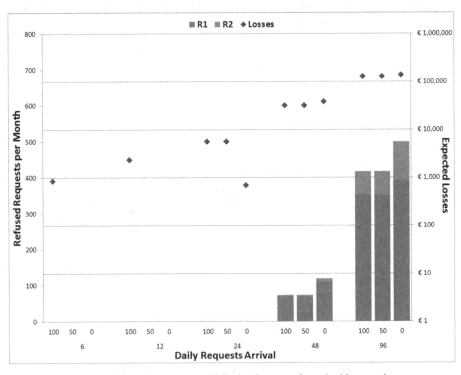

Fig. 4. Monthly Refused Requests and Missing Incomes for a double capacity system

6.3   Brokering Service Price Variation

As a second variation to the conditions of the reference scenario, we analyze the impact of varying the price of brokering service C_S without influencing[10] the number of

---

[10] In fact, any decision that affects the price, in free trade arrangements, can have repercussions on the number of requests received by the law of demand/supply. We did not discuss these issues, and we assume that the number of requests is invariant respect to the cost factor.

accepted requests. To perform a simulation somehow significant, we estimate values that could be reasonably attributed to C_S without excessively affecting the price of the service. For example, let us consider two requests R_2 and E_2 that require the same type of system resources (see Table 3), but committed to a different time and to a different cost (see Sections 3 and 5.3). From these data, we collect an average thus determined:

- $p_{R2\text{-Private}} = 168h * 0.5\ \text{€/h} + C_S\ \text{€} = 96\ \text{€} + C_S\ \text{€}$

- $p_{E2\text{-Private}} = 36h\ * 0.2\ \text{€/h} + C_S\ \text{€} = 7,2\ \text{€} + C_S\ \text{€}$

- $p_{E2\text{-Public}}$ $\qquad\qquad = C_S\ \text{€}$

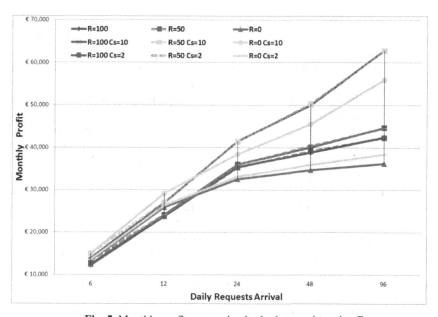

Fig. 5. Monthly profits at varying brokering service price C_s

The above values have been calculated by considering an average time of a week and 36 hours for the two requests. In the reference case we have so far considered, $C_S = 1$ implies that the impact in percentage terms of C_S on the total cost paid by the customer (equal to the PP income) who submits a request R_2 is about 1%. For a E_2 request the C_S impact is about 14% if E_2 is run in PP (as can happen for the SR and MO strategies) or 100% if E_2 is running on public Cloud. Thus, in the case of R_2 the brokering service charge is marginal in relation to the price paid, while become more relevant in the case of E_2. With these observations in mind, we considered two alternative hypotheses staring C_S to €2 and €10. In fact, considering R_2 requests, an increase of 1000% might seem appropriate for a client and definitely beneficial for PP, achieving an increase in revenues of about 10%. While in the case of E_2 a brokering price of €10 would offer clearly more detrimental (most of the price is fixed cost).

A minor increase of 100% for example (i.e. €2), it would be more satisfying for a client E_2 and, after all, also for PP, but would be uninteresting for R_2 requests that would have a marginal gain by about 2%. Probably the correct situation is differentiating the offer, regarding the cost of the service, by type of application required. However to give a demonstration of significance we checked out the two hypotheses by simulating variation of expected gains in both cases: $C_S = €2$ and $C_S = €10$. In Figure 5, one can see the results in the two scenarios and their comparison with the reference case for all three brokering strategies.

7   Conclusions and Future Works

In the context of an Italian research framework aimed to transfer ICT advancements from research centers towards ICT SMEs we presented the design of a brokering tool for hybrid Clouds capable to respond adequately to QoS constraints raised by two specific use cases. Based on the reservation of a quota of private Cloud resources for high-level QoS applications the brokering tool transparently manages the allocation between the public or private Cloud infrastructures depending on the QoS expectations and the workload of in-house resources.

The analysis of the various what-if scenarios allowed us to highlight the behavior of three scheduling strategies in relation to the two metrics considered, i.e. user's satisfaction and the private Cloud provider profit, taking into account the operational conditions. The main goal is to get a solution that gives the best values for both metrics without sacrificing excessively one or the other. As we see the role of the parameter R, which distinguishes the percentage of resources reserved to high-level QoS applications (i.e. R_{12}), heavily discriminates the evolution of objective functions at varying the expected loads of the system. We observed that until to system utilization factors within saturation, the Max Occupation strategy better responds to maximization objectives. However, MO it is outperformed by SR and FE when system begin saturates, due to their ability of preserving a quota of private resources to more profitable R_{12} requests. Moreover at low arrival rate SR is always better than the conservative FE for both the two metrics considered. A similar pattern occurred when varying system configuration. We noticed that doubling the capacity of the private cloud, allows realizing profits almost double (for all values of R) at higher load factors. Especially Max Occupation outperformed the other two for values within the system's saturation (between 24 and 48 daily arrivals). In this case, the larger cluster availability can be majorly allocated to requests E and R_3 without penalizing the R_{12} ones, in terms of rejection and then of user satisfaction. The choice of sizing the system belongs, of course, of a detailed cost-benefit analysis, which also includes aspects of formation of the cost of the service, and is outside the contents of this paper.

To summarize, the comparison of the policies pointed out that MO is better than SR and FE, beneath system saturation, while SR is preferable at higher rates with respect to MO (equaled by FE) and outperforms FE at low rates. Before to conclude we want to observe that, if we would take into account cost related aspects, and in particular energy ones, FE could partially compensate its relatively poor profits, by allowing minor energy expenditures. For this reason we think it profitable, as next development of this work, to analyze the energy figures of the three heuristics, and further evaluate the adoption of energy-efficient allocation techniques thus to study their impact on profit without compromising the user satisfaction.

Acknowledgments. This work has been supported by project grant pos. 138 "RE-THINK", under Regione Liguria Program POR-FESR 2007-2013 Action. 1.2.2 "Industrial Research and Experimental Development".

References

1. Armbrust, M., Fox, A., et al.: A View of Cloud Computing. ACM Communications 53(4), 50–58 (2010)
2. Buyya, R., Broberg, J., Goscinski, A.M. (eds.): Cloud Computing: Principles and Paradigms. Wiley Press (2011)
3. Ferretti, S., Ghini, S., Panzieri, F., Pellegrini, M., Turrini, E.: QoS–aware Clouds. In: IEEE Proceedings of Cloud Computing (CLOUD 2010), pp. 321–328 (2010)
4. Sim, K.M.: Towards Complex Negotiation for Cloud Economy. In: Bellavista, P., Chang, R.-S., Chao, H.-C., Lin, S.-F., Sloot, P.M.A. (eds.) GPC 2010. LNCS, vol. 6104, pp. 395–406. Springer, Heidelberg (2010)
5. Garg, S.K., Buyya, R.: Market-Oriented Resource Management and Scheduling: A Taxonomy and Survey. Cooperative Networking, 277–306 (2011)
6. Courcoubetis, C., Dramitinos, M., Rayna, T., Soursos, S., Stamoulis, G.D.: Market Mechanisms for Trading Grid Resources. In: Altmann, J., Neumann, D., Fahringer, T. (eds.) GECON 2008. LNCS, vol. 5206, pp. 58–72. Springer, Heidelberg (2008)
7. Kashef, M.M., Altmann, J.: A Cost Model for Hybrid Clouds. In: Vanmechelen, K., Altmann, J., Rana, O.F. (eds.) GECON 2011. LNCS, vol. 7150, pp. 46–60. Springer, Heidelberg (2012)
8. Prodan, R., Wieczorek, M., Fard, M.H.: Double Auction-based Scheduling of Scientific Applications in Distributed Grid and Cloud Environments. J. Grid Comput. 9(4), 531–548 (2011)
9. Li, J., Peng, J., Zhang, W.: A Scheduling Algorithm for Private Clouds. Journal of Convergence Information Technology 6(7) (2011)
10. Garg, S.K., Yeo, C.S., Anandasivam, A., Buyya, R.: Environment-conscious scheduling of HPC applications on distributed Cloud-oriented data centers. J. Parallel Distrib. Comput. 71(6), 732–749 (2011)
11. Agarwal, A., Anderson, M., Armstrong, P., Charbonneau, A., Fransham, K., Gable, I., Harris, D., Impey, R., Leavett-Brown, C., Paterson, M., Penfold-Brown, D., Podaima, W., Vliet, M.: Simulation and user analysis of BaBar data in a distributed cloud. In: Proceedings of the International Symposium on Grids and Clouds and the Open Grid Forum, Proceedings of Science (ISGC 2011 & OGF 31), vol. 086 (2011)
12. Nou, R., Kounev, S., Torres, J.: Building Online Performance Models of Grid Middleware with Fine-Grained Load-Balancing: A Globus Toolkit Case Study. In: Wolter, K. (ed.) EPEW 2007. LNCS, vol. 4748, pp. 125–140. Springer, Heidelberg (2007)

A Mixed-Methods Research Approach to Investigate the Transition from on-Premise to on-Demand Software Delivery

Francesco Novelli

SAP Research, Darmstadt, Germany
francesco.novelli@sap.com

Abstract. Verdicts on the advisability for software vendors to adopt on-demand delivery models are widespread in the business and technology press. Incumbent software vendors, in particular, are prompted to transition to on-demand and cannibalize their on-premise customer-base, in order to supposedly enjoy market expansion, economies of scale and revenue predictability. Yet, academic research addressing this strategic move is scarce. Relying on a mixed-methods research approach, I examined the transition of two software companies which originally entered the market as on-premise vendors and turned into pure on-demand players over time. Specifically, I performed a qualitative analysis of financial reports and transcripts to identify possible milestones in the course of the transition, followed by an econometric analysis of quarterly financial results to shed some light on the impact such milestones may have had on the vendors' performances.

Keywords: on-demand, software-as-a-service, cannibalization, mixed-methods research, intervention analysis.

1 Introduction

The appearance of a technological or organizational innovation should always be scrutinized closely by market leaders, for overlooking disruptive changes may seed their demise [1]. The rise of the on-demand delivery model in the enterprise software market is increasingly regarded as a case in point and has indeed exhibited some of the defining attributes of disruptive technologies. The first generation of on-demand solutions (so-called Application Service Providers) was underperforming in comparison with on-premise counterparts, both in responding to customers' needs and in generating the high-margins software vendors were used to. Moreover, it targeted the fringe price-sensitive market segments (medium-size companies). The following generation of on-demand software solutions – now commonly called Software-as-a-Service (SaaS) – has been bridging the performance gap, increasingly appealing to the mainstream business software customers (viz., to large enterprises), yet remaining less profitable than packaged software.

K. Vanmechelen, J. Altmann, and O.F. Rana (Eds.): GECON 2012, LNCS 7714, pp. 212–222, 2012.
© Springer-Verlag Berlin Heidelberg 2012

The above-mentioned interpretation is a basic tenet of the plethora of verdicts from the business and technology press prompting incumbents to transition to on-demand and cannibalize their customer-base on the premise of certain advantages: market expansion, economies of scale, and revenue predictability. Yet, academic research which would rigorously verify these claims and examine the nature and the consequences of such a strategic move is scarce. A vendor's transition from an on-premise to an on-demand delivery model is, therefore, a topical theme for academics and practioners alike. Relying on a mixed-methods research strategy, I conducted an explorative study focusing on two of the very few software companies which already turned into pure on-demand players after an on-premise market debut. Specifically, I used qualitative analysis to identify the milestones within such a transition and the most salient organizational issues they raise, and time-series econometric analysis to assess the statistical significance of their impact on the vendors' financial performances.

After reveving the relevant literature (section 2), and detailing my research approach and data (sections 3 and 4), I describe the transition as it emerges from the qualitative analysis (section 5). The econometric analysis and its findings are then illustrated (section 6) and put in perspective with the outcome of the qualitative data analysis, and the limitations and possible extentions of this work (section 7), before concluding.

2   Related Work

During the late 90s and early 2000s, three concurrent phenomena paved the way to on-demand. First, enabling technologies such as server-based computing and the Internet became widely accepted [2]. Second, on the demand side, large enterprises manifested the intention to reconsider their IT-sourcing strategies in order to reduce overheads and focus on core competences [2]. Third, on the supply side, software vendors grew conscious of the middle-market's hunger for affordable enterprise software [3].

As a response to such demands, the Application Service Providing model (ASP) was introduced: renting and remotely accessing a software solution hosted and managed by a third party (outside of the customer's premises). Over time, the Software-as-a-Service (SaaS) moniker displaced ASP, but whether something substantially differentiates SaaS from ASP is a source of debate. I will adopt today's seemingly more common view that the distinguishing characteristic of SaaS from ASP be multi-tenancy – i.e., the one-to-many cardinality between software instances and software customers [4]. Multi-tenancy supposedly yields economies of scale while increasing the development cost [5].

The economics of on-demand software have attracted the scholars' interest from both a theoretical and an empirical point of view. From a microeconomic perspective, on-demand software shares the characteristics and complexity of both services and information goods. Therefore, analytical approaches must rely on simplifying assumptions and abstract the differences between on-demand and on-premise.

In a duopolistic model where the SaaS provider can guarantee customers lower implementation/installation costs than its on-premise rival but must bear the expenses for the needed IT capacity, quality is showed to have a more decisive role in the long run than the lower costs [6]. With different modeling choices (abstracting all but the licensing terms), it has been shown that, in a monopoly setting, in the presence of network externalities, renting is more profitable than selling [7]. Besides, a SaaS monopolist has an incentive to invest more in software quality than an on-premise one and, whenever its cost of quality is not much greater than the latter's, will earn a higher profit [8].

The economics of on-demand have also been investigated empirically. An analysis of the quarterly financial results of a sample of software companies (with 158 firm-quarter observations of SaaS companies between 1994 and 2006) revealed that on-demand providers had significantly higher costs of goods sold and higher levels of sales, general and administrative costs (i.e., lower gross and operating margins) than their on-premise peers [9]. The estimation of Cobb-Douglas production functions from the annual financial results of another sample (with 284 firm-year observations of SaaS vendors between 2002 and 2007) has revealed significant *diseconomies* of scale in the on-demand model as opposed to the on-premise or hybrid one [10].

A second relevant stream of research is that around the marketing phenomenon of cannibalization. In a narrow sense, sales cannibalization is the diversion of sales from existing products toward a newly introduced-one [12]. It is traditionally presented as the consequence of erroneously marketing a new product too closely with old ones and their established markets [13]. However, cannibalization may be tolerated or even deliberately pursued to reduce the dependence on a single market segment, to preempt or retaliate a competitor's entry, to attack the competitor, to take advantage of new distribution channels, or to replace a product while retaining its market share [14].

To my knowledge, the *transition* from on-premise to on-demand has barely been touched upon by scholars, and only from a software engineering perspective: traditional software engineering practices devised in the on-premise paradigm cannot support the service-oriented business model and need to be re-aligned with it [11]. Moreover, the "willingness to cannibalize" established products and related assets has been found to be an organizational trait which distinguishes enduring market leaders [15], but strategies of deliberate cannibalization are a rather underinvestigated topic. As a unifying note for the two research themes: higher-than-average cannibalization rates and the ability to successfully introduce a new product already during the growth phase of the previous one have been found a distinctive feature of successful software vendors [16].

3   Research Methodology

To comprehensively investigate the transition from on-premise to on-demand, I relied on a mixed-methods research approach combining qualitative and quantitative data analysis. The qualitative component consisted in the interpretation and analysis of publicly available written accounts on the way the transition was conceived and conducted by the two organizations. This encompassed coding and systematic comparisons of codes and quotations. An initial series of codes was derived from the literature and iteratively revised while coding the texts. Relevant paragraphs in the SEC filings were preliminarily identified through computer-aided lexical search. The coding techniques employed were Descriptive, Simultaneous, Hypothesis, and, to a lesser extent, In-Vivo coding [17]. Codes, coded passages, and thematically-related sets thereof were systematically compared across vendors, speakers, and publication dates to identify the transition milestones and to extract the qualitative input for the quantitative phase.

The econometric part of the study was structured into an *exploratory* and a *confirmatory* data analysis stage as suggested in [18]. The exploratory analysis consists in detective work to reveal the main statistical characteristics of the time series and, in the context of my mixed-methods research, bridges the qualitative and quantitative research phases. It does not assume a formal model fitted to the data, but instead relies on instruments such as time-plots, smoothers, and autocorrelograms. In the confirmatory data analysis, clues from the qualitative data analysis and the exploratory procedures are rigorously verified by estimating appropriate econometric models. In particular, intervention models allow for a formal test of a change in the mean of a time series [18]. In its most general form (see [19] for a more detailed account), an intervention model has the following structure:

$$y_t = a_0 + A(L)y_{t-1} + c_0 z_t + B(L)\varepsilon_t \tag{1}$$

where the response variable y_t is the product of an auto-regressive moving-average process (whose two components are respectively $A(L)y_{t-1}$ and $B(L)\varepsilon_t$) plus an intervention term $c_0 z_t$. The intervention series z_t is a dummy variable, of the same length of y_t, modeling the occurrence of the intervention. It assumes a value of 1 if the intervention is taking place (or is in effect), and a value of 0 otherwise (i.e., intervention not yet started or stopped). The coefficient c_0 is the intervention's impact effect.

It should be now clearer why the qualitative component is an important preliminary step to the subsequent quantitative analysis: it enables to devise circumstantiated hypothesis around candidate interventions produced by the transition, which might have impacted the vendors' cost and revenue generating stochastic processes. In other words, it suggests possible shapes and anchor-dates for the indicator series to be used in the intervention models. Besides, it provides an historical perspective on the organizational and technological context in which decisions and events took place.

4   Data

All documents and numerical observations are from secondary data collection. The software vendors considered for this study are the US public companies Ariba (provider of solutions for enterprise spend management and sourcing) and Concur Technologies (provider of employee spend management solutions). The documents are SEC filings (available from the vendors' own corporate websites) or transcripts of interviews and earnings calls with the participation of senior managers from the two vendors (published on specialized websites). A detailed description of the data can be found in Table 1.

Table 1. Data employed in the study

	Data	Ariba	Concur Technologies
Qualitative	SEC filings (10Q / 10K / others)	47 / 22 / 122	41 / 14 / 1
	Earnings call transcripts	11	21
	Interview transcripts	22	7
Quantitative	Observations (per time series)	53	56
	Time span	Q2 1999 – Q2 2012	Q3 1998 – Q2 2012

Four time-series for each vendor were constructed from the collected quarterly observations: sales revenue (SR), gross profit margin (GM, gross profit over sales revenue), operating profit margin (OM, operating profit over sales revenue), and asset turn (AT, sales revenue over total assets). Sales revenue is an absolute measure of business scale; the profit margins summarize a vendor's ability to make a profit from its operations; the asset turn testifies of the vendor's efficiency in employing its assets. Revenue figures were converted to constant dollars using the Producer Price Index for Software Application Publishing of the US Bureau of Labor Statistics.

5   Qualitative Analysis

Analyzing the transcripts and financial reports, it is possible to elicit some generic phases and milestones which may characterize the transition from on-premise vendor to pure on-demand service provider (cf. Figure 1 and Table 2 throughout the following paragraphs). An initial phase poses the basis for the decision to transform the business and is therefore called *gestation*. Senior managers from both vendors declare that the strategy was mainly elaborated as a response to the way organizations were expected to buy enterprise software in the future, especially the middle market, seen as an untapped source of growth. Both firms had *ante-litteram* on-demand offerings in the market already (i.e., web-based, hosted, or ASP) which, though amounting to a minority of revenues, exposed the vendors early on to distinctive on-demand characteristics and challenges: scalability, subscription-pricing, potential cannibalization of license revenues and reduction of cash flows, integration requirements, and continuous enhancement.

The formalization and internal dissemination of the decision to embrace on-demand as the main delivery model for the company's future represents the beginning of the *transformation* phase. This phase affects all of the company's assets: the developed IT artifacts as well as the organizational capabilities needed to market, deploy and service them. Apparently, the vendors realized early the need for a multi-tenant architecture underlying the new on-demand business, and built it mostly organically, re-engineering pre-existent technology and establishing new hosting organizations.

Acquisitions and merges with ASP/SaaS pioneers, however, also played a role in making the needed technological assets and organizational capabilities available (the 2004 merge of Ariba with FreeMarket and the 2002 acquisition of Captura by Concur in particular). The underlying multi-tenant platform is not the only technological novelty. Since subscriptions move the revenue barycenter farther away in time compared with traditional licensing, on-demand products must be built to simplify and thus speed up deployments, so as to accelerate revenue recognition.

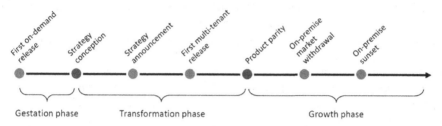

Fig. 1. Generalized timeline of a vendor's transition from on-premise to on-demand

The primacy of platform and product development efforts lasts approximately until the first multi-tenant on-demand application or module is launched, shortly following or coinciding with the public announcement of the strategy shift to all external stakeholders (customers, analysts, investors, etc.). The most prominent goal then becomes adapting the organization. This is judged an even greater challenge than the technologic transformation, and it namely impacts the company's leadership as well (e.g., all but two executives were replaced at Concur over 9 months after the decision to transition was taken). In particular, services and sales must bear the most radical changes.

In the transition to on-demand both the service mix and the nature of individual services change. Consulting services must be optimized for the deployments' higher volume and lower average complexity and length. Specialized services and expertise must be added to complement a solution which grows commoditized in its technological component. As a case in point, Ariba's system integration services, mainly linked to on-premise installations, have declined as professional services around sourcing and spending have increased. A customer management department must be established, which focuses on customers' satisfaction to drive usage – a recurrent theme, probably owing to the transaction-based pricing employed by both providers. With regard to sales, under the on-demand paradigm these tend to be more transactional, with shorter cycles and lower upfront commitment than on-premise. Therefore, salesmen should quickly close many small opportunities and build from there in a so-called "land and expand" model instead of aiming at only few large deals as they used to with on-premise products.

As the transition progresses, a fundamental turning point is reached when the on-demand solutions equal the on-premise counterparts' performances: product parity. As Ariba's senior management put it: *"This is the milestone that marks our successful transformation to an on-demand company. [...] we are entering the growth phase for subscription and on-demand software"* (notice the In-Vivo coding in the excerpt).

Starting from product parity, the on-premise business is overtaken. The on-demand organization rides the learning curve and builds capacity to sustain growth. Amongst the vendor's challenges at this stage, organizational aspects are once more predominant: a bottleneck may namely arise whenever the balance between the capacities of the sales, deployment, and research and development organizations is lost.

The way legacy on-premise applications and their customers are managed in the growth phase deserves closer examination. Ariba and Concur have ceased offering on-premise solutions to new customers, and revenues from perpetual-licenses have accordingly grown smaller until the corresponding GAAP financial measure stopped being reported altogether. Nevertheless, this now finite universe of on-premise customers appears resilient – caught in the lock-in effect of sunk costs and customizations – and spontaneous conversions to on-demand are qualified as the exception rather than the norm (*"we do see a handful of customers go to on-demand [...] but it is not strategic and it is not significant"*). Nonetheless, self-cannibalization is expected to increase with the growing acceptance of SaaS and the aging of past IT investments.

Ariba devotes on-premise customers a business unit and last delivered a new on-premise software release in the third quarter of 2008. Concur stated in 2010 being in the process of "sunsetting" some legacy systems and migrating their customers to the on-demand platform. However, this is a delicate move from a competitive point of view, and, therefore, the disclosed information is merely sufficient to sketch the transition's end. Interestingly, Ariba managers declare that they refrain from any such self-cannibalization plan, although it would supposedly be attractive to both the customer (through total cost of ownership reduction) and Ariba (the subscription fee being higher than the maintenance one).

Table 2. Historical timeline of the examined vendors' transition

Milestone	Concur Technologies	Ariba
First on-demand release (i.e., web-based or ASP)	October 1999 (Concur eWorkplace.com; ASP)	April 1999 (Ariba Supplier Network; web-based)
Strategy conception	March 2000	May 2004
Strategy announcement	June 2000	November 2005
First multi-tenant release	not disclosed; est. 2000 – 2003	October 2005
Product parity	not disclosed; est. 2003 – 2007	April 2008
On-premise market withdrawal	2010[*]	Q1 2008[*]
On-premise sunset	Q1 2011, ongoing[*]	not disclosed

[*] Approximations based on the publicly disclosed information.

Theoretically, any of the above-mentioned transition milestones may represent a candidate intervention which could alter the stochastic processes underlying the vendors' performances. In particular, the specific dates in Table 2 could anchor indicator series with a variety of patterns: a step function with a sudden level change coincident with the identified date, a gradually increasing or decaying level change, a temporary level change, a trend change. A perusal of the time series is thus required.

6   Econometric Analysis

In the *exploratory* stage of the econometric analysis, the collected observations were visually inspected to determine the stochastic processes' main characteristics and detect apparent interventions. Given space constraints, only few illustrative examples of the undertaken procedures are given, summarizing the main findings.

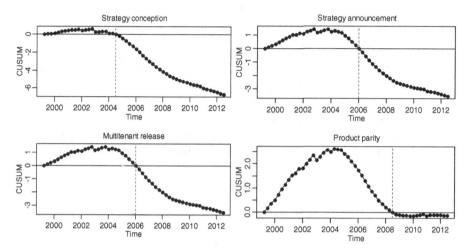

Fig. 2. Cusum charts for candidate interventions in Ariba's GM series

Level changes unambiguously relating to a transition milestone are not easy to identify on time-plots alone, for other complex nonstationary components (seasonality, deterministic and stochastic trends) may confound their effects. An exploratory investigation tool specifically suited for intervention analysis is the "cusum chart": a plot of the cumulative sum over time calculated for a tentative intervention date (see [18] for a formal account). The cusum follows an upward (downward) slope whenever the mean increases (decreases), and a sudden change in direction or steepness may signal the occurrence of an intervention.

Consider the cusum charts in Figure 2, used to investigate the effect of four transition milestones on Ariba's GM series. While strategy announcement and release of a fully-multitenant software version do not seem to produce any effect (there is no apparent change in the cusum in correspondence with the intervention date), strategy conception and product parity *might* be turning points in the profit-generating process (a change in the cusum may be spotted). Transition milestones identified as interventions by such exploratory procedures are gathered in Table 3.

In the *confirmatory* stage of data analysis, econometric models are fitted to the time series, and the interventions' significance could thus be statistically assessed. For every time-series/milestone pair, I estimated intervention models with an array of alternative ARIMA configurations (in particular: AR1, AR2, MA1, MA2, ARMA11, and constrained AR2 and MA2 – with and without first-differencing). For each intervention, three possible effects were simultaneously estimated, that is, three shapes of z_t were used in the response equations (cf. Eq. 1): pulse, step, and trend. Formally:

$$y_t = a_0 + A(L)y_{t-1} + c_0 z_{0t} + c_1 z_{1t} + c_2 z_{1t}(t - T + 1) + B(L)\varepsilon_t \qquad (2)$$

where the c's are the intervention terms' coefficients, whose significance would corroborate the transition milestones' impact in the vendors' performances. z_{0t} is a pulse indicator series entirely made up of 0's, except for a 1 at time T (the intervention date). z_{1t} is a step indicator series made up of 0's until T, and then 1's thereafter.

This main round of estimations served the two purposes of selecting the significant effects among the three considered for each intervention/time-series pair, and of screening the best fitting ARIMA configurations. Subsequently, the insignificant terms were removed from the equations before re-estimating the more parsimonious models. The first round of estimations resulted in discarding most candidate interventions (not producing any statistically significant impact), and keeping a few which produce multiple concurrent (significant) effects. Results of the second round of estimations are showed in Table 4.

Table 3. Detected interventions from the exploratory data analysis

	Series	Ariba				Concur Technologies			
		SR	GM	OM	AT	SR	GM	OM	AT
Milestones	First on-demand release				✓		✓		
	Strategy conception	✓	✓		✓		✓		
	Strategy announcement			✓			✓	✓	
	First multi-tenant release			✓		✓			
	Product parity	✓	✓						✓
	On-prem. market withdrawal								
	On-premise sunset	N/A	N/A	N/A	N/A				

Table 4. Detected interventions from the confirmatory data analysis

Series		Significant intervention	Pulse effect* $\hat{c}_0$	Step effect* $\hat{c}_1$	Trend effect* $\hat{c}_2$	ARIMA best fitting conf.
Ariba	SR	None				AR1
	GM	Strategy conception	- 0.37124	0.05527	- 0.00275	ARIMA(0,1,1)
	OM	None				ARIMA(0,2,1)
	AT	First on-demand release	3.03762	- 4.69899	0.03697	ARMA11
Concur Tech.	SR	First on-demand release	- 0.37914	- 0.16106	- 0.1263	MA2
	GM	Strategy announcement	- 3.75797	- 0.39184	0.00723	ARMA11
	OM	Strategy announcement	- 6.14422	0.16008		MA2
	AT	First on-demand release	0.50136	0.23668	- 0.00654	ARIMA(0,2,1); constrained

* significant at 5% level at least.

7 Discussion of the Findings

The processes underlying the on-demand transformation are complex and difficult to manage for a vendor, both from a technological and from an organizational point of view. The latter is an often overlooked aspect shaded by the attention on technological topics, such as multi-tenancy. Yet, the deep changes affecting sales and consulting organizations are amongst the most relevant issues emerging from the qualitative analysis.

Some of the identified transition milestones do appear to produce changes in the vendors' cost and revenue generating processes – changes which can be visually spotted in the time series and confirmed as statistically significant by appropriate econometric procedures. Interestingly, some milestones act on multiple levels and impact in contrasting ways the short-term performances (pulse effect), the long-term ones (step effect), and the rate of change (trend effect) – a further testimony of the high complexity involved in the transformation. Surprisingly, despite the attention that on-demand attracts on the premise of expanding the market, no significant stimulation of total revenues could be detected in correspondence with any milestone. Moreover, early on-demand experiences (ASP, web-based solutions, etc.) seem to play an unexpected important role: this first milestone has triple significant impacts on the efficiency of assets utilization of both vendors and on the sales revenue of one. Profitability is negatively impacted in the short-term, as hypothesized in the literature (and intuitively reasonable considering the bearing of incremental responsibilities by the vendor). On the long-term the verdict is less clear.

A number of limitations must be acknowledged. First of all, the low number of companies in the sample may hamper generalizability. Moreover, the causal relationship between milestones and financial performances should be examined further, for there may be other phenomena acting in the background, either confounding or amplifying the effects ascribed to the milestones. With regard to the identified interventions, interactions and simultaneity were not investigated, and pattern of gradual or lagged change could be introduced.

8 Conclusion

Incumbent software vendors are often prompted to transition without ado to on-demand, but academic research around this transformation and its consequences is scarce. I employed a mixed-methods research approach to exploratively study the transition of two of the very few software companies which already turned into pure on-demand players from on-premise. Specifically, based on a qualitative analysis of reports and transcripts documenting the transition, I sketched the main phases composing such a transition and elicited the most salient organizational issues they raise. Relying on an econometric analysis of their quarterly performances, I then assessed the impact statistically ascribable to these milestones.

Acknowledgments. This work was partially financed by the European Commission under grant agreement 285248 (project FI-WARE).

References

1. Christensen, C.M.: The Innovator's Dilemma: When New Technologies Cause Great Firms to Fail. Harvard Business Press, Boston (1997)
2. Kern, T., Kreijger, J., Willcocks, L.: Exploring ASP as Sourcing Strategy: Theoretical Perspectives, Propositions for Practice. The Journal of Strategic Information Systems 11, 153–177 (2002)
3. Currie, W.: Delivering Business Critical Information Systems as a Service: a Taxonomy of Application Service Providers. In: Proceedings of the 1st International Conference on Systems Thinking in Management, Geelong (2000)
4. Stuckenberg, S., Beiermeister, S.: Software as a Service Development: Driving Forces of Process Change. In: Proceedings of the 16th Pacific Asia Conference on Information Systems, Ho Chi Minh City (2012)
5. Katzan, H.: Cloud Software Service: Concepts, Technology, Economics. Science 1, 256–269 (2010)
6. Fan, M., Kumar, S., Whinston, A.B.: Short-term and Long-term Competition between Providers of Shrink-wrap Software and Software as a service. European Journal of Operational Research 196, 661–671 (2009)
7. Choudhary, V., Tomak, K., Chaturvedi, A.: Economic Benefits of Renting Software. Journal of Organizational Computing and Electronic Commerce 8, 277–305 (1998)
8. Choudhary, V.: Comparison of Software Quality under Perpetual Licensing and Software as a service. Journal of Management Information Systems 24, 141–165 (2007)
9. Hall, T.W.: Is SOA Superior? Evidence from SaaS Financial Statements
10. Huang, K.-W., Wang, M.: Firm-Level Productivity Analysis for Software as a Service Companies. Information Systems (2009)
11. Olsen, E.: Transitioning to Software as a Service: Realigning Software Engineering Practices with the new Business Model. In: IEEE International Conference on Service Operations and Logistics, and Informatics, Shanghai, pp. 266–271 (2006)
12. Heskett, J.L.: Marketing. Macmillan, New York (1976)
13. Copulsky, W.: Cannibalism in the Marketplace. Journal of Marketing 40, 103–105 (1976)
14. Traylor, M.: Cannibalism in Multibrand Firms. The Journal of Consumer Marketing 3, 69–75 (1986)
15. Tellis, G.J., Golder, P.N.: Will and Vision: How Latecomers Grow to Dominate Markets. McGraw-Hill, New York (2002)
16. Hoch, D.J., Roeding, C.R., Purkert, G.: Secrets of Software Success: Management Insights from 100 Software Firms around the World. Harvard Business Press, Boston (2000)
17. Saldaña, J.: The Coding Manual for Qualitative Researchers. Sage Publications Ltd., Los Angeles (2009)
18. Hipel, K.W., McLeod, A.I.: Time Series Modeling of Water Resources and Environmental Systems. Elsevier, Amsterdam (1994)
19. Enders, W.: Applied Econometric Time Series, 3rd edn. John Wiley and Sons, Inc., New York (2010)

Towards a Federated Cloud Ecosystem: Enabling Managed Cloud Service Consumption

Dirk Thatmann, Mathias Slawik, Sebastian Zickau, and Axel Küpper

Technische Universität Berlin
Service-centric Networking
{d.thatmann,mathias.slawik,sebastian.zickau,axel.kuepper}@tu-berlin.de

Abstract. While cloud computing has seen widespread usage, there exist domains where the diminishing of management capabilities associated with cloud computing prevent adoption. One such domain is the health sector, which is the focus of the TRESOR[1] project. Enabling cloud computing usage under strict compliance constraints such as enterprise policies and legal regulations is the goal of TRESOR. The main approach consists of a distributed cloud proxy, acting as a trusted mediator between cloud consumers and service providers. In this paper we analyze issues which arise within the TRESOR context and show how an architecture for a proposed ecosystem bypasses these issues. The practicability of our solution is shown by a proof of concept proxy implementation. As all components of the architecture will be part of our proposed cloud ecosystem, we provide a holistic and generic proposal to regain management capabilities in cloud computing.

Keywords: Cloud Computing, Cloud Proxy, REST, SLA, Regulatory Compliance, Cloud Broker, Marketplace.

1 Introduction

Cloud computing promises many advantages. Widely it is recognized as a viable way to reduce operational costs. These cost reductions are opposed by some pitfalls, for example, lack of convenience by missing features, no industry standards and therefore non-interoperable solutions, insufficient compliance to legal requirements, and missing security and privacy functionality resulting in untrustworthy relationships [1].

We have identified disadvantages and risks of cloud computing which are the main reasons for the hindered adoption of cloud computing within sensitive domains, such as the health sector. These disadvantages and risks can be summarized as follows:

Privacy, Legal, and Compliance Issues. Most cloud computing solutions incorporate outsourcing over organizational and sometimes country borders. Within sensitive domains there are many guarantees, which have to be given

---

[1] **TR**usted **E**cosystem for **S**tandardized and **O**pen cloud-based **R**esources.

K. Vanmechelen, J. Altmann, and O.F. Rana (Eds.): GECON 2012, LNCS 7714, pp. 223–233, 2012.

regarding data privacy, legal compliance, and secure auditing. Some of them are reflected within acts, such as Payment Card Industry - Data Security Standards (PCI DSS), Sarbanes-Oxley (SOX) or Health Insurance Portability and Accountability Act (HIPAA). Special care has to be taken that the outsourcing provider fulfills these requirements [2] [3] [4]. Furthermore, hardware virtualization, storage abstraction, multi-tenancy, and container technologies allow flexible utility computing models, but sometimes introduce these issues themselves [5] [6] [2]. Also, laws and provisions are traditionally confined to national borders. As globally distributed cloud computing environments make these borders indistinct, the risk for enterprises not being compliant to these requirements is increasing.

Transparency. The inability to asses critical aspects, such as the mean time to repair (MTTR), is often caused by the fact that the cloud provider's contingency procedures, such as backup, restore or disaster recovery are not transparent to the cloud computing consumer. As with most other IT services, migrating to and using cloud computing services introduces follow-up costs, as shown in [7] and [8]. Some of these costs are hidden, for example, costs for making services compliant to regulations, backup, restore, and disaster recovery procedures.

High Integration Efforts. Within enterprise architectures, the means of integrating heterogeneous systems are manifold. Generalized, homogeneous, and invariable cloud computing services raise the integration effort of existing enterprise infrastructure, such as existing user databases or single sign on solutions, considerably.

Lock-In Effects. Lock-in effects arise from the lack of industry standards enforcement and make migration to other providers difficult. The bankruptcy of a cloud service provider could have severe consequences if important enterprise services are hosted in the cloud.

Addressing Cloud Computing Disadvantages and Risks. To address these shortcomings, we propose a distributed cloud proxy for monitoring and controlling the cloud service consumption. This control is necessary to enable compliance to all privacy, legal, and regulatory issues regarding the service consumption. As the proxy is comparable to an application layer gateway for cloud computing services it reduces the integration effort, as it is able to integrate existing user databases for a manifold of different services. Common lock-in effects, such as dependencies on vendor tools or proprietary protocols are avoided, as the proxy will provide open APIs and is based on the widespread HTTP protocol applied within a REST-based architecture.

A cloud service description language formalizes aspects of cloud services on many levels, for example, technical interfaces, legal constraints, and business models. This description language will enhance the transparency of cloud services from different viewpoints like service-level agreements (SLAs), compliance, and price models. Additionally, it is used by a cloud service broker to connect clients and providers of cloud services within a cloud service marketplace.

In the following chapter we show how the distributed proxy addresses theses issues. In chapter 3 we present a proof of concept implementation of the proxy and an assessment of our prototype. The paper concludes with a related work chapter and a summary and outlook.

2   The Cloud Proxy

The following subsections present some details of the cloud proxy. This includes its distribution and security, compliance and location-aware features, and its reliance on the REST architectural style. The last subsection explains, how the proxy relates to other proposed components of the cloud ecosystem.

2.1   The Cloud Proxy Distribution

The integration of existing enterprise systems, such as an Active Directory, into 3rd party services is easier and more secure if the communication is not extended to a public cloud environment. Furthermore, some management capabilities have to be realized by a 3rd party, independent from the cloud service client and the cloud service provider. This is especially true for the monitoring of SLAs: as pointed out by Koller et al. [9] an independent party can monitor and enforce SLAs more trustfully than the participating parties could do by themselves.

The management of cloud service consumption through a cloud proxy enables the service provider to rely on implicit guarantees - such as the correct client authentication or that all policies of service clients are met. Cloud services, which are accessed through the proxy, are released from the duty of implementing some AAA functionality, because the proxy can either locally authenticate users by using a simple password database or rely on existing single sign-on (SSO) solutions, such as Kerberos [10]. With all these factors in mind, we propose a distribution of the cloud proxy between the service client, a trusted, independent 3rd party, and the service provider.

In Figure 1 our distributed proxy and the functionality of the individual components are shown. The proxy is distributed between the service client organizations, a trusted party, and the service provider. All service consumption is managed by the distributed proxy and encrypted through a trusted cloud transfer protocol (see Section 2.4). The client proxy integrates local systems, such as user databases (e.g., LDAP, Active Directory). The trusted cloud proxy monitors and controls the connections from the client to 3rd party services.

2.2   Location-Aware Features

The cloud ecosystem includes novel approaches regarding location-aware cloud computing, which can be divided into four main categories:

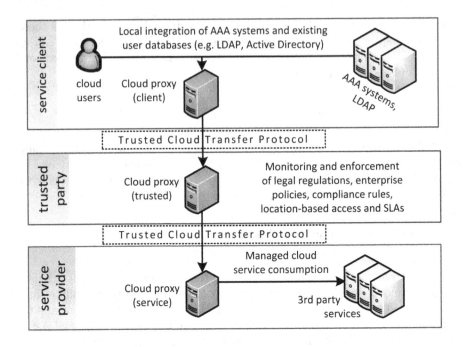

Fig. 1. The cloud proxy distribution

Access Control. We will reintroduce the former access restrictions of the physical boundary, for example, the enterprise premises, by enabling location-based access control for TRESOR services. Furthermore, we enable cloud service consumers to specify versatile policies to enable compliant and managed access to cloud services based on location information. This enhances existing concepts regarding location-based access control such as those proposed by Ardagna et al. [11]. The location information, which is used for enforcing location-based access control, can also be used by the cloud services to adapt their functionality based on the position of the consumers, thus realizing location-aware computing.

Compliance. As the proposed description language for TRESOR will include location information, e.g., the position of cloud computing resources, clients can assess the compliance of cloud services to regulations based on service locations such as EU data privacy laws.

Pricing. As traffic, maintenance, and hardware costs are not the same globally, the provisioning costs of cloud services may vary. To reflect these differing costs, the ecosystem allows the definition of different price models for service consumers based on countries or regions. As the ecosystem processes location information it can put these pricing models into practice.

2.3 Relying on REST

We identify the REST [12] architectural style as the prevalent[2] style for cloud service implementations. Many concepts of REST are suitable for using them to enable control over the data flow, for example the addressing of resources by URIs. The cloud proxy could easily match resource URIs with a set of patterns and connected access authorization rules. Unlike the SOAP/RPC-style, where each application may specify its own resource addressing scheme, this mechanism is applicable for all REST-based cloud services.

Meaningful REST URIs also enable operation and resource-based logging and accounting. Furthermore, HTTP includes information, which could be integrated into the SLA monitoring, for example, the HTTP status code. To make use of these advantages, all functional modules of the distributed proxy work with REST-based cloud services.

2.4 Trusted Cloud Transfer Protocol

The HTTP protocol separates the HTTP header, consisting of meta information about the request, from the HTTP body, which often contains sensitive application data [14]. To implement control and management functions within the distributed cloud proxy, only meta information about a request are needed and not the full message body.

Figure 2 shows the distributed cloud proxy, the connected systems, and their role within the Trusted Cloud Transfer Protocol (TCTP). All messages between the distributed cloud proxy instances are encrypted using TLS. To prevent the trusted party to access the content of all messages, we propose to use TLS not only for transport encryption, but additionally for encrypting the HTTP body between the service client and service provider. This enables direct control over the data flow without compromising end-to-end encryption of sensitive application data. As all out-of-band communication is prohibited, the trusted proxy and service proxy can rely on and trust the transmitted TRESOR identity.

2.5 Monitoring of SLA Compliance

Most cloud providers only offer simple SLAs, such as the "Annual Uptime Percentage" SLA of Amazon EC2 [15]. Emeakaroha et al. propose enhanced cloud computing SLAs, such as *mean time to repair* (MTTR) or *mean time between failure* (MTBF), which is also an aspect of the proposed framework of Dobson et al [16]. As our proxy combines in-band and out-of-band information, it can provide similar SLAs in order to allow the definition of complex SLA requirements:

In-Band Information. The TCTP protocol enables access to the HTTP header of messages sent to the cloud proxy, which convey relevant SLA information, e.g., status codes, request URIs, user identities or location information.

---

[2] The largest directory of public cloud APIs identifies 70% of all 6.931 listed as being based on REST. [13].

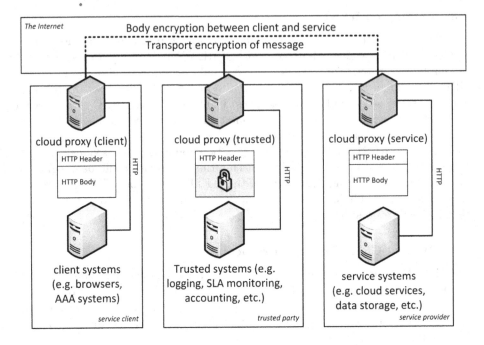

Fig. 2. The TCTP (Trusted Cloud Transfer Protocol) scheme

Out-of-Band Information. In addition, some SLA information has to be gathered differently, i.e. through agents [17], plug-ins for external XaaS services or other APIs.

2.6   Further Components of the Cloud Ecosystem

The TRESOR proxy is interconnected with many other components, which are are briefly described in the following paragraphs, as they are not in the focus of this paper.

The Cloud Service Description Language. The cloud service description language is a future aspect of the cloud ecosystem and will formalize technical, compliance, and business aspects. For the technical aspects, we will consider existing languages for inclusion, e.g., WSDL [18], USDL [19] or Linked-USDL [20]. Our formalization of SLAs will be based on the groundwork of ITIL's SLA definition. Besides the common areas, our focus lies on: Compliance with regulations by law, enterprise policy mappings, and enhanced network connection agreements. To enable service brokering and a marketplace, the cloud description language will incorporate business aspects, such as pricing information and payment models.

Service Broker and Marketplace. The proposed cloud service description language for TRESOR allows clients and providers to formalize their requirements and capabilities. The TRESOR broker then matches and suggests compatible cloud services based on these formalization. This automation considerably lowers the effort for clients to discover and select cloud services, which are compatible to the client requirements as this is now a manual and sometimes time consuming task.

Menychtas et al. [21] identify four major phases of electronic marketplaces. All processes within these areas are implemented and enriched by TRESOR components. The *information phase* is enhanced through the detailing within the cloud service description language. The description language also includes pricing information, which are the basis for the *negotiation and price setting phase*. The cloud broker matching result is cryptographically signed to form a legal agreement between service provider and consumer within the *Contracting phase*. As all communication is managed by the cloud proxy, it can implement independent metering functionality, which is used during the *settlement phase*.

3   Proof of Concept

In the following, a proof of concept implementation of the cloud proxy is presented. On the basis of this implementation we make a preliminary analysis of the impact of our proposed cloud architecture.

3.1   Technology

The proxy uses non-blocking and asynchronous functions to enable highly scalable I/O operations using the Java New I/O (NIO) API [22]. To provide abstractions for the low-level functions of the Java New I/O API, we use the Grizzly Framework [23]. The Grizzly Framework has shown impressive performance characteristics, as shown in [24]. The Grizzly Framework also contains supporting implementations for processing HTTP packets and a customizable TLS engine, which assists us in the implementation of the Trusted Cloud Transfer Protocol (TCTP).

For modularization we rely on the industry standard OSGi [25]. As OSGi application server platform we chose Eclipse Virgo [26]. Eclipse Virgo eases the deployment effort, as the application OSGi modules, can be independently updated at runtime - a major requirement for central architectural components.

3.2   Architecture

The proof of concept architecture consists of two bundles: the *proxy model*, which contains a preliminary configuration, authentication, and an SLA model, and the *proxy core*, which reads a model instance and configures a proxy runtime object. For the proof of concept, we implemented the following functionality:

Authentication. The proxy matches URI patterns to authentication rules and authenticates users through a password database.

Relaying Identities. After users are authenticated, the proxy relays their identities to the downstream proxies by using a special HTTP header. In the future, it could also relay roles to enable role-based access control (RBAC).

Routing and SSL. The proxies can encrypt traffic using SSL and route incoming messages as defined by the proxy model.

Monitoring of SLA Compliance. The Proxy monitors simple SLAs, e.g., logging application errors and comparing them to a defined maximum allowed percentage.

3.3   Evaluation

In this chapter, we evaluate the performance characteristics and the integration effort of the cloud proxy prototype.

Performance Analysis. For performance analysis, the homepage of a simple Ruby on Rails web application is accessed through the Apache JMeter [27] load test tool. The application runs on a Linux server (Debian 6.0) with an Intel Core i7 930 CPU, 24 GByte RAM and is accessed using a HP EliteBook 8440p notebook PC (Core i7 620M, 8GByte RAM).

We compare the direct communication with the service with the communication through one instance of the proxy regarding the application throughput (requests per minute) and the CPU usage on the client computer to show the impact of the proxy processing on the application access. We varied the number of JMeter threads to simulate different parallel workloads. To cut out network impacts, the proxy is running on the machine used for accessing the service and furthermore, SSL is deactivated to exclude encryption overhead.

Our results are shown in Figure 3. We see that the Proxy impacts the throughput 9% at most. The server CPU starts to saturate when using 50 parallel threads. The overall application throughput does not increase significantly if the

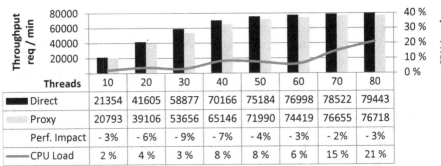

Threads	10	20	30	40	50	60	70	80
Direct	21354	41605	58877	70166	75184	76998	78522	79443
Proxy	20793	39106	53656	65146	71990	74419	76655	76718
Perf. Impact	- 3%	- 6%	- 9%	- 7%	- 4%	- 3%	- 2%	- 3%
CPU Load	2 %	4 %	3 %	8 %	8 %	6 %	15 %	21 %

Fig. 3. Impact of the cloud proxy prototype on the application throughput

number of threads is increased. At this stage of the implementation we see that the chosen technology does not impact the overall performance of the proxy in a substantial way.

Integrating the Proxy Authentication. We modified a sample Ruby on Rails application to use the relayed identity of a service user to analyze how the proxy authentication could be integrated into existing cloud services. Our evaluation shows that it is very easy to modify such a contemporary RESTful web application to use the supplied proxy authentication information. If this holds true for other web frameworks, this mechanism could therefore lead to reduced implementation efforts for proxy-compatible applications.

4   Related Work

The approach of a multi-role distributed proxy is in line with the idea of Weissman et al. [28] which states that "enabling proxies to assume multiple roles is key to the performance and reliability of distributed data-intensive multi-cloud applications". In order to follow this idea a representation of SLAs is needed, which the distributed cloud proxy will be enforcing. A number of such representations is available, for example, OWL ([29], [16]), WSLA ([30], [31]), and RDF ([32] and [33]).

Many works depict cloud proxies with additional roles, for example, mitigating constraints of mobile devices [34] or realizing a certificate-less re-encryption scheme [35].

5   Summary and Outlook

In this paper we have presented a distributed cloud proxy with the goal of regaining management capabilities within cloud computing environments. As compliance rules will be formalized through a cloud service description language, the cloud proxy allows compliant and managed cloud service consumption. This enables novel cloud computing services within sensitive domains with many compliance regulations, such as the health sector. The solution is also considerably more secure as no authentication information is sent to any system outside of the client organization. The preliminary analysis of the cloud proxy prototype shows the applicability of our approach regarding performance characteristics and integration effort. Future work will include the extension of the cloud proxy, implementing the other components of the cloud ecosystem, and the provisioning of initial services in collaboration with associated project partners from health care institutions.

Acknowledgements. The work presented in this paper was performed in the context of the TRESOR project. TRESOR is funded by the German Federal Ministry of Economics and Technology (BMWi).

References

1. Zhang, Q., Cheng, L., Boutaba, R.: Cloud computing: state-of-the-art and research challenges. Journal of Internet Services and Applications 1, 7–18 (2010)
2. Sengupta, S., Kaulgud, V., Sharma, V.: Cloud Computing Security–Trends and Research Directions. In: 2011 IEEE World Congress on Services (SERVICES), pp. 524–531 (July 2011)
3. Gonzalez, R., Gasco, J., Llopis, J.: Information Systems Outsourcing Reasons and Risks: An Empirical Study. Industrial Management and Data Systems 110(2), 284–303 (2009)
4. Chen, L., Hoang, D.: Novel Data Protection Model in Healthcare Cloud. In: 2011 IEEE 13th International Conference on High Performance Computing and Communications (HPCC), pp. 550–555 (September 2011)
5. Brandic, I., Dustdar, S., Anstett, T., Schumm, D., Leymann, F., Konrad, R.: Compliant Cloud Computing (C3): Architecture and Language Support for User-Driven Compliance Management in Clouds. In: 2010 IEEE 3rd International Conference on Cloud Computing (CLOUD), pp. 244–251 (July 2010)
6. Armbrust, M., Fox, A., Griffith, R., Joseph, A.D., Katz, R., Konwinski, A., Lee, G., Patterson, D., Rabkin, A., Stoica, I., Zaharia, M.: A view of cloud computing. Commun. ACM 53(4), 50–58 (2010)
7. Kashef, M.M., Altmann, J.: A Cost Model for Hybrid Clouds. In: Vanmechelen, K., Altmann, J., Rana, O.F. (eds.) GECON 2011. LNCS, vol. 7150, pp. 46–60. Springer, Heidelberg (2012)
8. Gmach, D., Rolia, J., Cherkasova, L.: Comparing efficiency and costs of cloud computing models. In: 2012 IEEE Network Operations and Management Symposium (NOMS), pp. 647–650 (April 2012)
9. Koller, B., Schubert, L.: Towards autonomous SLA management using a proxy-like approach. Multiagent Grid Syst. 3(3), 313–325 (2007)
10. Neuman, C., Yu, T., Hartman, S., Raeburn, K.: The Kerberos Network Authentication Service (V5). RFC 4120 (Proposed Standard), Updated by RFCs 4537, 5021, 5896, 6111, 6112, 6113, 6649 (July 2005)
11. Ardagna, C.A., Cremonini, M., De Capitani di Vimercati, S., Samarati, P.: Access Control in Location-Based Services. In: Bettini, C., Jajodia, S., Samarati, P., Wang, X.S. (eds.) Privacy in Location-Based Applications. LNCS, vol. 5599, pp. 106–126. Springer, Heidelberg (2009)
12. Fielding, R.T.: Architectural Styles and the Design of Network-based Software Architectures. Doctoral dissertation, University of California, Irvine (2000)
13. Programmable Web: Protocol usage by APIs (2012), http://www.programmableweb.com/images/charts/TopProtocolsAlltime.png
14. Fielding, R., Gettys, J., Mogul, J., Frystyk, H., Masinter, L., Leach, P., Berners-Lee, T.: Hypertext Transfer Protocol – HTTP/1.1. RFC 2616 (Draft Standard), Updated by RFCs 2817, 5785, 6266, 6585 (June 1999)
15. Amazon Web Services LLC: Amazon EC2 SLA (2008), http://aws.amazon.com/en/ec2-sla/
16. Dobson, G., Sanchez-Macian, A.: Towards unified QoS/SLA ontologies. In: Proceedings of Third International Workshop on Semantic and Dynamic Web Processes, SDWP 2006 (2006)
17. Emeakaroha, V.C., Brandic, I., Maurer, M., Dustdar, S.: Low level Metrics to High level SLAs - LoM2HiS framework: Bridging the gap between monitored metrics and SLA parameters in cloud environments. In: 2010 International Conference on High Performance Computing and Simulation (HPCS), June 28-July 2, pp. 48–54 (2010)

18. Christensen, E., Curbera, F., Meredith, G., Weerawarana, S.: Web Services Description Language (2001), http://www.w3.org/TR/wsdl
19. Oberle, D., Barros, A., Kylau, U., Heinzl, S.: A unified description language for human to automated services (in press, 2012)
20. Carlos Pedrinaci, T.L.: Linked USDL (2012), http://www.linked-usdl.org/
21. Menychtas, A., Gomez, S.G., Giessmann, A., Gatzioura, A., Stanoevska, K., Vogel, J., Moulos, V.: A Marketplace Framework for Trading Cloud-Based Services. In: Vanmechelen, K., Altmann, J., Rana, O.F. (eds.) GECON 2011. LNCS, vol. 7150, pp. 76–89. Springer, Heidelberg (2012)
22. Reinhold, M.: New I/O APIs for the JavaTM Platform (2002), http://www.jcp.org/en/jsr/detail?id=51
23. java.net: index.html - Java.net (2012), http://grizzly.java.net/
24. Mkrtchyan, T.: dCache: implementing a high-end NFSv4.1 service using a Java NIO framework. Computing in High Energy and Nuclear Physics, CHEP (2012)
25. OSGi Alliance: OSGi Alliance — Main / OSGi Alliance (2012), http://www.osgi.org/Main/HomePage
26. The Eclipse Foundation: Virgo - Home (2012), http://www.eclipse.org/virgo/
27. Apache Software Foundation: Apache JMeter (2012), http://jmeter.apache.org/
28. Weissman, J., Ramakrishnan, S.: Using Proxies to Accelerate Cloud Applications. In: Proceedings of HotCloud 2009 - Workshop on Hot Topics in Cloud Computing (2009)
29. Dobson, G., Lock, R., Sommerville, I.: QoSOnt: a QoS ontology for service-centric systems. In: 31st EUROMICRO Conference on Software Engineering and Advanced Applications, pp. 80–87 (September 2005)
30. Brandic, I., Music, D., Leitner, P., Dustdar, S.: VieSLAF Framework: Enabling Adaptive and Versatile SLA-Management. In: Altmann, J., Buyya, R., Rana, O.F. (eds.) GECON 2009. LNCS, vol. 5745, pp. 60–73. Springer, Heidelberg (2009)
31. Emeakaroha, V.C., Ferreto, T.C., Netto, M.A.S., Brandic, I., Rose, C.A.D.: CASViD: Application Level Monitoring for SLA Violation Detection in Clouds. In: Proceedings of the 36th Annual IEEE Computer and Application International Conference (COMPSAC 2012), Izmir, Turkey (2012)
32. Chaudhary, T.C.S., Kumar, V., Bhise, M.: Service Level Agreement parameter matching in Cloud Computing. In: Proceedings of the World Congress on Information and Communication Technologies 2011. IEEE (2011)
33. Leidig, T., Momm, C.: USDL Service Level Agreements (April 2012), http://www.linked-usdl.org/ns/usdl-sla
34. Zhu, W., Luo, C., Wang, J., Li, S.: Multimedia Cloud Computing. IEEE Signal Processing Magazine 28(3), 59–69 (2011)
35. Wu, X., Xu, L., Zhang, X.: Poster: a certificateless proxy re-encryption scheme for cloud-based data sharing. In: Proceedings of the 18th ACM Conference on Computer and Communications Security, CCS 2011, pp. 869–872. ACM, New York (2011)

Business Models for Semantic Content Providers

Monika Kaczmarek and Agata Filipowska

Department of Information Systems,
Faculty of Informatics and Electronic Commerce,
Poznan University of Economics
al. Niepodleglosci 10, 61-875 Poznan, Poland
{m.kaczmarek,a.filipowska}@kie.ue.poznan.pl
http://www.kie.ue.poznan.pl

Abstract. The Semantic Web, being the next phase in the evolution of the Web, relies on the existence of semantic annotations i.e., the documents describing the data and information using ontologies. The major barrier in the development of the Semantic Internet is that the process of creating semantic annotations is complex and labour-intensive. The lack of semantically annotated data on the one hand, and the need to create, disseminate and use standards for data description in the Semantic Web on the other, have created a niche on the market for suppliers of the semantic content. The purpose of this paper is to present business models of the semantic content providers and discuss the benefits and challenges in the delivery of semantically annotated artefacts.

Keywords: Semantic Internet, content providers, business models.

1 Introduction

A business model is a conceptualization of the logic standing behind providing value by a company. Whenever we observe a shift in the economy paradigm and emergence of new technologies, a discussion on the applicability of the already defined business models appears. A good example may be the emergence of the Internet and new business models that needed to be defined in order to take advantage of new possibilities and to address new challenges [1–4]. The impact of ICT development on business may be summarized as follows [5]:

- more and more networking organizations as affordable and easy to get ICT technologies have reduced transaction and coordination costs, i.e., costs of collaboration and costs of providing customized products and services,
- possibility to offer completely new and innovative products and services relying on various information components or new technologies, very often provided by multiple companies collaborating to achieve a common goal,
- possibility to reach customers in new and innovative ways and through a multitude of channels,
- possibility to conduct business on a global scale,
- emergence of new pricing and revenue mechanisms.

K. Vanmechelen, J. Altmann, and O.F. Rana (Eds.): GECON 2012, LNCS 7714, pp. 234–244, 2012.
© Springer-Verlag Berlin Heidelberg 2012

Progress and achievements in the ICT field as well as increased highly the number of possible business configurations, caused choices made by managers to be even more difficult and complex. Therefore, with the new paradigms and trends in ICT, such as e.g., the appearance of the Semantic Web, new business models adjusting the existing concepts to the new settings are needed.

The Semantic Web, being a major step in the evolution of the Web [6], aims at making the content of the Web not only machine processable, but also *understandable* by using semantic annotations. A semantic annotation is machine *understandable*, if it is explicit, formal, and unambiguous [7] (i.e., publicly accessible, agreeable and identifiable) and this goal is usually reached by using ontologies [8]. However, the process of creating the semantically annotated content still constitutes a challenge and requires an involvement of a human with a degree of knowledge about ontologies. In addition to the problem of incentivizing users to create semantic content, there is still a lack of convincing semantic applications for users and companies as well as a lack of semantic content (and semantic content providers) that could be used by the applications.

In order to facilitate the adoption of the semantic technologies, the semantic community must present advantages of using proposed approaches in the business context and provide convincing business models for business partners. Thus, the main goal of this paper is to provide arguments in a discussion on the possible business models that could support the semantic content creation process. Within this paper, we propose a business model design template that can guide organizations while making decisions regarding the usage or creation of semantically annotated content. The discussed issues are to point out to all interested players the potential and expected benefits of application of semantic content and thus, facilitate their adoption. The work conducted was driven by the design science paradigm postulated in [9].

In order to realize the above discussed goal, the paper is structured as follows. First, the specific aspects connected with the semantic content providers, their classification are presented. Then, the general concept of a business model is discussed together with the challenges related to its definition process as well as the analysis of the operations model (what?), actors involved (who?) as well as possible value creation opportunities for the content providers (why?). Next, the developed business model design template is presented and discussed. Finally, the paper concludes with summarising remarks.

2   Semantic Content Providers

In the Internet – a Web of Data [10] – we assume existence of two target groups:

- content providers (information providers), who publish data and meta-data on the Web,
- content consumers, who first decide whether or not to accept the data offered (quality and trust related issues)[11] and then consume it.

Having a look at the semantic data providers, we may further divide them into:

- not-fully fledged semantic data providers or owners – providers or owners of data sources with well defined, unambiguous structure, however, not provided in a RDF[1] format;
- fully-fledged semantic data providers – providing any kind of data in a machine-readable format through deferenceable URIs (Uniform Resource Identifiers), SPARQL endpoints or RDF dumps (this category encompasses also linked data providers, so e.g., DBpedia);
- semantic data application providers (i.e., service providers) – in this case semantic data is processed/consumed by some application and a human or machine readable output is created. This category encompasses also the providers of semantic services.

These categories may be flexibly assigned to a data provider, all at the same time. The role that a provider is assuming, influences the business model followed.

There exist quite a few data providers on the market. In addition, to the classification presented above, they may also be divided into Web 1.0 content providers and Linked Data [10] providers. According to the scope of knowledge data they offer represents, we may distinguish providers of domain specific and general resources. Table 1 presents a few examples of semantic data providers and maps them into the distinguished categories.

Table 1. Semantic Data Providers - examples

Type / Scope of knowledge	General Resources	Domain specific resources
Not-fully fledged semantic data providers	Wikipedia	various topic specific databases
Semantic data providers	Freebase, DBpedia Cyc/OpenCyc, Yago or Wordnet	GeoNames and other domain specific elements of Linked Data cloud

To summarize, semantic content production may be related to two different areas of company activities: where information is a product offered by a company or the information concerns the main product of the company and is a way of promoting this product. Within next section we focus on the business models and current achievements in this area as well as specific aspects of business models in case of content providers.

3   Business Models of (Semantic) Content Providers - Concept and Challenges

A business model, being a conceptualization of the logic standing behind providing value by a company, specifies the following features [4, 12, 13]: major flows

---

[1] RDF - Resource Description Framework.

of product, information, and money; major benefits to participants; roles and relationships among organization's consumer, customers, allies and suppliers.

A business model does not focus on processes, but instead on the value exchange and the value creation among actors. However, similarly to the business process model, a business model, being a simplification of the complex reality [14], also provides an understanding of the current business or helps to plan how a business should look like. However, the business model defines, how company makes money (or value in general) by specifying where it is positioned in the value chain [4].

In the context of content providers, regarding the **Who pays?** question – there are three categories of actors that may provide payments, namely:

- content consumers – being the main stream of revenue, providing payments at the time of consumption; however, other mechanisms can also be applied relying on deferred and indirect reciprocity, following [15] they encompass loans and subscription fees (deferred reciprocation); gratis access for limited time or functionality, but after some time for a specific fee (conditional deferred reciprocation) and debt factoring (indirect reciprocation);
- content providers – being obliged by a mission statement (e.g., government agencies and Linked Open Data paradigm) or by legal obligation (e.g., companies and their financial statements);
- third parties – here the most common examples are:
  - advertising and sponsoring – advertisers and sponsors perceive enough benefit in exposure, brand building or referrals of customers to pay for the goods or services [15];
  - patronage – benefits for the payer are psychological in nature – as in case of Wikipedia or DBpedia;
  - subsiding encompassing transfer payments, e.g., within or between organizations.

For what? – we pay for:

- content and services – also their specific features such as accuracy and precision or timeliness;
- value-add – updates of information/content, customization, as well as adding some expertise to the content, proving to be more beneficial for the consumer; this includes also so called differentiated products [15];
- complementary goods and services – e.g., training, advice on application as well as activities required by the consumers to sustain a prior investment.

Thus, as the creation, publishing and maintaining content (and it is even more challenging in case of semantic content), takes time and a lot of effort, the following table summarizes the economic incentives – i.e., the direct or indirect revenue model, the companies may have in order to become a semantic content provider (see table 2). Please note, that the semantic content may be delivered in two ways as raw data or as an application.

Table 2. Direct and indirect revenue models

Model	Revenue Type	Comment
Subscription	Direct	Paying for the access to the content or services (semantic content driven applications). Although, usually the basic access to the semantic data is usually for free, one may pay for[2]: **full access** - access to richer, more detailed data; **timely access** – paying for an access to the most recent or current version; **archival access** - paying for having more data to analyse and explore; **unlimited access** - paying for access within the specific time frame, frequency of accesses or number of concurrent ones; **convenient access** - paying for access to the data through a specific mechanism. Some of these models are directly connected to the value-added based revenue model.
Value-Added	Direct	Semantic data enhanced applications, additional aggregation, personalization
Advertising and affiliate links	Direct and Indirect	Sell advertising around the data-driven applications and services providing access to data as well as e-commerce affiliated links embedded in the presented data
Branding and positioning	Indirect	Using semantic data and ontologies to shape the market and build the position
Sponsorship	Direct	A semantic data provider may be funded to do so.

Why? – this deals with the motivation the person paying has and it may encompass the following:

– perceived value – encompassing such categories as: quality, uniqueness, lowest available price, speed of gaining an access to the product or service,
– other such as necessity, fear (e.g., against court-actions), conscience (e.g., shareware approach) or duty and fairness (e.g., buying a legal copy of content I have already tried and like).

Much research has been devoted to the attempt to define the elements that a business model consists of by distinguishing building blocks and relations between them e.g., [14, 16–18]. However, up till today, among researchers and practitioners there is still no agreement regarding neither the scope nor definition of the elements that should be taken into account while describing the business model followed by a company. One of the most interesting conceptualizations of business model's components is, in our opinion, the one offered

---

[2] http://www.ldodds.com/blog/2010/01/
thoughts-on-linked-data-business-models/

by Osterwalder [5], who provides a synthesis of different approaches and suggests a single reference model. Osterwalder distinguishes four building blocks: Infrastructure, Offering, Customers and Finances. The structure proposed by Osterwalder is in fact a business model design template, which allows enterprises to describe their business model. However, if we would like to apply this business model design template to the Semantic Web world, we would fail, as it needs first to be adjusted to the specific needs of semantic content life-cycle management processes in order to become a useful tool also in this area. In case of semantic technologies, elements of a business model should get a semantic flavour including elements specific for the Semantic Technologies domain. This concerns not only different offering (object type) or the offering channel, but also the introduction of the non-monetary aspects regarding the reputation or role played within the community. The traditional economic approach to definition of business models is no longer the case [19]. The main issue is related to information features, and between them information scarcity that undermines the typical model. The new values that appear besides the traditional revenue and profit are, i.e., reputation, business relationships, social responsibility, environment footprint. And finally, what also greatly influences the business models of companies is the massive customization. This means that not only the products should be personalized based on individual preferences but also technology that facilitates this personalization will be human-centric.

Within the next section we focus on the developed business model design template and its validation.

4   Business Model for Semantic Content Providers

The business model described within this article was developed taking into account the previous research in this field. Therefore, firstly an extensive state of the art review has been performed. Then, the business model dimensions together with sub-dimensions were defined. This definition allowed for further instantiation of the business model developed. The business model created was validated based on various case studies. This enabled for further extension of the business model and delivery of the result presented in the article.

4.1   Business Model Overview

The business model for the semantic data and service provider enables defining how an organization may create its business value in the Semantic Web domain. This enables for definition of a value object (product or service) and the way of earning money (or gaining non-monetary benefits) by providing or selling this value object.

The dimensions of the business models that were adopted to describe the business model are as follows:

- **offering** – related to the selling object and the offering distribution channel,

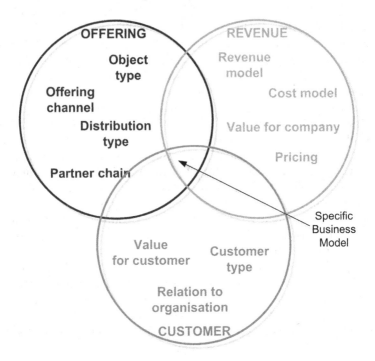

Fig. 1. Business Model Overview

- **revenue** – defining the monetary and non-monetary aspects,
- **customer** – showing the customer perspective on the business model including the value perceived or relation to the offering organisation.

Worth to notice is that besides of classical elements that have to be addressed within the business model related to the partner network, costs and revenues, the business model for semantic data and services should also take into account the intangible issues. The Semantic Web technologies are still in their early maturity phase, therefore, the companies besides gaining the real income, build their reputation in the field thus, increasing their value as perceived by the community. For this reason, the business model proposed incorporates also the appropriate "non monetary" sub-dimension.

The following sections present the proposed dimensions and the sub-dimensions and discuss their potential values.

4.2   Offering

This business model dimension describes a product or service that creates the value for a customer (an object). Therefore, the object as well as the channel through which the object is offered to the customer must be described.

To provide a sufficient level of details, the following sub-dimensions were identified:

- **Object Type:** Description of an object being offered to the customer. The object is of value to the customer. In the semantic data and service domain, the following object types were identified: conceptualization, knowledge base, querying engine, integration of data from diverse sources, semantic application, supporting tools (for developers) and consulting. These object types may be standardised or customised taking into account different requirements that may appear.
- **Offering Channel:** The offering channel describes the way the customer may access the offering. In case of semantic data or services, that is an intangible product, the offering channels identified are: querying interface, website, documentation, online/traditional consulting, data dumps and application. The offering channel is closely related to the object type, as each new object demands definition of a new offering channel. Moreover, not all channels are applicable in all cases, e.g., consulting may not be offered through the querying interface.
- **Distribution Type:** Describes the way the customer is addressed by the company. The contact of the customer with an offering organisation may encompass the following forms: cooperation, alliance or buyer/seller agreement model. The alliance, similarly to cooperation is set to *"advance the common goals and to secure common interests"*[3], however, it may be more formal than traditional cooperation, having one party managing the cooperation. The organisation may be also a part of the value-added chain. In this case, the organisation either is a seller of the solution delivered by the whole value chain or a contributor to a solution offered by another party, e.g., by offering data or services.
- **Partner Chain:** Describes the method the offering is provided to the customers. The organisation may distribute its offering directly or indirectly to customers. The direct partner chain means that customers contact and collaborate with the organisation itself; third-party collaboration means making the product available via the third party. The last sub-dimension of the partner chain is the cross-sales, meaning selling the data or services in a data or service bundle or simply together with an another product.

4.3 Revenue

This dimension of the business model depicts how an organization gains value (in monetary and non-monetary terms) while delivering its data or services to clients. The revenue may be generated directly based on income from a customer or indirectly from another stakeholder that prices the offering. This dimension is to describe the revenue, the cost model and the pricing method.

---

[3] http://en.wikipedia.org/wiki/Alliance

The following sub-dimensions were differentiated:

- **Revenue model** that describes the method the customer uses while paying for the offering. The revenue may be created by selling or licensing the offering object. Some organizations, provide its offering for free on the community-access basis, what is also included in our business model. Some other revenue models cover subscription, usage fee, licensing, advertisements, donation-based or asset sale, being the traditional revenue models in the ICT.
- The **pricing** describes the way the price for the value object is determined. The price may be fixed (stable, however there might be certain price groups differentiated) or dynamic (depending on some features of the offering). The fixed pricing model describes also the situation, when the content or services are offered for free. The price may be set directly (in most cases) or indirectly (depending on some additional features, what may be the case, e.g., in cross-sales).
- The **cost model** explains the way the expenses are accounted in the organisation. Besides of the accounting method used, this sub-dimension focuses on explaining the management of costs incurred while delivering the offering. In traditional approaches, the cost model is cost-driven. In case of intangible objects or when the offering is hard to account its value, the value-driven cost model should be applied.
- **Value for company** (non-monetary value) that describes the value the company has as perceived by the community. This value does not emerge from the accounting procedures, i.e., difference between the income and the costs. This value is related to company reputation, social responsibility, branding and corporate image and role played within the community. This sub-dimension explains, e.g., the DBpedia model, where the financial flows enable for functioning with necessary investments only, building however a brand that makes DBpedia more valuable than the total assets it possesses.

4.4 Customer

The customer is the third dimension of the business model and the object for which the offering is of value. The offering to be valuable, must be aligned to the customer's requirements. This dimension encompasses:

- **Value for Customer:** This sub-dimension defines the real benefit for a customer from buying or using the offering object. The following features were differentiated: cost decrease, quality increase, access to knowledge, pleasure, robustness, interoperability, time reduction and increase in quality. These features are twofold, as the access to knowledge granted by using the semantic data or services is an enabler of all other values listed (except from pleasure). Moreover, access to knowledge may be also understood in terms of the education possibilities. Finally, sometimes the users will benefit from semantic application without noticing that they are semantically powered.

- **Customer Type:** This sub-dimension defined the types of customers potentially interested in the offering.
- **Relation to the Organisation** describes, how an organization interacts with its customer and how the customer is being offered with the value object. Initially, the following relation models were distinguished: community, agents, business partner, individual user and contributor.

In order to verify, whether the developed business model design template is aligned with the assumptions and usable for business entities, it was validated on examples of various organizations delivering semantic data and services. Due to the limited space, the validation results are not presented in this paper, but may be found in [20].

5   Conclusions

This article discusses the issue of business models for the semantic content creation. The notion of a business model relates to the Porter's concept of value chain investigating the issue of value creation at a company level. The value chain is to define elements of the business that contribute to the life-cycle of a product delivering value to a customer. A business model goes one step further, focusing not only on issues such as supply, demand, margin or revenue, but also presenting the relations of the company with its environment and trying to identify value of these relations.

The Internet and its popularity contributed greatly to definition of new business models, that also influenced the business models in the traditional world. The Semantic Web will cause another change. Introduction of Semantics may bring a desired level of automation, and change the way people work with different applications. However, to fulfill this vision, we firstly need to deal with challenges regarding semantic content delivery and application. And here the human involvement seems to be inevitable. Therefore, the current business models for the Future Internet in the area of the semantic content creation have to take into account the user involvement.

Semantic content providers, as all enterprises, need to identify customers or customer-segments, recognize their needs, then to structure offers that satisfy those needs and deliver perceived value over the free-sources by differentiating products. The differentiation in case of the content may be performed in various ways (e.g., bundling with products from strategic partners, improved search-facilities). The semantic content production may be related to two different areas of company activities: where information is a product offered by a company or the information concerns the main product of the company and is a way of promoting this product. This greatly influences the definition of the business model.

This article is one of the inputs to research work on business models for the Future Internet, presenting the Semantic Data and Services point of view in the discussion. This work however, is still an ongoing effort and the research team involved will advance certain elements of the business model providing insights into the business model for the Future Internet.

Acknowledgments. This work has been partially funded by the FP7 project INSEMTIVES under EU Objective 4.3 (grant no. FP7-231181).

References

1. Timmers, P.: Business models for electronic markets. Journal on Electronic Markets 8(2), 3–8 (1998)
2. Tapscott, D., Lowy, A., Ticoll, D.: Digital Capital - Harnessing the Power of Business Webs. Harvard Business School Press, Boston (2000)
3. Wood, G.: Do we need new economics for the new economy? Bank Accounting & Finance 14(1), 76–80 (2000)
4. Rappa, M.: Managing the digital enterprise - Business models on the Web. PhD thesis (2001)
5. Osterwalder, A.: The Business Model Ontology - a proposition in a design science approach. PhD thesis (2004)
6. Berners-Lee, T., Hendler, J., Lassila, O.: The semantic web. Scientific American 284(5), 34–43 (2001)
7. Andrews, P., Zaihrayeu, I., Pane, J., Autayeu, A., Nozhchev, M.: Insemtives - deliverable 2.4 - report on the refinement of the proposed models, methods and semantic search (2011)
8. Uschold, M., Grüninger, M.: Ontologies: principles, methods, and applications. Knowledge Engineering Review 11(2), 93–155 (1996)
9. Hevner, A., March, S., Park, J., Ram, S.: Design science in information systems research. Management Information Systems Quarterly 28(1), 75–106 (2004)
10. Bizer, C., Heath, T., Berners-Lee, T.: Linked data - the story so far. Int. J. Semantic Web Inf. Syst. 5(3), 1–22 (2009)
11. Carroll, J.J., Bizer, C., Hayes, P., Stickler, P.: Named graphs, provenance and trust. In: Proceedings of the 14th International Conference on World Wide Web, WWW 2005, pp. 613–622. ACM, New York (2005)
12. Weil, P., Vitale, M.: What it infrastructure capabilities are needed to implement e-business models. MIS Quarterly 1(1), 17–34 (2002)
13. Osterwalder, A., Pigneur, Y., Tucci, C.: Clarifying business models: Origins, present and future of the concept. Communications of AIS 16(1), 751–775 (2005)
14. Staehler, P.: Business models as an unit of analysis for strategizing. In: International Workshop on Business Models (2002)
15. Clarke, R.: Business models to support content commons. SCRIPT-ed 4(1), 59–71 (2007)
16. Mahadevan, B.: Business models for internet-based e-commerce: An anatomy. California Management Review 42(4), 55–69 (2000)
17. Afuah, A., Tucci, C.: Internet Business Models and Strategies. McGraw Hill, Boston (2003)
18. Alt, R., Zimmermann, H.: Introduction to special section - business models. Electronic Markets 11(1), 3–9 (2001)
19. Missikoff, M., Drissi, S., Giesecke, R., Grilo, A., Li, M.S., Werth, D.: Future internet enterprise systems (fines) – research roadmap (2010)
20. Filipowska, A., Kaczmarek, M.: Business models for the life-cycle management of semantically annotated content and services, fp7 insemtives deliverable 8.6. Technical report (2012)

Author Index

Altmann, Jörn   139
Al Zahr, Sawsan   29
Assunção, Marcos D.   182

Bañares, José Ángel   61
Broeckhove, Jan   46

Clematis, Andrea   197
Cliff, Dave   16

D'Agostino, Daniele   197
Depoorter, Wim   46
Díaz Sánchez, Felipe   29
Djemame, Karim   76
Doumith, Elias A.   29

Falkner, Jürgen   169
Filipowska, Agata   234

Gagnaire, Maurice   29
Galizia, Antonella   197
Gogouvitis, Spyridon V.   114
Guitart, Jordi   154

Haile, Netsanet   139
Haller, Armin   102
Hans, Ronny   91

Kaczmarek, Monika   234
Karl, Holger   125
Kasper, Harriet   169
Katsaros, Gregory   114
Kavanagh, Richard   76
Kett, Holger   169
Koch, Fernando   182
Künsemöller, Jörn   125
Küpper, Axel   223
Kyriazis, Dimosthenis   114

Lampe, Ulrich   91
Lu, Kuan   1

Macías, Mario   154
Mangini, Matteo   197
Menzel, Michael   102

Nepal, Surya   102
Netto, Marco A.S.   182
Novelli, Francesco   212

Pham, Congduc   61

Quarati, Alfonso   197

Rana, Omer F.   61
Ranjan, Rajiv   102
Rogers, Owen   16

Schuller, Dieter   91
Siebenhaar, Melanie   91
Slawik, Mathias   223
Steinmetz, Ralf   91

Talyansky, Roman   114
Thatmann, Dirk   223
Tolosana-Calasanz, Rafael   61

Vanmechelen, Kurt   46
Varvarigou, Theodora   114
Voulodimos, Athanasios   114

Weisbecker, Anette   169
Wieder, Philipp   1

Yahyapour, Ramin   1
Yaqub, Edwin   1

Zhang, Miranda   102
Zickau, Sebastian   223